GOOD COMPANY

GOOD COMPANY

A STUDY OF NYAKYUSA
AGE-VILLAGES

by

MONICA WILSON

BEACON PRESS   BOSTON

First published in 1951 by the Oxford University Press
for the International African Institute
First published as a Beacon Paperback in 1963
by arrangement with the original publisher
Printed in the United States of America
International Standard Book Number: 0–8070–4699–X
Fourth printing, July 1971

PREFACE

THE material presented in this book was collected by my late husband, Godfrey Wilson, and myself, between 1934 and 1938; he then being a Fellow of the Rockefeller Foundation, and I a Research Fellow of the International African Institute. Godfrey Wilson was in the field from September 1934 to December 1935 (with one month's break) and again from September 1936 to January 1938; the interval having been spent in London, digesting material. I did not begin work until March 1935, and was invalided out of the Territory with malaria for six months in 1937, so that I only spent a total of twenty months in the field. We had three main centres of work: Mwaya on the Lake-shore plain, Isumba in Selya, and Ilolo on the plateau near the Moravian mission of Rungwe; and either together or singly we stayed for some time in Kinga country on the Livingstone mountains, in Ngonde, at Lubaga, near LiKyala, at the White Fathers' station of Makete, on the Lupa gold-fields, in the Government station of Tukuyu, and at the Church of Scotland mission station, Livingstonia (Kondowe), to which youths from Ngonde and a few from Nyakyusa go to be educated (cf. Maps II and III). At one time or another we walked through almost all the district except for the Ndali hills: that expedition, long planned, was repeatedly prevented by attacks of malaria. At Mwaya and Isumba we were lent disused mission houses close to villages; in Ilolo we lived in a Nyakyusa-style house built for us in the main thoroughfare of the village; when camping we pitched our tent within the village usually near the homestead of the chief or headman.

As will be seen, the Nyakyusa are an extremely democratic people, and we lived in democratic fashion with Nyakyusa dropping in to visit, and sharing with us tea, or occasionally more solid meals, at all times of the day. We in turn were welcomed and fed in our friends' houses. After the first few months the atmosphere was extremely cordial, and the Nyakyusa took immense pains to explain their customs and to invite us to events which they thought would interest us. We both learnt to speak Nyakyusa and took notes largely in the language.

We got a great deal of help from two Nyakyusa clerks, Leonard Mwaisumo (now dead) and John Brown Mwaikambo. Mwaisumo laboured to teach us the language (for there is no published grammar or dictionary in Nyakyusa) as well as the conventions of the country, and he wrote many valuable texts. Mwaikambo (who joined us after Mwaisumo had been appointed clerk to the Appeal Court of the district) was also invaluable in writing texts, which gave both his own account of events and those of people he interviewed. Mwaisumo was a commoner; Mwaikambo the son of a chief. Both men were Christians; both had passed Standard VII, and spoke reasonably good English. To mention others by name is perhaps invidious, but we cannot omit these: the great rain-maker, Kasitile, an old man and a conservative, who formally introduced Godfrey Wilson to his ancestors, and opened his heart on matters of ritual; Mwakionde, famous as a doctor and maker of lions, a regular Silenus in his joviality and consumption of beer; Mwandesi, an ancient chief recognized by the Nyakyusa themselves as their foremost authority on history, and Mwaipopo, the chief in whose country we lived in Selya (see Plate V); Mwambuputa, Kakuju, Nsusa, and Mwafula, village headmen and conservatives; Fibombe, a Christian elder (see Plate VI); Porokoto, the pagan (but sceptical) chief of Ilolo, and his sister Martha, a leading woman in Rungwe congregation. Our house-boy Angombwike, and his wife Ndimbomi (see Plate IX) were also admirable informants. Both were Christian, but Angombwike came from a family of pagan doctors, his mother Mwangoka being one of the foremost practitioners in Selya, and herself an excellent informant. These are but a few among many able informants, for we were instructed in *iki-Nyakyusa*, that is, Nyakyusa language and culture, by people of varying status from all over the district.

To the Europeans of Rungwe district and Ngonde we also owe a great debt for warm hospitality, professional help, and a friendly tolerance of the eccentricities of anthropologists. We spent delightful week-ends in Tukuyu, Karonga, and Mwakelili, the guests of one and another of our European friends, who are too many to mention all by name. We must however acknowledge our particular obligation to Mr. P. M. Huggins, District Officer of Rungwe when we arrived, and Mrs. Huggins; Mr. Fox-Strangeways, sometime District Commissioner at Karonga, and Mrs.

Fox-Strangeways; the late Mr. Eustace of the Tanganyika Agricultural Department, and Mrs. Eustace; the Rev. and Mrs. Marx of the Moravian mission at Rungwe; the Rev. and Mrs. Faulds of the Church of Scotland mission at Karonga; the Rev. and Mrs. Galbraith of Livingstonia; Mr. Godfried Schuler, a planter, and his wife; and the Officers of the King's African Rifles then stationed at Masoko.

When planning work among the Nyakyusa, we were guided by Lord Lugard, who had lively recollections of 'the north-enders', and by the Rev. D. R. and Mrs. MacKenzie, missionaries of the Church of Scotland in the area for many years. Mr. MacKenzie had published *The Spirit-Ridden Konde* in 1925, and was deeply interested in the Nyakyusa-Ngonde people; he lent us manuscript notes on the language and gave us the most generous encouragement.

Godfrey Wilson was concerned to make a general sociological study of the Nyakyusa, while I had been commissioned by the International African Institute to study particularly the effects of Christian missions on the community; in practice we found it profitable each to work primarily with our own sex, though we did not do so exclusively. Nyakyusa men proved better informants than women, largely, we think, because the men all had a training in logic, gained in discussion in the villages and in court. Women lacked this training and, except for doctors and those who had had some schooling, they found it difficult to give an account of their customs. The pagan women were markedly less coherent than conservative Pondo women (among whom I had previously worked[1]), a difference which I attribute to the narrow scope for leadership among the women in the traditional Nyakyusa society. And the difference between conservative pagan Nyakyusa women (doctors excepted) and Christians who had had some schooling was very noticeable.

Material on pagan and Christian, as well as that on men and women, overlapped at every point; and shortly after leaving the field we agreed that to describe pagan and Christian groups separately would distort the facts very seriously, and that we would collaborate in writing three books on Nyakyusa kinship, Nyakyusa villages, and Nyakyusa chiefdoms, including in each of

[1] Monica Hunter, *Reaction to Conquest: Effects of Contact with Europeans on the Pondo of South Africa* (1936).

them an analysis of pagan and Christian differences. Godfrey Wilson died on active service before the writing of these books was begun, and I am thus solely responsible for the form of this volume, but the material is from the field notes of us both. Portions of Chapter I, and a few paragraphs in other chapters have been quoted (with minor emendations) from articles already published by him. Throughout the book the present tense refers to the period 1934–8 when the material was collected.

The problem of combining adequate documentation with lucidity has not yet been solved in anthropology: either monographs are so loaded with texts and case records as to be almost unreadable, or else they are impressionistic, and the student is left wondering just what evidence there is for the author's conclusions. We have attempted to meet this difficulty by publishing certain relevant documents in a separate section. These documents represent only a small selection of the field notes used, but at least they illustrate the type of evidence on which our argument is based. Many of them are translations of texts written in Nyakyusa by Mwaisumu and Mwaikambo from their own knowledge, or at the dictation of others.

The maps have been drawn by my friend and colleague at Rhodes University College, Professor J. V. L. Rennie, to whom I am much indebted for the time and trouble he has lavished on them. The map of Rungwe District is based on one compiled by Mr. R. de Z. Hall, and traced by Mr. G. D. Arthur, which was given me by the courtesy of the Survey Department of Tanganyika.

Finally, I am indebted to Dr. Audrey Richards, Professor Meyer Fortes, and Professor Dover Wilson for reading this manuscript and making many valuable suggestions.

Rhodes University College,
Grahamstown, 1949.

ACKNOWLEDGEMENT

THE field material on which this study was based was collected under the auspices of the Rockefeller Foundation and the International African Institute,

CONTENTS

CONTENTS

ILLUSTRATIONS

(Photographs by the author)

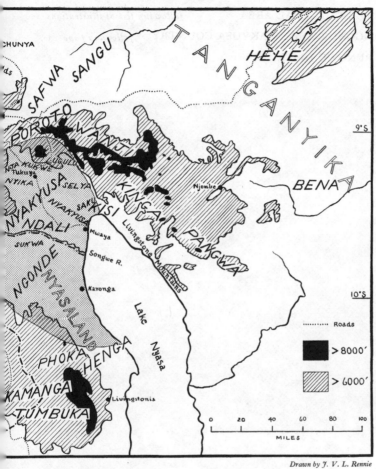

Drawn by J. V. L. Rennie

MAP I.   THE CULTURAL AREA

fine dot stipple indicates the approximate area occupied by the Nyakyusa-Ngonde people and groups dominated by them.

MAPS

CHAPTER I

INTRODUCTORY

a. The cultural area

THE Nyakyusa and Ngonde[1] are a Bantu-speaking people who live at the north-west corner of Lake Nyasa, on the marshy plain at the head of the Lake, and in the hills that rise steeply to the north and west of it. They straddle the Songwe river which divides Tanganyika from Nyasaland. The area is enclosed by the Lake itself, the escarpment of the Livingstone mountains on the north-east and the Poroto mountains on the north-west. To the west the boundaries are less clearly defined, but coincide pretty closely with the boundary of Rungwe district and with the water-shed which separates Nyasaland from Northern Rhodesia. To the south the boundary is that of Chief Mwafulira's country, which lies some twenty miles south of Karonga (see Map I). Most of the area is thus situated between 9° and 10° S., and 33° and 34° E. It covers approximately 4,500 square miles and the population is about 235,000.[2]

Within this area there are local differences in language and custom. The dominant groups are the *Nyakyusa*, who live in Tanganyika on the Lake-shore plain and up into the hills as far as Rungwe mission, and the people of *Ngonde* who live on the Lake-shore plain in Nyasaland. These two groups speak dialects which, though differing somewhat in vocabulary and pronunciation, are easily understood by speakers from both, and their social structure is essentially similar. The main difference is that in Ngonde a

[1] The old men say *Nkhonde*, and the name appears in most of the literature as *Konde*.

[2] The area of Tukuyu district is 1,866 square miles, and the area subject to the Kyungu, the paramount chief of Ngonde, is 2,687 square miles. The Tanganyika census of 1931 gives the population of Rungwe district as 195,062: this was believed in the district to be an over-estimate. The population of Ngonde is approximately 40,000. For the southern boundary of the Ngonde people in 1881 see James Stewart, 'Lake Nyassa and the Water Route to the Lake Region of Central Africa', *Proceedings of the Royal Geographical Society, New Series*, Vol. III, 1881. He states that nine miles north of Mount Waller is a marsh; south of it are the Tumbuka, north of it the 'Chungu' (i.e. Ngonde).

centralized chieftainship[1] developed with the development of the ivory trade, whereas among the Nyakyusa (who were geographically much more isolated) nearly a hundred small chiefdoms maintained their independence until the European conquest. In their economy, their kinship system, their age-village organization and their rituals, however, the people of Ngonde are very similar to the Nyakyusa.

The Nyakyusa themselves may be sub-divided into those living on the Lake-shore plain (*MuNgonde*), those around *Masoko*, those to the east under the Livingstone mountains in *Selya* and *Saku*, and those to the north, viz. the *Kukwe* and *Lugulu*. The last two groups differ appreciably in dialect and custom from the others, but all speak dialects which are mutually intelligible.[2]

There are also a number of small groups with old langugages of their own which, though related to that of the Nyakyusa and Ngonde, are more or less unintelligible to them; and they have equally distinct cultures. These include the *Penja* on the plateau to the west of the Kukwe; a small group of *Nyika* on the same plateau; the *Ndali* in the hills to the north of the Songwe; the *Sukwa* to the south of them; the *Lambya* and *Wenya* further west; small groups of *Henga* and *Mambwe* on the western border of Ngonde, and the *Kisi*, a people famous as potters and fishermen, who live on the north-east shore of the Lake. Most of these people are now, we are told, being rapidly assimilated to the Nyakyusa and Ngonde in speech and in law, but we have little

---

[1] Godfrey Wilson, *The Constitution of Ngonde*, Rhodes-Livingstone Papers No. 3, 1939.

[2] The term *Nyakyusa* means primarily the people of the Lake plain in Tanganyika, and those around Masoko, but it is now used by extension to include those in Selya and Saku, together with the Kukwe. We use 'Nyakyusa proper', for those on the Lake plain and around Masoko. The terms *Ngonde* and *Mwamba* are a source of some confusion because their meaning varies with the location of the speaker, and the meaning of Ngonde also varies with the prefix used. The primary meaning of *Aba-Ngonde* is 'the people of the plains' but anyone travelling in the direction of the sacred hill Mbande, on which the Kyungu (the paramount chief of Ngonde) lived is spoken of as going *KuNgonde*, whether he start from nearby, or from as far away as Tukuyu (cf. Godfrey Wilson, op. cit., p. 7). *MuNgonde* is generally used by the Nyakyusa for the Lake-shore plain of Tanganyika. In this book we use *Ngonde* for the area of the Kyungu's supremacy, and avoid *MuNgonde*. *AbaMwamba* means by derivation 'the hill people', but is generally used for 'the people to the north'. The Ngonde of Karonga call those on the plain around Mwaya *BaMwamba*, the men of Mwaya apply the name not to themselves, but to the people of Selya, while the people of Selya apply it to those in the hills to the north of them. We therefore avoid the term.

first-hand knowledge of them. On the coast they are classed with Nyakyusa and Ngonde as *Sokile*, a nickname derived from the traditional Nyakyusa greeting.

This book is concerned with the Nyakyusa.[1] What it contains is true in general terms for the people of Ngonde, but how far it is applicable to the smaller groups cited we are not certain. The Ndali, Sukwa, and Penja, are said to have long had an age-village organization; and Henga, Nyika and Kisi living inter-mingled with Ngonde and Nyakyusa have adopted it; but of the customs of the Wenya and Lambya we know little. Dr. Kerr Cross and Monteith Fotheringham, who travelled extensively in the area before 1890, reported that the Ndali and Sukwa (of Misuku) were very similar to the Nyakyusa and Ngonde people, but that the Lambya were different, practising shifting *citemene* cultivation, and living in stockaded villages.[2]

According to their own traditions the Nyakyusa and Ngonde chiefs (who trace descent from common ancestors) came ten generations ago from Kinga country, on the Livingstone mountains, and found the Rungwe and North Nyasa country already occupied. They established themselves as chiefs and have since been in-creasing the area of their occupation. The Kinga also affirm that their chiefs are related to those of the Nyakyusa and Ngonde, and they join with the Nyakyusa in sacrifice to common ancestors at Lubaga and LiKyala (see Map III), but the Kinga culture is quite distinct from that of the Nyakyusa and Ngonde; we stayed long enough in Kinga country to convince ourselves that the Kinga live in kinship villages and not in age-villages, and that they differ from the Nyakyusa in many other respects.

There seems little doubt that the Nyakyusa and Ngonde people have been expanding in an area not uninhabited, but sparsely inhabited, and that the assimilation of the Penja and other groups now proceeding is no new phenomenon, but part of a process which has long been going on. Within recent years over 2,000

---

[1] The Nyakyusa as here defined numbered 159,044 in Rungwe district at the 1931 census, and 3,732 outside the district; the Ndali 22,834, the Lambya (within Rungwe district, and not including those in Nyasaland) 12,403, and the Kisi (in Njombe district) 2,115. *Tanganyika Territory, Census of the Native Population, 1931.*

[2] D. Kerr-Cross, 'Geographical Notes on the Country between Lakes Nyassa, Rukwa, and Tanganyika, *The Scottish Geographical Magazine*, Vol. VI (1890), p. 286; L. M. Fotheringham, *Adventures in Nyassaland* (1891), pp. 129-33. Nyondo was a Lambya chief, cf. Godfrey Wilson, op. cit., p. 10.

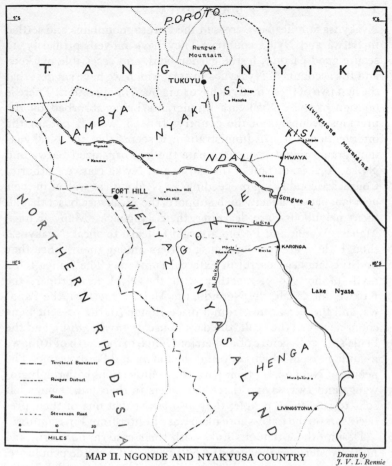

MAP II. NGONDE AND NYAKYUSA COUNTRY

Drawn by
J. V. L. Rennie

Nyakyusa families have crossed the Poroto mountains and settled in Safwa and Nyika country. They have moved, primarily, to secure good pasture, fertile garden land, and accessible markets; and the accounts of Nyakyusa history which we have suggest that the first two of these motives have long been in operation. There is no sign of these Nyakyusa immigrants being absorbed by the previous occupants of the country. Indeed, were it not for the intervention of the Administration, it seems that the Nyakyusa immigrants might soon dominate the less organized Safwa and Nyika. As it is, certain of the Safwa and Nyika Native Authority Courts are conducting proceedings in Nyakyusa as well as in their own languages,[1] a fact which supports the Nyakyusa boast that all their neighbours are learning their language. Many Kinga, Mahasi, Wanji, and Poroto are said to learn to speak Nyakyusa, though there are few Nyakyusa settlers among them, since they find the language useful in external contacts.[2] The Kinga tell a myth of how they, together with the Nyakyusa proper, the Kukwe, the Ndali, the Ngonde, the Mahasi, the Kisi, the Pangwa, and the Bena came from a place Ilongo (in the present Bena country) which they call 'the dark house' (*nyumba nditu*), and the Penja speak of a centre of dispersion, Kina, to the north of Rungwe mountain, from which they and the Safwa and Poroto came. The people of Ngonde, for their part, trace connections with the Inamwanga and Iwa, saying that their chiefs in their journeyings left sons to rule these people; they also assert that one of their predecessors on the Lake-shore plain was a hunter from Fipa country.[3]

Despite these tenuous links with their eastern, northern, and north-western neighbours, the Nyakyusa and Ngonde people are, as we have said, culturally quite distinct from them. The Nyakyusa themselves are emphatic that their culture differs from the cultures of the Kinga, the Safwa, the Poroto, and the Nyika—a statement which our own observation, and the evidence of other writers, confirm.[4] And the Ngonde differ in many respects both

[1] R. de Z. Hall, 'Local Migration in Tanganyika', *African Studies*, 4 (1945). 2,100 families had moved before 1938; 3,000 by 1941.

[2] This is despite the fact that Swahili is the official vernacular for Tanganyika, being the medium of instruction in Government primary schools, and the language used by the Administration.

[3] Godfrey Wilson, op. cit., p. 10.

[4] E. Kootz-Kretschmer, *Die Safwa* (1926); J. Thomson, *To the Central African Lakes and Back* (1881), Vol. I, pp. 46–52; R. de Z. Hall, op. cit.; D. Kerr-Cross, op. cit.

from the Inamwanga and Iwa to the north-west and the Henga to
the south. The affinities of the Inamwanga and Iwa appear to be
with the Mambwe,[1] while the Henga are an offshoot of the Tumbuka-Kamanga people who took refuge from the Ngoni in
Ngonde.[2] Of the Phoka who live high up in the hills south-west
of Ngonde we know almost nothing, except that they are skilled
cultivators, and their language is closely related to Tumbuka.

The cultural group consisting of the Nyakyusa and Ngonde
people, together with small groups in Rungwe district and
Ngonde largely absorbed by them, and including the Nyakyusa
immigrants in Mbeya district, probably numbers about a quarter
of a million.

Of the more distant cultural affinities of this group we know
nothing: there are no consistent similarities in culture between it
and any other known group. The elaborate age-organization, and
the great ceremony of handing over secular power to the next
generation, which is held every thirty years or so, suggest East
African connections, while the girls' puberty and marriage ceremony (*ubusungu*) is in many ways similar to the *cisungu* ceremony
of the Bemba;[3] and the witchcraft beliefs are like those of the
Azande[4] and the Lovale.[5]

b. Environment and economy

The Nyakyusa-Ngonde country is fertile, well watered and, to
European eyes, spectacularly beautiful, with its arc of high mountains and sparkling lakes. The Nyakyusa valley forms part of the

[1] F. F. R. Boileau and L. A. Wallace, 'The Nyasa-Tanganyika Plateau', *The
Geographical Journal*, Vol. XIII (1899); J. C. C. Coxhead, 'The Native Tribes
of North-Eastern Rhodesia, their Laws and Customs', *Royal Anthropological
Institute, Occasional Paper*, No. 5, 1914; C. Goldsbury and H. Sheane, *The
Great Plateau of Northern Rhodesia* (1911).

[2] F. D. Lugard, *The Rise of our East African Empire* (1893), Vol. I, p. 52;
M. Sanderson, 'Some Marriage Customs of the WaHenga, Nyasaland', *Journal
of the African Society*, Vol. XXII (1922-3); T. Cullen Young, 'The WaHenga
of North Nyasaland', *Journal of the African Society*, Vol. XXIII (1923-4);
'Tribal Intermixture in Northern Nyasaland', *J.R.A.I.*, Vol. LXIII (1933);
'Habits and Customs of the Olden Days among the Tumbuka-Kamanga
People', *Bantu Studies*, Vol. X (1936).

[3] A. I. Richards, *Bemba Marriage and Present Economic Conditions*, Rhodes-
Livingstone Papers, No. 4. (1940).

[4] E. E. Evans-Pritchard, *Witchcraft, Oracles and Magic among the Azande*
(1937).

[5] C. M. N. White, 'Witchcraft, Divination and Magic among the Balovale
Tribes', *Africa*, Vol. XVIII (1948), pp. 81-104.

Great Rift valley, walled in on the east by the Livingstone mountains, which rise to 10,000 feet, and on the west by the rather lower Ndali hills. It is blocked to the north-west by Rungwe volcano and the Poroto mountains; the volcano rises from the floor of the Rift to nearly 10,000 feet, and the lowest pass over the Poroto mountains is 8,000 feet. Scattered throughout the hills are a number of small lakes formed in the craters of old volcanoes, each one like a jewel set in the green of field and pasture.

The rainfall in this valley is very heavy, averaging over 100 inches in the year, and innumerable streams rush down the mountain slopes, flooding parts of the plain during the torrential rains of March and April. The dry season is short—it scarcely exists in the hills—and such a rainfall, combined with skilful cultivation and stock-breeding, makes a large population possible. The average density for Rungwe district is over eighty persons to the square mile; the population is most concentrated on the Lakeshore plain, but stretches up into the hills to 6,000 feet. South of the Songwe the rainfall is much less—at Karonga it averages only 45 inches a year—and the country supports a smaller population, the average density for Ngonde being less than fifteen persons to the square mile.

The Nyakyusa grow a variety of crops of which the chief are bananas and plantains, finger millet, maize, cow-peas, coco-yams, cassava, sweet potatoes, ground-nuts, curcurbits and, recently, rice and coffee. They also breed short-horned, humped, cattle which are carefully stalled at night, and hand-dressed to keep them free from ticks. Banana plantations stretch mile upon mile through the plain and along the crests of the ridges.[1] In them are hidden the villages, often so close together that the boundaries between them are not obvious. On the fringes of the bananas are the tilled fields, and beyond the fields the open pasture land. Unlike most of their neighbours in Central Africa the Nyakyusa practise fixed, not shifting, cultivation, and the land is kept in good heart by green manuring, rotation of crops, and periodic fallows.[2] Only in the cultivation of finger millet, cow-peas, and pumpkins,

[1] J. F. Elton, *The Lakes and Mountains of Eastern and Central Africa* (1879), pp. 330-1, and D. Kerr-Cross, op. cit., pp. 285-6, comment on their great extent.
[2] According to the Nyakyusa themselves the productivity of their fields is slowly diminishing. Most of them attribute this to the neglect of traditional rituals. We do not know how far their observations are objective, and how far they are biased by the tendency to glorify the past. D. H. Thwaites, in his article

planted at the break of the rains, and of the new crop, rice, is a seed-bed of ash prepared, and then it is grass and scrub which is burned; they do not fell or pollard trees to provide ash. For other crops there is no burning; the weeds are hoed in green instead; and, at a second hoeing before planting, the earth is piled into ridges or mounds to ensure drainage. Formerly, it is said, the chiefs insisted that the ridges on slopes should be made contour-wise, and recently this law has been revived. Elton, the first European to travel through the area, observed that there was 'terraced cultivation everywhere';[1] and the ridges do in fact look like terracing from a distance.

Hoeing is the work of men and boys; only quite recently have a few women, whose husbands are away in European employment, begun to hoe for themselves. And most men hoe for three or four hours a day during the greater part of the year, for crops are planted in succession. Neither old age nor high status excuses a man from this duty. Even the chief Mwaipopo, who was already grown up when the Europeans arrived in his country, hoed regularly in his fields during the years 1935–8. Iron hoes were made by Nyakyusa smiths from iron obtained from the Kinga,[2] but they were scarce, and some men had to use wooden hoes such as many of the women still have for weeding (*vide* Plate VII). The women are solely responsible for sowing, weeding, and reaping.

Cattle are fairly numerous:[3] few men over twenty-five nowa-days own none, and many older men have four or five cows in their stalls. Long ago, we were told, cattle were scarcer, some men having to marry without them, but Cotterill (1876)[4] and Kerr-Cross (1890)[5] both said 'cattle abound' in Nyakyusa coun-

---

on 'Wanyakyusa Agriculture' (*The East African Agricultural Journal*, April 1944), states that 'though the soil is not being eroded to any great extent it is still being impoverished'.

[1] Elton, op. cit., pp. 326, 330.

[2] Thomson, op. cit., Vol. I, pp. 272–3. Possibly iron was also obtained from the west. Kerr Cross (op. cit. p. 289) saw large foundries in Nyika country before 1890. cf. Elton, op. cit., p. 321 and map at the end.

[3] No census of the cattle in the district had been taken when we were among the Nyakyusa. D. H. Thwaites, op. cit., states that, 'The number of cattle in the district (Rungwe) in the 1941 census was about 2.3 head per taxpayer or 55 head per square mile'.

[4] H. B. Cotterill, 'On the Nyasa and a Journey from the North End to Zanzibar', *Proceedings of the Royal Geographical Society*, Vol. XXII (1878).

[5] D. Kerr-Cross, 'Crater-lakes north of Lake Nyassa', *The Geographical Journal*, Vol. V (1895), p. 119.

try, and Lugard speaks of 'enormous herds' in 1888[1] which a rinderpest epidemic decimated in 1892.[2] A few Kukwe keep one or two sheep, but we saw no goats at all in Rungwe district,[3] and neither sheep nor goats figure in ritual: cattle and fowls provide flesh for sacrifice. Every woman keeps fowls, as every man seeks to own cattle.

With curds and meat from their cattle, with fowls, fish, bananas, grain, pulses, roots and curcurbits, as well as bean tops and pumpkin tops, and—less generally—fruit, the Nyakyusa are exceptionally well fed. Since the dry season is so short and two crops of maize and pulses are grown in the year, there are no 'hunger months' such as the Bemba and many other African peoples experience. Shortages and famine occur, but rarely. All the early travellers comment on the quantities of food available in Nyakyusa country.[4]

c. Relations with the outside world

Perhaps the most significant fact in the history of the Nyakyusa is their long isolation, which is mainly the result of their geographical position. Surrounded on three sides by high mountains, and on the fourth by the stormy head waters of the Lake,[5] the district was largely cut off from the outside world. Slave caravans passed to the north, the west, and the south, but never through Nyakyusa country; and though they were repeatedly attacked by the Sangu, who are said to have raided as far as the Nyasa plain,[6] and several times by the Ngoni, the Nyakyusa repulsed both peoples. Certain of the Kukwe chiefs were forced for a period to pay tribute to the Sangu chief, Merere; but according to their own account none did so for long, and some never paid at all. Kerr-Cross comments on the contrast before 1890 between the unfortified villages of the Nyakyusa and Ndali, and those of the Lambya and Nyika, who, living in open country and harried

---

[1] Lugard, op. cit., p. 131.

[2] H. H. Johnston, *British Central Africa* (1897), p. 430; D. Kerr-Cross, op. cit., p. 119.

[3] Fotheringham, *op. cit.*, pp. 1, 25, mentions goats in Ngonde.

[4] See especially, Thomson, op. cit., Vol. I, pp. 268, 274; Lugard, op. cit., Vol. I, p. 131.

[5] In 1946 a Lake steamer, the *Vipya*, sank in a storm near Karonga with heavy loss of life.

[6] Kerr Cross, op. cit., pp. 119–29.

by the Arabs and Bemba, built their huts within a stockade.[1] According to Thomson, the Nyakyusa were unaware even of the existence of Lake Tanganyika in 1879 and their more distant eastern neighbours, the Pangwa, Bena, and Hehe had no communication with them.[2]

Unlike the Nyakyusa, the people of Ngonde were trading with the coast long before the arrival of the Europeans, a fact which had a profound effect on their political institutions;[3] but even they did not suffer from the attacks of slavers until *after* Europeans were established in Karonga.

From the point of view of the Nyakyusa-Ngonde people the Europeans came just in time. It was the establishment of British control in Nyasaland which prevented the complete destruction of the people of Ngonde by the slavers, and it is likely that the Nyakyusa also were saved by European intervention, for the raids of Arab slavers and their Sangu allies were becoming serious in Kukwe country in 1889[4] before the German annexation.

The first Europeans known to have sighted Nyakyusa country were a party from the Livingstonia mission (then established at the south of Lake Nyasa) who circumnavigated the Lake in the mission steamer, the *Ilala*, in 1875. They anchored off the north shore but did not land.[5] Two years later, the same steamer sailed by two famous missionaries, Dr. Stewart (of Lovedale) and Dr. Laws (of Livingstonia), landed Frederick Elton, H.B.M. Consul at Mozambique, and a party near the Mbaka mouth.[6] Elton and his party travelled through Selya and Kukwe country to the fort of the Sangu chief, Merere, and thence started for the coast. Elton died on the road, but some of the others got through.[7] In 1879 Joseph Thomson (aged 20), alone with his carriers, travelled through Hehe and Bena country, crossed the Livingstone moun-

---

[1] D. Kerr-Cross, 'Geographical Notes on the Country between Lakes Nyassa, Rukwa, and Tanganyika', *The Scottish Geographical Magazine*, Vol. VI (1890), pp. 286-7; Fotheringham, op. cit., pp. 13-5; 269.

[2] Thomson, op. cit., pp. 248, 276.

[3] Godfrey Wilson, op. cit., *passim*.

[4] Fotheringham, op. cit., pp. 238-41, 288. The Sangu had previously been occupied in a prolonged war with the Hehe. cf. Elton, op. cit., p. 374; Thomson, op. cit., Vol. I, pp. 229-34.

[5] E. D. Young, 'On a recent Sojourn at Lake Nyassa', *Proceedings of the Royal Geographical Society*, Vol. XXI (1877), pp. 230-1.

[6] J. Stewart, 'The Second Circumnavigation of Lake Nyassa', *Proceedings of the Royal Geographical Society*, 1879, pp. 289-304.

[7] Elton, op. cit., pp. 318-44; Cotterill, op. cit.

tains to the north-east corner of Nyasa, and went on through Nyakyusa country to Lake Tanganyika.[1]

Despite the isolation of the Nyakyusa and their own fear of travelling in foreign chiefdoms, they were not inhospitable to these white strangers: Elton and all his party (some of whom were delayed by illness and travelled separately), and later Thomson, walked up the Nyakyusa valley in safety though it was 'teaming with armed warriors', who carried 'most cruel-looking spears'. Elton remarks that 'the people of Konde, though not unfriendly, are passively obstructive, and being in want of nothing are disinclined to render any services whatsoever to strangers'.[2] But Thomson appears to have been on the best of terms with the Nyakyusa he met. The Kukwe fled from their villages at Thomson's approach, but were usually persuaded to return.[3]

After these journeys of discovery, mission work and trade developed quickly. The African Lakes Corporation, a company formed to develop legitimate trade in Central Africa as a means of combating the slave trade, established a station at Karonga; and a road was surveyed from Karonga through to Lake Tanganyika.[4] Out-stations of the Livingstonia mission were set up at Chirenji (Mwini Wanda) in the hills north-west of Karonga, and at Kararamuka near Tukuyu.[5] Meantime, an Arab slaver, Mlozi, had settled in Ngonde, and a protracted struggle ensued between him and his Henga allies on the one side, and the people of Ngonde and the Europeans on the other, during which many Ngonde were enslaved or killed and their villages destroyed. Five thousand Nyakyusa spearmen came to the aid of the Europeans but, being more concerned with loot than with the defeat of the Arabs, they returned home with the goods they had taken instead of pursuing Mlozi and his men when they had the chance to do so.[6] Lord (then Captain) Lugard was for some months in command of the exiguous European force and its allies, and nearly

---

[1] Thomson, op. cit., Vol. I, pp. 260-86.

[2] Elton, op. cit., p. 332.

[3] Thomson, op. cit., Vol. I, pp. 281-2.

[4] Fotheringham, op. cit.; F. L. M. Moir, *After Livingstone* (1923).

[5] D. Kerr-Cross, 'Geographical Notes on the Country between Lakes Nyassa, Rukwa, and Tanganyika', *Scottish Geographical Magazine*, Vol. VI, 1890, pp. 281-93.

[6] Fotheringham, op. cit., pp. 117-23.

died of wounds and fever. Because the Europeans lacked arms
the war dragged on,[1] and the power of the slavers was finally
broken only in 1895, when Sir Harry Johnston came up the Lake
with a well-armed force.[2]

German missionaries of the Berlin and Moravian missions
arrived in 1891, and established themselves at a number of
stations in Nyakyusa country.[3] The Songwe had by that time
been agreed upon as the boundary between Nyasaland and German East Africa, and the German administration followed hard
on the heels of the missionaries.[4] Twenty years later war broke
out between England and Germany; there was fighting throughout Rungwe district, and many Nyakyusa were impressed as
carriers. The absorption of the Nyakyusa into a world society
was considerably accelerated by war.

d. The form of Nyakyusa society

Not only was the Nyakyusa valley long isolated from the outside world, but it was divided into a number of small, independent chiefdoms, whose members had few dealings with people
beyond their own chiefdoms and those immediately adjoining.
Each family produced for its own needs, so that trade was the
merest trickle; and marriage outside the boundaries of the chiefdom was discouraged, since beyond the jurisdiction of one's own
chief there was no security for life and property. A plea against a
man of a neighbouring chiefdom might not be heard by the
defendant's chief. Nyakyusa men enlarged to us on the dangers
and difficulties of travelling even twenty miles from home,
before the coming of the Europeans; a journey from Selya to
Tukuyu (twenty-five miles) was said to take three days, because
travellers had to seek cover so often.

The number and size of chiefdoms varied; for a continuous
process of splitting, together with periodical conquest and re-
absorption, was going on and, as we have seen, the area of Nyakyusa occupation was expanding. In 1938 the Nyakyusa themselves

---

[1] Lugard, op. cit., Vol. I, pp. 51–167.
[2] H. H. Johnston, British Central Africa (1897), p. 143.
[3] A. Merensky, Deutsche Arbeit am Njassa (1894); J. T. Hamilton, Twenty Years
of Pioneer Missions in Nyasaland (1912).
[4] F. Fülleborn, Deutsch Ost-Afrika, Band IX (1906).

recognized over 100 chiefdoms, mustering anything from 100 to 3,000 adult men apiece.

Although no centralized political authority existed before the German occupation, certain groups of chiefdoms joined in common rituals directed to common ancestors. We traced four such centres of worship among the Nyakyusa; the most important being Lubaga, in the middle of the valley, where Kinga priests (from the top of the Livingstone mountains) join with many Nyakyusa chiefdoms in sacrifice to Lwembe, who is claimed as the ancestor both of the chiefs of the Nyakyusa proper, and of the Kinga. At LiKyala, on the Lake-shore plain, Kinga also join in sacrifice with the surrounding Nyakyusa chiefdoms. In Ngonde the chief connected with a similar centre of worship, Mbande, developed far-reaching secular as well as religious powers; and by the time the Europeans arrived he was established as a paramount chief with the title of the Kyungu. This development was directly connected with the fact that Ngonde traded with the outside world, and that their Kyungu, through his control of ivory, was able also to control the guns and cloth which came into the country:[1] the Nyakyusa, remaining isolated, remained politically disunited.

Besides sacrificing to a distant ancestor in company with the representatives of a large group of chiefdoms, two or more chiefs who are neighbours participate in a sacrifice at the grove in which their common father, or grandfather, is buried. Thus common worship links both large groups of chiefdoms, whose chiefs are more or less distantly related, and small groups of contiguous chiefdoms whose chiefs are close kinsmen. The sacrifices made are to the chiefs of immediately preceding generations, and to certain great heroes of the distant past, such as Lwembe and Kyala.

All these sacrifices are believed to bring rain and fertility, for the well-being of each chiefdom is thought to be bound up with the health of the chief and the goodwill of his ancestors.

The Nyakyusa are all agreed that their chiefs, *abanyafyale*, are 'strangers' who came down from the Livingstone mountains eight or ten generations ago, and found the valley already occupied by people who had no knowledge of fire, but ate their food raw. The chiefs brought fire with them—some say, cattle also;

[1] Godfrey Wilson, op. cit., pp. 9, 39-48.

and by virtue of this great benefit were accepted as chiefs. Such is the myth (*vide infra*, p. 26). It is remembered that the chiefs of different groups such as the Nyakyusa proper, the Kukwe, the Lugulu, and the Saku arrived at different times, but of the proportion of the immigrants to the former occupants, and of the proportion of men to women in the invading groups, we learnt nothing. Some suggest that the chiefs were lighter in colour than the previous inhabitants of the valley,[1] and the term *abatitu*, 'black people', is used for commoners as contrasted with chiefs. But chiefs intermarry freely with commoners and there is no observable difference in physical type between them and their people to-day. The Nyakyusa are without a clan system, and though kinship with a chief may be remembered for three (or perhaps even four) generations, the body of 'kinsmen of the chief' is not defined as it is in tribes which have a 'royal clan' like the Bemba or Pondo. Moreover, among the Nyakyusa the chief's advisers are never his kinsmen, but commoners. Sons or grandsons of a chief are ineligible as village headmen, who are the counsellors of the chief, and who had in the past very great control over him. The contrast is made between chiefs, *abanyafyale*, on the one hand, and commoners, *amafumu*, on the other, and the leaders of villages, chosen each generation by their predecessors (*vide infra*, p. 23), are the *amafumu par excellence*.[2] Words from this -*fumu* root mean 'chief' in various central Bantu languages (Bemba, Tumbuka, Nyanja); and it is tempting to suppose that the *amafumu* were the old chiefs conquered by the invading *abanyafyale*, but that is only a supposition. The important point for the contemporary social structure is that the village leaders are *commoners*; that their position is not hereditary, since they are selected afresh each generation; and that formerly they had very great power over the chief. This power has diminished considerably with the development of European administration. The Nyakyusa, indeed, were astounded to be told that the British

[1] cf. Godfrey Wilson, op. cit., p. 10 (footnote).

[2] For this reason *ulifumu* was translated by Godfrey Wilson as 'great commoner', in 'An Introduction to Nyakyusa Society', *Bantu Studies*, Vol. X (1936), and other papers, but this translation has considerable difficulties, and I have preferred to translate *ulifumu* as 'village headman' in the contexts in which it means the leader of the village, and 'commoner' or 'villager' in other contexts. It must be clearly understood that 'village headman' as used in this book means something quite different from 'headman' as used by the Administration (*vide infra*, p. 258).

constitution (about which they asked many questions) was a democratic one; for, they said, the Administration always supported the chiefs against the commoners.

The villages to which commoner leaders are appointed differ from all other Bantu villages of which we have knowledge in that they consist of groups of age-mates, not groups of kinsmen; boys build with contemporaries and remain with them through life; girls join the villages of their husbands at marriage; therefore relatives, other than husband and wife and young children, do not live together. Nevertheless kinship ties are important, for property circulates within the kinship group rather than within the village, and kinsmen are believed to be mystically interdependent, in a way in which fellow villagers are not. The most prized possession of the Nyakyusa are cattle, for cattle enable a man to marry, to live in comfort, to gain prestige by feasting his friends; and cattle pass along the roads of kinship. They pass between brothers, and half-brothers, and the sons of brothers; between fathers and sons; and between affines. Kinsmen also participate in common rituals, praying to common ancestors, and seeking protection from mystical dangers which are thought to travel, like cattle, along the roads of kinship. Ever fearful lest a quarrel among them should bring misfortune on all, they strive to live in harmony.

The range of kinship recognized varies somewhat with the status of the family concerned and the proximity and personalities of its members, but, generally speaking, economic and religious co-operation link the descendants of a common grandfather, and marriage between the descendants of a common great-grandfather is excluded. A legal marriage is effected by the passage of cattle from the groom's group to the bride's, and it is this passage which is said to create kinship (*ubukamu*), with the consequent mystical interdependence, between a man and his wife, and between the one partner in a marriage and the close kinsmen of the other. Polygyny is the ideal of every pagan, and it is made possible by the ten years' difference in the average marriage age of men and women. Girls are betrothed very young and finally join their husbands at puberty, while few pagan men marry under twenty-five. Inherited cattle are controlled by the older generation and polygyny is the prerogative of age. For property passes not directly from father to son, but from brother to brother, through each group of full brothers, until, when the last full brother is dead, and the son of the eldest is an adult, the family stock comes to him. Thus few men under forty (other than chiefs) have more than one wife. Of 3,000 tax-payers (presumed to be 18 years and over) in Selya, 34 per cent were bachelors, 37 per cent monogamists, and 29 per cent polygynists. Plural marriages breed wealth, for the polygynist is likely to command the labour of many sons as well as several wives, and in due course he expects to receive the marriage cattle of many daughters.

Social status turns primarily on age, sex, and the control and distribution of wealth. As we have seen, the position of a chief is hereditary, but kinship with a chief does not carry office, nor are the kinsmen of chiefs conspicuously wealthy. Every man in turn hopes to control the property attaching to the house into which he was born, and all who live long enough do so. But there is a delayed right of primogeniture, for the senior son of a senior son inherits the bulk of the family stock when it passes to his generation, and the eldest of each group of full brothers has a special claim to the cattle coming in from the marriages of his sisters.

Seniority, whether within the context of the lineage, or of the hierarchy of age-villages, is something respected in itself, but wealth carries authority and prestige only in so far as it is used generously, in hospitality: one man is great and distinguished (*nsisya*) because he feeds people, another of little account because he is poor or mean.

Women occupy a position very subordinate to men in Nyakyusa society. They play no part in public life, except in so far as the two great wives of a chief, and the first wife of a village headman co-operate with their husbands in rituals; and in the relationship of husband and wife, as well as in that of father and daughter, a woman is expected to show obedience and respect. Her deference is expressed conventionally in her crouching to greet men (*vide* Plate IX), and in her use of the submissive *taa* ('Yes, my lord') when addressed by them. Having no great chiefs and little regard for rank, Nyakyusa men show no trace of subservience in their manner to each other, but they expect a meek compliance from all women. The only relationships with a male in which a woman may in some measure assert herself are those which she has with a brother, and with a brother's sons. Leader-

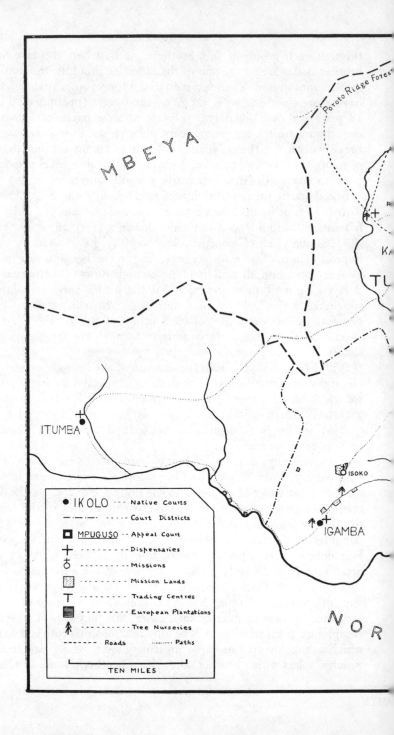

MBEYA

Poroto Ridge Forest

KA

TU

ITUMEA

IKOLO ···· Native Courts
—·—·— ····· Court Districts
☐ MPUGUSO ·· Appeal Court
✝ ·········· Dispensaries
⚲ ·········· Missions
▦ ·········· Mission Lands
T ·········· Trading Centres
▦ ·········· European Plantations
↟ ·········· Tree Nurseries
------- Roads   ········ Paths

TEN MILES

ISOKO

IGAMBA

NOR

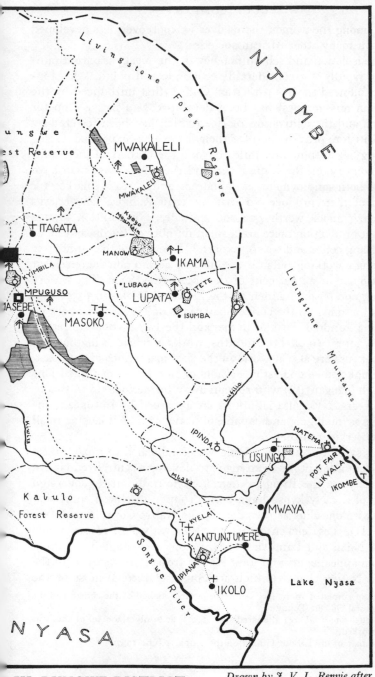

III. RUNGWE DISTRICT

Drawn by J. V. L. Rennie after R. de Z. Hall and G. D. Archer

ship among the women themselves is, moreover, less developed than in many other African societies.

The isolation and self-sufficiency of the Nyakyusa are diminishing rapidly, for considerable economic and political development followed the 1914–18 war. Coffee (first introduced by the German missionaries) has been developed as a native crop for export, and the cultivation of rice (which had been fostered by the British to provide food for their troops) has expanded. Gold-digging began some fifty miles beyond the borders of the Nyakyusa country, on the Lupa river, and there Nyakyusa men have found both employment as labourers and a ready market for much of their produce, so that by 1936 Rungwe district was exporting goods worth £24,000 annually.[1] In addition to this peasant production there are a small number of European estates producing coffee and tea for export.[2] We estimate the number of Nyakyusa working outside the district as migrant labourers at about 8,000 or 25 per cent of the able-bodied men. There were about 7,000 Nyakyusa men on the Lupa gold-fields in 1937,[3] and a small number on the coffee plantations of Mbozi. These are all within a hundred miles of home; and the Lupa labourers return usually after two or three months' work. A considerable number of Nyakyusa are also at work on the sisal plantations of the coast, and employed as domestic servants or in other semi-skilled jobs through Tanganyika, who remain away for periods up to two or three years. Nyakyusa labourers are regarded by European employers as intelligent and capable of heavy work, but lacking in all the subservient virtues.

The system of Indirect Rule was established in 1926, and a consistent attempt has been made to develop a centralized Native Authority for the Rungwe district. The traditionally sovereign chiefs of the Nyakyusa have been grouped in eleven court districts with one chief as president of the Native Court in each (see Map III); these eleven chiefs, together with the two presidents of the Ndali and Lambya courts, belong to a single federation, with an appeal court and joint Native treasury of its own. In the eleven Native Courts (which are courts of record) most of the

---

[1] Figure estimated on the basis of information supplied by the courtesy of the Agricultural Officer, Tukuyu.

[2] In 1938 the total area alienated was 26,c ac.; only 2,200 ac. of this was being worked.

[3] Estimate of the Labour Officer on th᷅ upa, 4 June 1937.

traditionally sovereign chiefs are entitled to sit with their village headmen, and assist the president and his village headmen in the hearing of cases. Much of the legal business previously transacted by each chief in his own country is now taken to court (*KwiKoroti*); but the power of village headmen to settle disputes by arbitration in their separate villages is still the basis of the legal system.

Though the Administration has worked through the traditional authorities it has consciously and deliberately modified the traditional system; and, as part of its policy of development, it has established schools, dispensaries, and nurseries for coffee-seedlings and other plants. There are three schools in Rungwe district receiving Government grants: one directly under the Administration, one under the Native Authority, and one a mission school. There are also a great number of 'bush schools', that is, mission village schools under uncertificated teachers giving instruction in the three R's and in religion. Over 19,000 children (12·6 per cent of the population served) are enrolled in the various schools; but 96 per cent of these are in 'bush schools', many of whom never learn even to read and write.

The structure of Nyakyusa society has been further complicated by the conversion of a substantial minority (16 per cent in 1938)[1] of the people to Christianity. The Christians form a group with values radically different from those of the pagans, on whom they react in innumerable ways.[2] The growth of this diversity in the society is a direct effect of its diminishing isolation.

To treat of Nyakyusa villages as if missions, or the Administration, or migrant labour and coffee export did not exist would simplify, but distort our analysis. We have therefore included some account of the differences in behaviour between pagan and Christian, of the effects of centralization on the position of village headmen, and of the influence of trade and migration on economic co-operation in the village. A discussion of the organization of schools and Christian congregations; of the development of courts of record, and 'court districts'; of the relation between

---

[1] Calculated from figures supplied by the courtesy of the missions and the independent African Churches working in the district.

[2] Moslems are very few and they have little influence on the community as a whole. These few are mostly Swahili traders, Ngoni settlers, or soldiers of the K.A.R. from Nyasaland. We heard of only two or three Nyakyusa who had turned Moslem.

chiefs and the Administration, and between Nyakyusa workers and their employers, falls outside the scope of this book.

e. . The subject of study

Nyakyusa society may be viewed as three circles of relationship —the relationships of kinship, village relationships, and relationships within and beyond the chiefdoms. This book is concerned with the second of these circles, that found within and between villages. Such relationships are not fully intelligible apart from the relationships of kinship and of the chiefdom, but a measure of abstraction is necessary—it is not possible to talk about everything at once. A sketch of kinship relationships has already been published;[1] a full account of them and of the relationships of chiefdoms has been planned; and the general theoretical approach has been set forth in *The Analysis of Social Change*[2] and in a paper entitled *Some Possibilities and Limitations of Anthropological Research*.[3]

The fundamental question we pose is *why age-villages?* Why should the Nyakyusa differ from all their neighbours of whom we have knowledge in the form of their villages? Why should they live with contemporaries, rather than kinsmen? The attempt to answer this leads us to discuss the characteristics of Nyakyusa society, which can be shown to be associated with the age-village organization, so that we can reformulate the question thus: *What are the pecularities of Nyakyusa society not found in neighbouring societies with kinship villages?* We know too little about the neighbouring societies to answer this question fully, but some indication of the Nyakyusa peculiarities is given, and an analysis of these compels us to consider the relation between Nyakyusa values and social structure.

[1] Monica Wilson, 'Nyakyusa Kinship' in *African Systems of Kinship and Marriage*, edited by A. R. Radcliffe-Brown and Daryll Forde, 1950.
[2] G. and M. Wilson, 1945.
[3] Monica Wilson, 1948.

I. CULTIVATION IN NYAKYUSA COUNTRY

In the foreground are bananas, coffee, and bamboos; in the middle ridges for sweet potatoes and mounds for maize. On the extreme right Rungwe volcano appears. The house is a modern style, and raised for drainage.

II. THE GENESIS OF A VILLAGE

Boys' huts built on the edge of their fathers' village

CHAPTER II

VILLAGE ORGANIZATION

NYAKYUSA villages (*ifipanga*)[1] are formed by groups of boys or men, all roughly of the same age, together with the wives and young children of those who are married. Women belong to the villages of their husbands, young children to those of their fathers. Girls live at home until they are betrothed, after which they visit their future husbands periodically, and soon after puberty each joins her husband in his village. Boys, who marry later in life, leave home at about the age of ten or eleven and set up villages of their own.

a. The genesis of the village

Between the ages of about six and eleven boys sleep at their fathers' houses and herd their fathers' cattle. This is a full-time, if not a very arduous, occupation. The cattle are driven out about an hour or two after sunrise and return to be milked about 1 p.m.; after an hour they are again driven out and do not come back until sunset. The cattle of a group of neighbours, usually five to ten,[2] are herded together by their young sons; and so these boys spend all day together for several years of their lives. This group of boys is the germ of the future age-village; it is a community with a common activity in the herding of the cattle, with a leader and laws and customs of its own.[3]

When the boys reach the age of ten or eleven, two important changes usually take place in their lives. Firstly, they leave the herding of cows to their younger brothers, and themselves begin the business of hoeing the fields which will occupy them until they die; secondly, they no longer sleep in the houses of their fathers but join an age-village of boys. Nowadays the two changes usually, but not always, take place at the same time, and well before puberty.

---

[1] cf. Xhosa *intanga*, 'a company of persons or animals of equal age'.

[2] The herd group is smaller in young men's villages where few are cattle-owners, and a very rich man occasionally herds his cattle alone.

[3] G. and M. Wilson, *The Analysis of Social Change*, pp. 51–3.

Before the establishment of peace by European authority, however, cattle were commonly herded by young men, armed, and
only the calves were entrusted to boys, who herded them near
the homesteads; therefore moving to a boys' village did not coincide with the change of occupation. Even to-day it is not uncommon for some boys who have reached puberty to be found
herding cattle. One we knew herded his father's cattle although
he had reached puberty, because he had no younger brothers old
enough to take over, and there were only five or six boys in his
herd-group altogether. There are also cases where special circumstances put the age of moving later. In one age-village the boys
leave home a little later than usual because there are leopards
about and it is dangerous for small boys to walk from the village
of their fathers to that of the boys, after dark.

When a number of the sons of a village of married men have
reached the right age, their fathers give hem a piece of land to
one side of the parent village on which to build. There they build
little huts of reeds for themselves, sufficiently well thatched to
keep out the heavy rain, and there they sleep (*vide* Plate II). The
building of the huts on this land begins in a playful manner,
before the boys move. While they are still herding cows and
sleeping at home they build miniature huts there in their spare
time, but do not sleep in them. When they move they build
slightly more substantial huts with better thatch. At the beginning, when a group of boys starts a new village, or when boys join
one already formed, they do not all have huts for themselves:
two or three friends share a hut. But later, as they grow older,
each builds for himself.

Until he marries each boy hoes his father's fields in his father's
village and eats food cooked by his own mother at his father's
house, but he sleeps with his friends. Thus between the time
when he leaves home and his marriage each is a member of two
villages: economically he still belongs to that of his father;
socially to that of his own contemporaries. Though bachelors eat
at their parents' home, it is very rarely that they do not eat in the
company of their own friends. A bachelor does not simply go
home to eat by himself, but a group of bachelors, friends living
in the same boys' village, go round together eating at the house
of each one's mother in turn.

In an age-village of married men there are always several

different herds of cattle; and it is not only those from the same group of herd-boys that set up a new village together, but all the sons of the age-village. Thus when a boy leaves the herd group he joins a larger community, including the friends of his own age who have herded cows with him, and many others as well. Every boys' village consists primarily of the sons of the member of an older village who originally gave the land for its building, but sons of other villages live there too.

The village begins with perhaps a dozen boys, and their younger brothers join them, one by one; but after some years, when the senior members of the boys' village are between sixteen and eighteen years old, the younger ones begin to be refused admittance to the village: 'they are children.' The young ones then either begin a new age-village of their own, or else join a village which has already been started by the sons of a nearby men's village a little junior to that of their own fathers. If you inquire who are the members of such and such a boys' village you are always told that they are the sons of a particular village of men, but detailed investigation reveals the presence of some sons of other men's villages as well. Brothers, half-brothers and other relatives are sometimes members of the same village, but more often not; and if they do belong to the same village that is because they are near each other in age, and were born in the same village, not because they are kinsmen.

The members of the older boys' village, which is now closed and no longer increases in numbers, begin to marry as they reach the age of about twenty-five. Getting married is often a gradual process; but it is not until he has his wife permanently with him that a young man can have fields of his own and eat the produce at his own place. The cultivation of land requires the co-operation of a man and woman, and cooking on any elaborate scale is a woman's business. As the young men marry their village expands. The site is not changed but the houses are built ever bigger and farther apart, and adjacent land is brought under cultivation. The boys' village with which we are best acquainted is in this transitional stage. It has fifty-three members altogether, the majority of whom are single; but some few are married, cultivate their own fields with their wives and eat food cooked by their wives in their own houses. Of those who are single some again are betrothed to girls who visit them from time to time, but each still cultivates his father's fields and eats at his father's home. In former days, we were told, the marriage age of men was even later than it is at present (*vide infra*, p. 80). 'Perhaps after twenty a boy would be betrothed, but to a young girl, and he would wait eight years before she grew up.'

From the time boys begin to herd they recognize one of their number as a leader. 'When we herd cows as boys', a friend told us, 'there is always one who is obeyed by his fellows whatever he says. No one chooses him, he gains his leadership and his prestige by bodily strength. For always, when we are boys together among the cows, we vie with one another and dispute about going to turn back straying cattle, or about fetching fire to cook the food we have brought with us. And so we start fighting, and we go on fighting until one of us beats all his fellows completely and so becomes the leader. And then it is he who sends others to turn back straying cattle, to fetch fire and to collect firewood. And he is greatly respected. He settles quarrels too. What we quarrel about most as boys is a particular insult: one says to another: "You are only a child, you are, I am your senior." This is always happening and then it is the part of the one who is leader to set those two on to fight. We all stand round and watch and the one who first cries is proved the child.'

Later, when the boys have built apart from their fathers, one of their number is often appointed by the headman of their fathers' village to settle disputes between them. Some boys' villages have no such appointed leader, but many of them do. Such appointments are, however, temporary. It is only when political authority is transferred to their generation that the young men's permanent leaders are chosen.

b. The 'coming out' ceremony

Eight or ten years after the young men of the senior boys' village of the chiefdom have begun to marry, their fathers hand over the government of the country to them. This transfer of authority is effected in an elaborate ceremony called the 'coming out' (*ubusoka*).

The 'coming out' is a series of legal acts by which the country of an old chief and his village headman (*amafumu*) is, with certain reservations, handed over into the possession and control of his two senior sons and their respective village headmen. These legal acts are accompanied by much pomp and ceremony. It is at once the initiation of all the youth of the chiefdom into public life, the constitution of two new political units and the proclamation of two new chiefs. It consists not only of a series of legal acts but of religious ritual as well, action being taken to increase the personal qualities appropriate in a chief and his village headmen by treatment with medicines.

The 'coming out' comprises six main events: firstly, the public recognition of a number of age-villages of young men, and the selection of headmen to lead them; secondly, the magical treatment of young chiefs and headmen to make them dignified and powerful; thirdly, the public recognition of the two young chiefs; fourthly, a cattle raid; fifthly, the establishment of the young age-villages on adequate land; and sixthly, the marriage of the young chiefs.

When the eldest sons of his contemporaries reach the age of about thirty-three to thirty-five years the old chief is approached by his village headmen who say: 'The sons have grown up, let us make the "coming out" for them.' After a period of delay, for he is unwilling to relinquish his own honour and power, the old chief agrees, and the 'coming out' takes place. He fears lest he may fall ill from 'the breath of men' should he delay too long (*vide infra*, p. 134). His two heirs, together with all the boys and young men, whether married or single, who arc sons of the old chief's contemporaries, are summoned to attend, according to their age-villages, at the old chief's principal house. When they arrive they wait there for several days, while the old village headmen discuss with their chief where to give the young men land, and whom they will select as headmen of the young villages. In many of the young village groups there are already leaders previously appointed by the village headmen of their fathers. If they have proved satisfactory their appointments are confirmed by the old village headmen; if not new ones are selected.

In selecting leaders of the young men's villages the old headmen look for men who are wealthy, who come from respected families, who have ability in judging cases, and are popular with their fellows; in the old days they looked also for courage and the ability to lead men in war. These qualities correspond to the village headman's functions. He should be hospitable to his neighbours, he judges their cases; he is their leader at ceremonies and in the old days he led them to war also. He represents their desires to the chief, and it is through him, and in consultation with him, that the chief gives orders. Besides this each headman (*ulifumu*) is believed to protect his own villagers from witchcraft, 'to watch over the country by night', to shield men and cattle from the spiritual forces of evil.[1] To fit them for this task, village headmen are treated with medicines at the 'coming out' to give them the power of seeing and fighting witches.

So important is this position of village headman that legal precautions are taken 'to prevent the village headman becoming a chief', as several informants have put it to us. It is illegal to choose a village headman from among the kinsmen of a chief, and it is illegal to elect the son of a village headman to that office in any age-village of his own contemporaries, though he may perhaps inherit the position in his father's village when his father dies.

To return to the 'coming out' ceremony: when the old men have made up their minds, one of them goes among the crowd of young men, and catches hold of those they have chosen in order of seniority: first the one who is to be leader of the senior village of the first son of the old chief, then the leader of the senior village of his second son, then the leader of the next senior village of the first son, and so on. There are commonly eight age-villages of young men; of these four will belong to the chiefdom of the first son, four to that of the second. The eight new village headmen are now publicly known, four in each new chiefdom.

The young chiefs, together with the senior headman of each, are then treated with medicines that they may be impressive (*nsisya*). From birth a chief undergoes periodical treatment to make him impressive (*nsisya*) 'that we commoners may tremble before him'. The treatment at the 'coming out' is directed towards the same end: 'We treat him, then he will be altogether a chief, men will respect him!' The village headmen now drink the

---

[1] The essential meaning of a word in one culture is often illuminated by the meaning of a word from the same stem among neighbouring people. In this connection it is significant that *ifumu* in Bemba and *mfumu* in Nyanja mean 'chief', but in Ankole *abafumu* means 'magicians' (including diviners) (*African Political Systems*, p. 145), and among the Sukuma *bafumu* is used in the same sense (*Africa*, Vol. XIX, p. 14). cf. H. H. Johnston, *A Comparative Study of the Bantu and Semi-Bantu Languages*, Vol. II, p. 270.

medicines of power for the first time, and these are thought to create or develop in them *amanga*, that is, the power of seeing and fighting witches (*vide infra*, pp. 96-102). To the senior headman of each young chief is handed a magic horn to attract people to the country. 'The horn is the luck of the chief that many people may come to build.' To each is given also a magic tail, which, it is believed, will enable him to dream of wars that are approaching and which, together with a magic spear, he carries into battle. 'The spear of the chieftainship is to fight battles with, it is manhood, strength.' The horn, the tail, and the spear are emblems of office handed on by the senior village headman of the old chief to the senior headmen of the young chiefs. They were treated periodically by a special doctor and a set was provided for each independent chiefdom at the coming out. The treatment of these emblems is now rarely undertaken—we were fortunate to see it once. The Nyakyusa say that since the country has been pacified, it has become unnecessary; its purpose was to secure success in war.

The next stage in the action is the one from which the whole institution takes its name: 'the coming out' (*ubusoka*). The two young chiefs are secluded for a few hours in the hut of the old chief's first wife, where they receive various forms of magical treatment, and when this is finished someone outside knocks at the door and cries 'Come out!' Then, to quote the words of a village headman who told us about his own 'coming out', 'The director of ceremonies said: "Get up!" The chiefs got up and came out (*basokile*)[1] of the house to us, and we, the crowd of young men, cried "Come on!" and welcomed them. Then we all ran shouting and calling the war cry towards the next chiefdom. In the old days we should have invaded that country to take cattle and to bring them back and eat them at the new huts which we build next. But that is finished now.' The senior headmen of the new chiefdom lead the charge, each grasping his war tail, his

---

[1] cf. the traditional Nyakyusa greeting (now archaic) '*Sokile!*' literally meaning 'You have come out (of the house)' i.e. 'Good morning!' This greeting was not confined to those who had been through the *ubusoka* ceremony.

A comparison of the meaning of the root in other Bantu languages is again suggestive. In Xhosa *ukusoka* means 'to install circumcised lads into manhood by giving them presents when they come out from their seclusion and are publicly acknowledged as men by the assembly of men' (Kropf, *A Kaffir English Dictionary*); *ubusoka* means bachelorhood, celibacy (of a circumcised man, not a boy).

spear, and magic horn. In this way the new chiefs are shown to their people.

Chiefs who are to be independent now separate, each moving off with his men to the place where the senior age-village of that chiefdom will eventually be built. All fire in the country is extinguished, even the fires in the homesteads of the old men, and in each of the new independent chiefdoms new fire is made, ceremonially, by the senior headman of the chiefdom and his fellow next in rank. One holds a lion-bone while the other twirls a medicated stick in a groove in the bone. The senior headman and his second each gives fire to the village headman immediately junior to him, and then the latter in turn to his immediate junior, until each of the headmen has fire. At this point the future division of each new chiefdom is foreshadowed, for the second senior headman in each new chiefdom is recognized as the leader of one side of the country. As each village headman lights his fire he calls: 'Come men of such and such a village to me!' and they take fire from him.

Since we are not primarily concerned with symbolism in this book we shall not enter at length into the interpretation of these events.[1] It must suffice to remind our readers of the Nyakyusa myth that their chiefs came down from the Livingstone mountains ten generations ago bringing fire with them, and that they found the previous inhabitants of the valley, who became their subjects, without fire, and eating their food raw. The extinguishing of the old fires and lighting of new is interpreted by the Nyakyusa as a symbol of the new chieftainship. A chief with whom we were well acquainted explained it thus: 'The fire is the fire of lordship (*umoto botwa*). The old chieftainship is coming to an end, the new has come. They extinguish the fires in all the homes, those of the young men and those of the old men, then they make new fire which is taken to every home. For formerly Mwangamilo [the old chief] would have had little power [after the 'coming out'], Mwakyusa and Reubeni [his sons] would have ruled.' But why fire? we asked. 'Because of old,' they relate, we chiefs came with fire, the commoners had not yet got it, they ate raw food only. When we came we slept in men's houses and we made fire and cooked food. Men were astonished, and said:

---

[1] A full analysis of the symbolism of one ritual necessitates a comparison of all the rituals of the society, which will be made in another book.

"Ha! what's this?" They were burned; so they said: "These are chiefs because they brought this fire." It is this they remember, even to-day. . . .' And another informant explained: 'The fire means (*kukuti*) that a new chief has come, he brings fire, we throw away the old fire in the house.'

Having lighted their fires the young men cut bamboos and build temporary shelters for themselves, making one or more huts according to their numbers. It is forbidden for them to sleep in old huts, nor may they build on the site on which they lived as boys. Usually their first huts are on what was formerly pasture land, and later their fathers move aside to make room for the new generation. On the new site the two senior headmen of the new chief, together with a doctor, plant with magical ritual two branches of a *ficus* (known in Nyakyusa as *iliyabe*)—a species which is important economically since the bark of saplings provides the traditional dress of Nyakyusa women. These trees, known as *ulupando* and *umpandapanda*, are planted where the future boundary will run between the two halves of the young chief's country, and the senior headman (who is leader of the senior half of the country) builds his house near where the *ulupando* has been planted. He and his colleague, together with the doctor, proceed, after planting the trees, to set up the hearth-stones of his hut. Again magic is performed. Nyakyusa informants were not agreed as to the symbolism of these trees, as they were about the symbolism of the new fire. The root *ukupanda* means to plant a crop, or to set up, or establish the hearth-stones of a house; it is used also for establishing, or treating, with medicines. Some informants interpreted the *ulupando* as the chief and *umpandapanda* as his wife, saying:'We are planting the chief and his wife.' Others said that the two trees represented the two senior headmen of the country, another that they represented the chief's two senior wives. What is certain is that *ulupando* is regarded as more important than *umpandapanda* and that both are taboo. No one may cut the trees. If anyone breaks the taboo it is believed that lions and leopards (closely associated with chiefs) will roar at night, and treatment by a doctor will be necessary to still them. It is also widely believed that the strength of the chief is associated with the growth of the trees. 'If these trees go dry the reign will not be successful, the chief will be defeated in war. If they flourish and grow the reign will be successful, the chief is a ruler.' It is relevant to add that cuttings of this tree strike easily in the soil and climate of Nyakyusa country. When a chief dies he is buried beside his trees, and gradually a thicket—a sacred grove—forms round them.

The young men spend much time feasting and dancing. Formerly not only did they raid cattle for food from neighbouring chiefdoms, but they also took cattle, milk, and bananas from their fathers' villages. And they still do the latter, for they say: 'We are now the owners of the country.' The milk and bananas are often sent by the old chief, but 'if the chief is stingy, they teach him a lesson by going and *taking* bananas, saying: "We are important people."' Great emphasis is laid on this right of the young men to take food: one group, the mates of the first heir of a senior chief, boasted to us: 'We came out with grandeur, we ate many men's cattle.'

After a month or two the members of each new village move off to build on a site of their own, and the wives of those who are married join them. Wives do not come to the first temporary shelters. The senior of the new villages remains on the site of the temporary shelters where fire was made, the ritual trees planted, and the hearth-stones of the senior headman established with magic. Gradually each member builds himself a permanent hut.

The old men move aside to make room for their sons. If land is short they may move on to the site on which a boys' village formerly was, or there may be other land available. Whatever the position, adequate land must be provided for the young men's villages. And, we were told, 'We old men are glad to move, we are glad our sons are so many and we leave the land to them.' Or again: 'The old men move because new fire has come; the young men have made themselves into new people, hence they cannot build on their old sites but on new ones. Perhaps the old men will succeed them, for they may build in the boys' village where their sons were, or if there is space they go elsewhere. But the old men rejoice greatly, for their sons have "come out".' Nevertheless there are sometimes disputes between villages of different generations regarding a particular site (*vide* Document, p. 188).

A few months after the 'coming out' each of the two young chiefs marries two wives. A young chief may be married already; but the two whom he now takes rank as his great wives (*abehe abakulumba*) and their eldest sons are his two heirs in the chieftainship. Young girls, daughters of neighbouring chiefs, are carried off with a show of force from their fathers' homes, by the young chief's men, who themselves later contribute to the herd of cows sent to regularize the position. The two great wives are thus married not solely with the cows of their husband, but also with those of the men whose sons their sons will one day rule. The duty of arranging the match lies with the village headmen of the old chief, and it is said that they are often guided in their choice by dreams.

The girls who are carried off are just about to reach puberty, and they stay at the house of one of the men of the old chief until their periods begin. When both have reached puberty they are initiated, not at their fathers' houses, as are ordinary girls, but in the country of their husband, and both together. At their initiation the old men and women of the country (contemporaries of the old retiring chief) play the part normally played by a girl's parents and their neighbours, while the young chief and his men take the usual part of a husband and his friends. And then, after the ceremonies are over, the two girls are given to the young chief as his wives. Houses are built for them separately, i.e. in the senior age-village of the new chiefdom for the first wife, in the next senior village for the second wife; and in this separation of dwelling place is already apparent the future division of the chiefdom between their sons.

Within the chiefdom, and among the wives and children of the chief two 'sides' (*imibafu*) are recognized. Usually, in each country there are, at its beginning, at least two age-villages and half the wives of the chief on either side. This distinction of two sides is important in succession, a son from each side eventually inheriting half the country.

From the time of the 'coming out' of the two young chiefs till the day of their own father's death there exists between him and them a delicate balance of prestige and power. Each of the three, traditionally, has judicial authority in his own age-villages, but appeals in difficult cases may be taken from either of the young chiefs and their village headmen to the old chief and his village headmen, while the religious duties of chieftainship are exercised entirely by the old chief. But in the old days it was the young chief who fought and fed men. 'Young chiefs used to lead their

men to funerals in other countries and start a fight, and raid
cattle. The old chief would say: "I am too old to lead people to
war and to funerals, and to feed men, I have no cattle, you have
the power to do these things now." It was the lusty young men
(*abatubwa*) who fought, not the old men.'

Formerly this transition period rarely lasted long, for the old
chief usually died shortly after the 'coming out' of his sons.
Success in war and probably also the fertility of the country were
believed to be dependent upon the virility of the chief. As one
informant put it: 'The old chiefs died because there was war: the
people would complain of an old chief saying: "He is too old,
when we fight we are beaten, he had better die. Perhaps the young
chief will help us." ' The old chief's death was commonly interpreted as due to 'the breath' (*vide infra*, p. 101) of his people who
loved his sons rather than himself, but we have evidence that
chiefs were sometimes ceremonially strangled by their village
headmen. Nowadays many chiefs survive for years after the
'coming out' of their sons, and relations between the generations
are consequently complicated, as we shall see later.

At the death of the old chief control of the villages of old men
passes to the two young chiefs and their village headmen, half to
each side. Village headmen of the old chief, relinquishing most of
their secular functions to their successors, enter upon new religious duties as priests in the sacrifices to the chief who has just
died, and this priesthood they hand on to their sons. The dead
chief's full brother is still the religious head of both chiefdoms,
but all the secular functions are now exercised by the young
chiefs, each in his own country. And the religious functions also
fall to them when all their father's full brothers are dead.

The 'coming out' ceremony has been described in some detail,
for it is the occasion when chiefdoms and villages are formally
established, and the future relations between them are made
clear. The splitting of the old chiefdom into two independent
halves; the division of every new chiefdom into two sides, each
under a senior headman; the boundaries, membership, and relations of the age-villages within each side—all are defined at this
ceremony. In the catching-hold of the village headmen, and in the
making of fire, the relative status of leaders and villages and the
membership of each village are shown. In the planting of the ritual
trees on the boundary between the two sides of the country, and

the establishment of the mother of an heir in each, the future division of the country is foreshadowed. Finally, it is the occasion on which power is formally handed over to the younger generation, and the success of the new headmen as war leaders is put to the test.

c. Relations between villages within one chiefdom

Within each chiefdom, then, there are two sides, each under a senior headman. On each side are two or more age-villages of contemporaries of the chief—men of the ruling generation. Attached to these villages are boys' villages made up of the younger brothers and sons of contemporaries of the chief. They live separately from their fathers and may have their own village leaders, but legally each boys' village is subject to the authority of the headman of its parent village. On each side there are also two or more villages of old men, contemporaries of the chief's father, whose headmen have ritual functions. Each village established at a 'coming out' ceremony has considerable autonomy under its own headman, but it is subject to the senior headman of the side it belongs to in two ways: cases not settled by a village headman go to the senior headman of the side, and a senior headman leads the villages of his side in war and communal hunts. Even villages of old men are subject to the authority of the senior headman of the ruling generation on the side of the country where they live. Boys and young men of the generation which had not yet 'come out' used to fight and hunt as village groups under the leadership of the senior headman (of their fathers' generation) on the side of the country to which they belonged. Whether or not each boys' village was also subject in war and chase, as in legal disputes, to the authority of the headman of its parent village is not clear. Certainly each boys' village formed a defined segment within any larger group.

To recapitulate, there are always villages of three generations in existence—those of contemporaries of the late chief, the headmen of which have ritual functions; those of mature men, contemporaries of the ruling chief, whose headmen have administrative and military functions; and those of boys and young men, contemporaries of the heir, who have not yet 'come out', and who fight under the leadership of their fathers' senior headman.

Sometimes, as we shall see presently, villages of a fourth generation exist also.

Each age-grade, or generation, covers a span of 30 to 35 years, and each village comprises an age-set with a span of 5 to 8 years, though this is longer in sub-chiefdoms (*vide infra*, p. 37). The average age of members in each grade varies with the date of the last 'coming out' ceremony. Just before the ceremony the elders with ritual functions are those over 65 or 70; the mature men of the ruling generation those between 35 and 65; and the 'boys' who have not yet come out, those between 10 and 35. Just after the ceremony the ruling generation consists of those between about 10 and 35, anyone over 35 being an elder. Those just too young to participate in one 'coming out' may be just too old to participate in the next. The village of Katumba in Mwaipopo's country was in this position: it had been created after the 'coming out' of the young chief Mwankuga, but informants were uncertain whether or not it would be established as a separate village at the 'coming out' of his heir Mwanyilu (*vide* Document, p. 183).

The two senior headmen of a new chiefdom are chosen from the two senior villages established at a 'coming out' ceremony, so that a commoner's chance of holding high office is greatest when he is just a little older than a chief's heirs. The senior village of one generation begets the senior villages of the next (*vide* Document, pp. 181-5). Thus, though the son of a village headman in one generation cannot become a village headman in the succeeding generation, there is a tendency for leadership within the chiefdom to pass from one *group* of men to their sons. Those who participate in a 'coming out' while very young tend to have least authority in the country, and are superseded when still under forty by the generation of their sons. The immediate contemporaries of a chief, i.e. those with whom he lives during boyhood, have a special bond with him all through life; and it may sometimes happen that when a chief dies young and is replaced by a brother (his own son being too young to inherit) a junior village comes into prominence because its members have been 'the companions' of the new chief. Bulindanajo in Mwaipopo's country was a village of this kind: Mwaipopo I had died young, and was succeeded by his brother Mwaipopo II ('Mwambene') who had 'come out' as a youth in Bulindanajo; and his immediate contemporaries from that village maintained a special bond with him.

Theoretically the territorial arrangement is one in which the villages of the ruling generation lie at the centre of the country, each surrounded by satellite villages of their sons, while smaller villages of old men lie on the boundaries. In practice—at least nowadays—the pattern is more complex, with old men's villages squeezed in between those of the ruling generation. From the time of its establishment as a separate chiefdom at the 'coming out', the future division of the country is adumbrated: there is a senior headman in each half of the country with villages subordinate to him, and the mother of an heir in each half. On the boundary between the halves stand the ritual trees, landmarks for all to see.

Age and locality coincide, while kinship cuts across local grouping, fathers and sons, and very often brothers, being in different villages. But kinsmen tend to be established in the same side of a country, and so to remain within one chiefdom. Kinship terms are extended in some measure to the villages of the chiefdom, which are classified as those of 'our fathers', 'our elder brothers', 'our young brothers', and 'our sons'. Women have no direct share in the age-organization: their membership of a village turns on their relationship to some man—father, husband, husband's heir—and the age-range of women within one village is very wide.

Villages vary considerably in size. Boys' villages, as we have seen, begin with a dozen members or less, and the villages of old men are often very small also; we knew one with only 10 households, another with 11. The villages of young and middle-aged men commonly vary between 20 and 50 households, with 30 as a fair average in the hills. In Mwaipopo's country there were 540 taxpayers on the roll and we recorded 19 established villages and 6 boys' villages.[1] Some members of the boys' villages, and some elderly men, were not on the tax-roll, so that the average was over 20 boys or men in each village. Villages in the plain are somewhat larger, averaging around 40 households.

Men's villages are usually subdivided into sections under the leadership of assistant headmen, appointed by the headman of the village. These assistants do not share in the 'coming out' cere-

---

[1] *Vide infra*, pp. 181 ff. The tax registers are no guide to the number of villages since in them several villages are commonly lumped together as one under a senior village headman.

mony, and are clearly distinguished from those who do. Indeed they may be appointed at a considerably later date. The qualities looked for in them, however, are similar to those looked for in the village headmen, namely, wisdom in dealing with men, generosity, wealth, and the respect of their neighbours. They are expected to settle disputes, to pass on the orders of their chief or village headman to the men under them, to entertain their neighbours, and 'to watch over the country by day and by night'. On the hot Lake-shore plain, where the cattle are brought in before noon to stand in the shade of the bananas and are protected from insects by the smoke of a fire specially kindled for the purpose, an assistant headman is called 'he of the heap of hot ashes' (*ugwakyemo*), implying that he is the leader of the group whose cattle are herded together. 'He of the heap of hot ashes' is responsible both for the cows and for their masters. 'If the cows give no milk he will call the ten friends and warn them that if there is a witch among them he will be driven away.' Again, the extent of an assistant headman's influence depends very largely on his personal popularity. 'The village headman chooses a man of wisdom and says: "Build here with your friends": he is there first, and, if he is charitable (*mololo*), more people will come.' Generally speaking the assistants are more important in the large villages of the plains than in the smaller villages of the hills.

The distinction between the sub-divisions of a village and two separate villages is theoretically quite clear for the villages of men, since each independent village has been formally established at a 'coming out' ceremony. But in practice the distinction is somewhat blurred; for large villages often split *after* the 'coming out' ceremony into sections which operate very much as independent villages. This became apparent when we analysed in detail the villages of Mwaipopo's chiefdom (*vide* Document pp. 181-5) and found, besides the nineteen established villages, five village-sections which were treated in many respects as independent villages. Boys' villages remain somewhat fluid until the 'coming out'; but those offshoots of a parent village which have been closed to younger brothers may be regarded as separate villages.

Boys build their huts close together and plant bananas round them (*vide* Plate II). Then, as they grow older and marry, they build larger huts and space them further apart; but the homestead

III. MEN'S VILLAGES HIDDEN IN BANANA GROVES AND FRINGED BY CULTIVATED LAND

A long hut is visible in the centre of the picture to the right, and an *umwali* tree on the left. In the cultivated land are oil-bearing *unsyunguti* trees

IV. A CHRISTIAN BOYS' VILLAGE BEING BUILT ROUND A SCHOOL

of a married man is close to those of his neighbours, his banana grove probably adjoining theirs, while the main garden-lands of the whole group are all together at a distance (*vide* Plate III). Boundaries between age-villages are thus not always apparent to a stranger. A solid hundred acres or so of houses and bananas may turn out to consist of two or three villages, each with its own organization, and each having a block of garden-lands separate from the others.

If any question arises about the village a man belongs to, the points discussed are: where he has built and where he cultivates —i.e. to what village the land he uses belongs; with whom he herds his cows; and which village headman he goes to in case of a dispute. Membership of a village is therefore defined primarily in terms of economic co-operation and political allegiance.

d. Moving

The age-system is somewhat modified by men moving from one village to another. When a man dies his heir frequently comes and lives where the dead man was living, so becoming a member of his age-village. A man's heir is his full brother next to him in age, and only when all the full brothers of a family have died does the property pass to the eldest son of the eldest brother. The difference in the ages of a man and his heir is often, therefore, only a few years; but even if the difference be great, and the heir many years younger than his new neighbours, he is now treated as their contemporary. He sits with them at ceremonies and he shares their rights at any division of meat.

Were all heirs to remove to the homesteads of those who had died, the villages of old men would, of course, continue to exist indefinitely. In fact they do not. In Mwaipopo's chiefdom there remained only one small village of old men, the grandfathers of the generation which had last 'come out'. Other villages of this grandfathers' generation were remembered by name; the heirs of former members sometimes used the old name; but they did not live together as a group; they were members of other villages of their own generation. Even the heir of the headman of each old village, who acted as a priest, lived in some other village. It was said that these grandfathers' villages would disappear even in name when Mwaipopo, the father of the young chief died. No villages of the great-grandfathers' generation survived, even ritually (*vide* Document, pp. 881–5).[1]

Men also move from one village to another and they do not always join a village of their exact contemporaries. A stranger may come and be granted land in a village even though he is considerably older or younger than the bulk of its members. Such movement from one village to another is now very considerable: we estimated that at least 80 per cent of the married men have at some time or other moved from the chiefdom in which they first cultivated gardens of their own. There is also movement from village to village within a chiefdom.

Everyone agreed that moving is not something new. In the past a convicted witch was expelled from his village, and sometimes from the chiefdom; thieves and adulterers were also expelled or fled to take refuge with another chief (*vide infra*, pp. 118–9). But it is probable that movement between villages has increased greatly since the imposition of European control. The main reason for moving nowadays is, as we have said, the fear of witchcraft. Subsidiary reasons are the desire to get suitable land for cultivating cash crops, the desire to be near some centre of employment (such as Tukuyu or Rungwe), and the desire to live with others of like mind, as fellow Christians or fellow pagans, fellow Moravians or fellow adherents of the 'Watch Tower' (*vide infra*, pp. 40–3).

Women move from one village to another even more often than men, for, not only do wives move with their husbands, but a girl commonly marries a man of a village other than that in which she grew up, and is later inherited by a kinsman of her dead husband who lives in yet another village. Since first wives are usually ten years younger than their husbands, and junior wives may be forty or fifty years younger, most women are inherited at least once during their lives, and some are inherited several times. The modern high divorce rate accelerates this long-established circulation of women from village to village.

---

[1] It is possible that the existence of villages of four generations was due to the fact that Mwaipopo continued to live long after the 'coming out' of his heir Mwankuga—a survival not usual in traditional practice (*vide supra*, p. 30).

e. Variation in the basic form of village organization

The splitting of a chiefdom into two at the 'coming out', the division of each country into two sides, the establishment of two age-villages of men in each half, and the development of two boys' villages attached to each village of men: all this division and sub-division into two equal parts creates the basic form of Nyakyusa political organization. But there are frequent variations from it. Formerly, in large chiefdoms sometimes three or even four sons went through the 'coming-out' ceremony, each with his own village headmen, and each setting up an independent chiefdom. Very often, we were told, a chief would build a separate royal homestead (*ikitangalala*) for his favourite wife, and her son would 'come out' with his two senior brothers and inherit a small country subordinate to one of them. Again, the division of an old chief's country into two was not always accepted by the young men concerned; quarrels and fighting between them were common and the position established at the 'coming out' was sometimes modified by war. If one of the two decisively defeated the other, he took all his brother's cattle and reduced him to a subordinate position. The land of the Nyakyusa is full of such minor chiefdoms; by the clerks who collect tax they are described as 'villages', but they are radically different from villages in their constitution; for, while they often consist only of a few score families, they are themselves articulated into age-villages, and have at their head not an elected village headman (*ulifumu*) but a hereditary chief (*umalafyale*). A minor chief marries in the ordinary way, like a commoner, and only one of his sons inherits his chieftainship; while his chiefdom, owing to its small size, is often simply divided into two villages, one for the old, one for the young men.

There is no separate 'coming out' ceremony for a minor chiefdom but the heir goes through the ceremony with his superior, remaining with him during and after the fire-making ceremony. His mates form one village under their own headman, who is subordinate to one of the two senior headmen of the new independent chief, taking fire from him. Great emphasis is laid on the fact that no separate fire, kindled by friction, is lighted for a subordinate chief.

In the chiefdom of Mwaipopo, with which we were well acquainted, there are three such minor chiefdoms. In one no heir survived; but the heirs in the other two went through the 'coming out' ceremony with their superior chiefs, and the young men from each of the three formed a separate village, attached to one or other of Mwaipopo's two heirs. How many generations these subordinate chiefdoms survive as separate groups is not certain: the three in Mwaipopo's country were chiefdoms of his junior brothers which had lost their independence to him. In his case four brothers had 'come out' together, and the senior had conquered the others. Probably at the coming out of Mwaipopo's grandson these subordinate chiefdoms will appear only as villages, and no heir from them will be treated as a chief.

This formation of subordinate chiefdoms is a traditional variation of the standard pattern still going on. There are further modifications which are modern.

f. Modern modifications

In 1926, as has been noted, the British Administration created new 'Native Authorities'. The traditionally independent chiefs of the Nyakyusa were grouped together into eleven court districts,[1] and in each district a 'Native Court' was set up, consisting of the various chiefs and their village headmen, under the hereditary presidency of one of the chiefs, who thereby became senior to all the others in that Court district. Salaries for chiefs were introduced, the senior chiefs receiving far higher salaries than the others; the meetings of each Court are now always held in the territory of the senior chief (*umalafyale unkulumba*), and to this Court has been transferred a great deal of the legal business which, before 1926, was transacted by each chief sitting with his own village headman in his own chiefdom. The chiefs themselves were consulted in the selection of the Court presidents, and those chosen were normally the chiefs with the greatest number of men in each particular Court district.

The introduction of salaries has had a profound effect upon the relative status of the two young chiefs who 'come out' together. When an ordinary chief, with a small salary, dies, the Government recognizes the first son alone as chief and pays the whole

---

[1] There are two other courts in Rungwe district for Ndali and Lambya.

salary to him. This reduces the second son to the position of a minor chief as effectively as a defeat in war might have done in the old days. But, while the action of warfare only occasionally led to the subordination of one of the brothers, this action of the Government does so invariably, and always subordinates the younger brother. When a senior chief dies, on the other hand, the salary is usually divided; the bulk of it goes to the first son, together with the position of senior chief, while the second son is given the salary of an ordinary chief.

Nevertheless, whether the junior brother is to become a chief in receipt of a salary or not, he still goes through the 'coming out' ceremony with his brother, and is apportioned villages and headmen. Even in a country in which there are several minor chiefs there still is the division into two, some being regarded as subordinate to the senior heir, and the others to the junior. Division of a chiefdom into two at the 'coming out' is the basic form which is maintained, at least ceremonially, despite all modifications.

The introduction of Courts and salaries has brought a new element into the relationship between the old chief and his heirs. Only one of them can receive the salary and they commonly dispute about it. Quarrels are particularly frequent over the position of senior chief, for the presidency of a Court carries with it a relatively large salary. Old senior chiefs cling to the position long after their sons have 'come out'. There is no compulsory superannuation of chiefs, and the traditional mechanism for getting rid of an old chief when his sons were ready to take over— strangulation by his councillors—no longer operates. The old headmen remain in power along with the old chief. Thus one effect of British Administration in Nyakyusa country has been to maintain the older generation in power much longer than was traditionally usual, and to delay the assumption of full responsibility for government by the younger generation..

Another modern change which has far-reaching effects is the omission in some chiefdoms of the 'coming out' ceremony. When there is no 'coming out' the old men do not move aside to make room for their sons, and consequently the territorial demarcation between villages of old and young becomes blurred. Among the neighbouring people of Ngonde the 'coming out' ceremony has been dropped. There boys still build apart from their fathers, and the villages of young and old are more or less separate, but as time goes on the demarcation between them becomes less and less clear. In most chiefdoms of the Nyakyusa the ceremony is still observed, but in the country of Porokoto, near Rungwe mission, it has not been performed for a generation, and there the territorial separation between young and old is much less definite than in other chiefdoms. The maintenance of the age-village system is ultimately dependent upon the moving aside of the old men in each generation to make room for their sons.

The reason commonly given for the omission of the ceremony in Ngonde is that since the country has become more densely populated there is no longer room for two chiefs to divide the country of their father. The old system of division was adapted to an expanding population in a relatively empty country; and the two young chiefs ordinarily ruled a greater area, and more men, than their father. Further, it is said, the ritual was in one aspect a preparation for war, and fighting between chiefdoms has ceased. These explanations are obviously not adequate, since the ceremony is still performed in Nyakyusa chiefdoms in which there is neither room for expansion, nor war. Its omission may be related rather to the general abandoning of traditional rituals in Ngonde. Forty-five per cent of the people of Ngonde, including many leading men, are professing Christians, and there is a very general scepticism of the efficacy of traditional rituals. This scepticism extends even to those who are not Church members.

In Porokoto's chiefdom the 'coming out' was omitted partly because of a dispute over the succession; but there, also, many of the traditional rituals are not regularly performed (as they are in other parts of Nyakyusa country), because the proportion of Christians is high since Porokoto's chiefdom adjoins the main Moravian mission station, Rungwe, and because pagan faith in these rituals has therefore been shaken. As Porokoto (who is not a professing Christian himself) put it, when explaining why he had not performed the twin ritual for his own twin daughters: 'We see that nothing happens to the Christians when they omit the rituals, so we begin to say "What value have they?" ' Thus not only are Christians forbidden by their Churches to participate in the ritual acts of the 'coming out' but pagans themselves begin to doubt their necessity.

The presence of Christians further complicates the traditional village organization since many of them live in separate Christian villages, or sections of villages. When the first German missionaries arrived among the Nyakyusa in 1891, they bought land from the chiefs and village headmen at the different points at which they decided to settle, and villages of Christian converts have grown up on this land. The nucleus of these villages consisted of Ngonde workmen who came from Karonga (where a Scots mission was already established) to help the Germans build their mission houses. Later, local Nyakyusa who came to work at the mission stations built there too, and a party of ninety slaves, rescued by the German administration from the Arab leader, Mlozi, were given into the care of the missionaries and settled on the land they had bought. These slaves were from other tribes, not Nyakyusa, and there was difficulty in repatriating them to their home villages. The foreigners and Nyakyusa who remained on mission land were those who accepted Christian teaching. Practically all the early converts were already working for the missionaries and living near them before their baptism, and later converts were encouraged to move out of their pagan villages and join the new villages of Christians on mission land. On the other hand, any who left the Church, or who were suspended for practising polygyny or for some other cause, were, and still are, liable to be turned off mission land by the missionary in charge. Thus these villages comprise only professing Christians.

In the villages on mission land there is a certain division of authority between Church and State. Up to 1914 such villages were treated as being outside the control of any chief. A Nyakyusa informant described the position thus: 'The missionaries said that they had bought their land and they would not admit any authority of the chief over it. They collected the taxes for the (German) Government themselves. The chief never sent into "European country" (*KiSungu*) for anything. The people there did not cook for him. The missionary used to be the chief in the European country; but since the English came it is different.' Under the system of Indirect Rule the administrative authority of chiefs over Africans living on mission-owned land is recognized; taxes are paid through the chief, and civil cases between Christians may be taken to the chief's court (*vide infra*, p. 138). But chiefs still treat Christians living on mission land rather differently from those living on land which has not been so allocated. They are, for example, chary of calling out Christians to carry loads when a Government official comes by wanting porters, or of sending their messengers into the mission villages when they require food for any purpose. The leaders of the villages on mission land are not headmen appointed at the 'coming out' (in which the Christian villages do not share), but 'elders' or 'peacemakers' appointed by the Church (usually the missionary and 'session'); and it is under such a leader that the members of a village on mission land rally when they are called out to co-operate in some activity, such as a pig hunt, in which each village acts as a unit.

Even on mission land, however, the traditional village organization and age-grouping are in some measure maintained. Boys leave their fathers' houses well before they reach puberty and build together a little distance away. There they are joined by younger brothers until the village is closed and the youngsters are told to start a new village of their own. Where there is plenty of land, as at Itete mission in Selya, the division between the generations is still quite clear, but where good building sites are scarce, as on Rungwe mission land, the divisions are blurred. As we have seen, the maintenance of clear territorial divisions between the generations depends upon the old men moving aside and leaving the greater part of the land for the more numerous ruling generation. Such a movement never occurs on mission land, which is not part of the land of any chief. It follows that territorial separation of age groups cannot there continue for long.

Many Nyakyusa Christians nowadays prefer not to live on mission land, on the ground that there is less security of tenure, and less opportunity to develop coffee planting, on mission land than off it (*vide infra*, p. 48). At the same time the Moravian and Berlin missions have ceased to press their early policy of gathering converts at mission stations,[1] so that more and more Christians are coming to live intermingled with pagan neighbours. Very often, however, Christians choose to gather in one section of a village: scholars who have decided to become Christians often get permission to build near their school; they choose to move out of the pagan villages in which they have been living in order to

---

[1] The Scots mission in Ngonde never sought to gather its converts into separate villages, recommending rather that Christians should remain in their own homes and influence their pagan neighbours.

build with Christian contemporaries, and sometimes the teacher is himself quite a young man and builds with them. Members of two independent churches, the Watch Tower[1] and the followers of Ngemela, have also built apart with fellow believers. Each such group has its own name, and a sense of unity, and its religious leader is recognized as the leader in secular affairs also, but politically it is a section of a larger pagan village of contemporaries. We know of no case in which a purely Christian group living off mission land has been given status as a village at the 'coming out'.

Since the same word, *ikipanga*,[2] is used both for a village and its sub-divisions the distinction between village and village-section is often not clear in ordinary speech, but it is apparent at the 'coming out', and in legal procedure.

[1] The Watch Tower (Jehovah's Witnesses) is of course a world organization, but Nyakyusa followers were organized under their own leaders and so far as we could discover were subject to no outside supervision between 1935 and 1938.

[2] *Ikipanga* is also used sometimes for the following of a chief, and nowadays for a congregation or church; cf. the Xhosa *ibandla*.

CHAPTER III

ECONOMIC CO-OPERATION

THE primary economic units in Nyakyusa society are the kinship groups—the elementary family, the cattle-owing lineage, and the group of cognates who co-operate in production and exchange many gifts, and among whom cattle circulate.[1] However, fellow villagers also work together, exchange food, and have a common interest in certain property.

a. Land

The village is the land-holding group. As we have seen, land is allocated to a boys' village, at its commencement, by the parent village, that is the village to which the fathers of most of the boys belong. Little boys' huts are usually to be seen going up on a strip of pasture-land, adjoining the block of banana groves which shroud their fathers' houses. The boys' land is primarily a building site, but very soon after moving into their huts they turn over the ground and plant banana suckers (*vide* Plate II). Bananas begin to bear very quickly, and so in a little more than a year after the establishment of a boys' village, its members have bananas of their own, which they cook for themselves and eat with their friends at odd times during the day. But they have, as yet, no fields, for the cultivation of fields requires the co-operation of a wife. Bachelors continue to eat their main meals at their parents' village. As the boys grow up and marry they begin to cultivate garden-land adjacent to their village. Some of these gardens are acquired by individuals from their own fathers and fathers-in-law, but whether there may also be a block grant of garden-land by the parent village as a whole to the boys' village as a whole we are not certain. In any case the land of boys' villages is limited, and at the 'coming out' the old men move aside and the young men enter their inheritance. The allotment to each village is

[1] cf. Monica Wilson, 'Nyakyusa Kinship' in *African Systems of Kinship and Marriage*, edited by A. R. Radcliffe Brown and Daryll Forde.

decided by the old village headmen and chief in consultation, at the commencement of the 'coming out' ceremony. This moving aside of the old men is an essential part of the ceremony and occurs even when there is unoccupied land available. For example, at the 'coming out' of Mwankuga, Mwaipopo's heir, the old men moved aside to make room for their sons, although there is a large area of unoccupied land in the chiefdom, which is slowly being colonized by Mwaipopo's men.

Although the main redistribution is at the 'coming out', later readjustments are common enough. If a particular men's village attracts many members, and these members become wealthy in wives and children, then it may be necessary for the old men to move aside a second time, to make yet more room for their sons. The senior headman of the side of the chiefdom concerned, in consultation with the chief and other village headmen, has the power to make equitable adjustments in the land holdings of the villages of his side. We watched one village, whose numbers had diminished, being moved to make more room for a junior one which had flourished. But so long as its members remain together, a village retains its name and identity, though its site may be moved more than once. 'A village', the Nyakyusa say, 'consists in men, not in land.'

Boundary disputes between villages of a chiefdom are not unusual. In the old days these often led to war. Nowadays they are taken before the Court, whence there is an appeal to the federal court, the District Officer, the Provincial Commissioner and thence to the High Court (cf. p. 137). One such case, which we observed, had dragged on for years because the chief concerned, who happened to be president of the Court, feared to give judgment lest he be bewitched by the village which lost the case (cf. Document p. 191).

The division of the land allotted to each village lies with the members of that village, under the leadership of their own headman. The village headman himself, and other prominent individuals in the group, get first choice of sites: a son does not have a prescriptive right to the building site and gardens of his father when the old men move aside for their sons. 'If you are prominent, and you like your father's old site, that's all right, the others agree; but if you are unimportant ("light"), no; one of the important men takes it; *you* have no power.' Certain building and garden sites are preferred to others, but the division of them at the 'coming out' does not appear to create much friction.

When the old men move they still maintain rights over what may be regarded as the major 'improvement' made on their old sites, that is, trees which they or others have planted. There are two species which were traditionally and still are of great value to the Nyakyusa, the bamboo and the *unsyunguti*. Bamboos are used for house-building, while the *unsyunguti* produces a fruit which is both delicious to eat and also full of seeds which are dried and crushed for ointment. As has been shown in a previous essay[1] rights over these trees are maintained when individuals move from one village to another. Similarly, when a whole village moves, rights over bamboos are maintained, the former owner returning to cut them himself if he chooses. But the less valuable *unsyunguti* crop is left to the occupier. As one old man put it: 'We don't send our wives back to harvest the *imisyunguti* trees lest the young men make love to them there.' Bamboos are felled by men. Further complications are now potentially created by the planting of coffee-trees, but we know of no case in which a 'coming out' has yet taken place in a chiefdom in which coffee has been extensively planted—the first coffee-planters were those living on mission land which is unaffected by the 'coming out' ceremony. Now that coffee planting is becoming general, however, the difficulties of moving whole villages will be much greater.

The only land which was traditionally excluded from the 'new deal' in each generation is the very scarce and valuable ground in the bottom of old volcanic craters. This land is owned by families, and is always claimed by a kinsman when the occupier dies or moves to another chiefdom. It may be that long ago the land in each particular crater was owned solely by members of some particular village, but now it is held by old families scattered all over the chiefdom in which it lies. Thus ordinary land, of which in the old days there was ample, was re-allotted in each generation, but the most valuable ground was passed down from father to son. We shall return to this point again in our last chapter.

As we have seen, movement of individuals from one village to another is very frequent. Normally land for building and gardens

[1] Godfrey Wilson, *The Land Rights of Individuals among the Nyakyusa*, pp. 43–5; Rhodes-Livingstone Papers No. 1, 1938.

is granted to a stranger by the villagers concerned, acting through their headman, not by the chief, who is usually informed, but seldom interferes. Only if a member of the chief's own family is moving within the chiefdom from one village to another, or if a very important stranger comes from outside, he may go to the chief and ask for a building plot, and the chief may then exercise his right of overlordship and grant the request. But this is a special and unusual case. It is villagers who grant land to an ordinary new-comer[1] and thereby accept him as one of themselves. His own wishes are taken into account whenever possible; if he sees a piece of ground which attracts him, and no one else has a claim to it, then it will be his.

We must emphasize the willingness with which strangers are received both by the villagers and the chief. Men are still scarcer than land in most places and the prestige and prosperity of villages and chiefdoms are increased by each addition to their membership. As we have said, part of the magical treatment at the 'coming out' is directly designed to attract followers to chiefs and village headmen. Strangers to a village are always given a house to sleep in while they are building their own and are usually given food as well, both formally by the chiefs and village headman and informally by the neighbours. This formal giving of food has lapsed in Porokoto's chiefdom, which adjoins Rungwe mission, and to which very considerable immigration has taken place in the last forty years; there the relative scarcity of land is reflected in a decline of hospitality to new-comers, though none have yet been refused land. But the usual custom still is to receive them generously.

The granting of land to a new-comer is subject to the rights of a villager who has moved but may return. As we have seen, moves from one village to another are frequent, and unless a man has been expelled for witchcraft or some other serious crime his building site and gardens are kept for him, at least for a time. Anyone who occupies them does so on the understanding that he must vacate them should the former owner, or his heir, return. Further, a man who moves retains certain rights over bamboos, *imisyunguti* and coffee-trees. The precise conditions under which individuals who have moved may reclaim their land have been discussed in *The Land Rights of Individuals among the Nyakyusa*,[2]

[1] cf. Godfrey Wilson, op. cit., p. 41.   [2] pp. 36–41.

and need not be recapitulated. The essential fact here is that the village is the group which allocates land to a new-comer, and which maintains the rights of individuals who have moved and who wish to return.

Once established in a village, a man can hoe any ground which has not yet been cultivated, and thereby make it his own.[1] No reference need be made to the headman and other villagers, provided that he does not encroach on land formerly cultivated by others, or on the main pasture land. There is no limit to the acreage he may use. Pasture-land is jointly owned by the whole village group and no individual has exclusive rights to any portion of it. Every member of a village has the right to graze his cattle on the village pastures, and this right may also be granted to an outsider by the village headman in consultation with his neighbours. But no one has the right to cut trees near the village (unless they are ones he has planted or inherited) without the permission of his fellow villagers. The death of one man we knew, the younger brother of a chief, was attributed to the fact that he had cut a branch from a self-sown tree growing in the arable land of a village in which he was a new-comer, without asking permission of his fellow villagers. It was said that 'the owners' of the village were angry and killed him because he had not asked their leave before lopping the tree. He had wanted the branch to make an axe-handle.

The land rights of Christians living in the chiefdoms are identical with those of their pagan fellows; but those who live on mission land are in a different position. They are tenants of the mission, paying an annual rent of 1s., and liable to be evicted by the missionary in charge if they leave the Church. A man so driven out loses the coffee-trees he has planted. One Christian informant remarked: 'We do not think it good to plant coffee on mission land because very often a man is turned out of the Church.' And at Rungwe mission even those moving voluntarily lose the coffee they have planted. Now all trees introduced by Europeans have been declared by the Federation of Chiefs to be the property of the planter, even though he has moved to a different chiefdom, and Christians feel that they have greater security of ownership in coffee planted in the chiefdoms than in that on mission land. The difficulties likely to arise at a 'coming out' are ignored, and

[1] Ibid., pp. 41–2.

it is implied that coffee planted in the chiefdoms will be inherited by a man's heirs. As a leading Christian woman put it: 'We like to build on this side of the river because the other is mission land, and if a man moves he loses the coffee and everything else he has planted there. . . . A man has children and he wishes his children to inherit what he has planted.' The number of coffee-trees each man may plant on mission land is also limited to 100, so that the development of large plantations, such as some astute Nyakyusa are undertaking, is impossible there.

b. Building

When a group of boys starts a new village two or three friends usually combine to erect a little hut and live in it together. As younger boys join the village the older ones instruct and help their juniors to build. Thus, although as they grow older each boy builds a hut for himself, the habit of co-operation with village-mates in construction is already established. Until they are married, boys do all the work on their huts for themselves, fetching their own reeds or bamboos for the frame, and cutting and carrying thatching grass. They usually leave their huts unmudded. Adult men, on the other hand, are helped by their wives and female relatives as well as by sons and sons-in-law, and one or two of their own village neighbours. Men fell the bamboos, construct the framework of the house, and thatch, while women cut and carry grass, carry bamboos, mould the mud bricks which are packed between the bamboo uprights, and plaster the hut inside. The wife for whom the hut is being built is responsible for the women's work, but she usually gets some help from her co-wives and women neighbours, as well as from her mother and sisters, and the mother and sisters of her husband. Sons and sons-in-law are expected to bring with them other young men, their village-mates. Co-operation is thus both with relatives and village neighbours—the neighbours of the couple building the hut, and of their sons and sons-in-law.

The huts of married men are built with immense care, for not only are substantial houses essential to comfort, and indeed a condition of survival, in this climate of torrential rains and cold winter mists, but the Nyakyusa take great pride in the appearance of their homesteads (*vide infra*, p. 77). The early European travellers in the area all comment on the excellently built huts and the cleanness of the villages.[1] Lord Lugard calls their huts 'the neatest and the most wonderfully built of any I have seen in Africa, excepting only the houses of the king and chiefs in Uganda.'[2] This high standard of building necessitates hard work and co-operation between a number of men and women.

c. Cultivation

The primary unit in cultivation is the elementary family consisting of a man, his wife and unmarried children or, in the case of a polygynous family, of the house group of a wife and her children, together with her husband, part of whose time is spent in hoeing her fields.[3] There is also, however, some co-operation with other relatives, and with village neighbours.

Unmarried sons hoe with their fathers and very often they bring one or more village-mates to work with them, making return, in due course, by working with these friends for their respective fathers. The boys who come are fed after hoeing, and should be fed generously, by the woman in whose fields they have worked. After his betrothal a young man comes in the same way with village-mates to hoe for his father-in-law, as well as continuing to hoe for his own father. Once his wife joins him they have their own fields, and the bulk of his time is spent in hoeing for her, but he still hoes one or two strips (*embaka*) for his own father and for his father-in-law. Such help is reciprocal, for his 'mothers' (i.e. his own mother and his father's other wives) and sisters, as well as the 'mothers' and sisters of his wife, will help his wife with her tasks of sowing, weeding, and reaping. From the point of view of village organization the essential fact is that young men working for fathers and fathers-in-law very frequently bring one or two village-mates with them. A typical hoeing group is made up of a man with his sons, and one or two village-mates of the sons.

Larger hoeing parties, to which not only youths, but also older men come, are fairly common, especially among the Kukwe.

[1] Elton, op. cit., p. 323; D. Kerr-Cross, 'Crater-lakes north of Lake Nyasa' in *The Geographical Journal*, Vol. V (1895), p. 116–7.

[2] F. D. Lugard, *The Rise of our East African Empire* (1893), Vol. I, p. 52.

[3] The respective rights of the husband and of each wife have been analysed by Godfrey Wilson, op. cit., pp. 16–29.

V. THE CHIEF MWAIPOPO

VI. FIBOMBE, A CHRISTIAN ELDER

To these come some of a man's village-mates and male relatives or special friends from other villages, as well as his sons and sons-in-law with their village-mates. At one such party we noted in the morning eight helpers, of which six were men, two being classificatory brothers of the owner and four of them friends. There were also two young sons of the owner working. In the afternoon a son-in-law came with a party of his village-mates. Such hoeing parties are not the concern of the whole village. Only those who have been specially invited, or very close friends of the owner of the field, come (the number usually ranging between ten and twenty), and some of those invited may be from other villages. It is difficult for one to whom an invitation has been sent to refuse. After work the guests are feasted. Traditionally they were given milk with bananas or beans (a prized food), but nowadays beer is expected. For the party noted above two pots of beer were provided, one being given to the older men and the other to the son-in-law with his friends. Christians, many of whom are forbidden to brew beer, provide meat, rice, or milk —all much prized foods. Possibly the proportion of men attending this type of work party has diminished as opportunity for paid employment has increased—we have no certain evidence.

Mutual assistance in cultivation turns on kinship and personal friendship: all the members of a village or a village-section are not obliged to work with a neighbour. But it is insisted that neighbours should keep in step with one another in cultivation. It will be remembered that their garden-lands are together, and each year different types of garden are hoed by groups of villagers— millet, cow-peas, and pumpkins in one place, potatoes in another, maize and beans in another, so that while the gardens of one particular household are scattered, each crop is in one or two blocks. Neighbours cultivating the same crop in adjoining fields should, according to Nyakyusa ideas, begin each process in cultivation together, and the whole village should keep in step. As one informant put it, 'in hoeing and planting one must be neither ahead of nor behind one's neighbours'.

The idea reaches its furthest development among the Kukwe in regard to three crops planted with the first rains, namely, finger millet, cow-peas, and pumpkins. Traditionally, no Kukwe man might begin to clear ground for these crops until his village headman had begun, or, if he lived in the village of a chief or in an immediately adjoining village, until his chief had begun. Members of other villages do not regard the chief, but wait only for their village headman to begin. Within the family, junior wives must follow senior wives, but there is no precedence between brothers. If two should live in the same village it does not matter which begins sowing first, provided both follow the leader, nor need a junior age-village wait on a senior one to begin. Not only must the headman of the village begin the clearing, but each process in cultivation must be initiated by him or his senior wife; thus clearing, raking, burning, planting, and reaping, are ceremonially begun, and the wife of the headman should be the first to wash her millet, and he the first to eat of the new crop. Further, once a process is initiated, the villagers should press on with their tasks so that all may finish about the same time.

Now the cultivation of millet, cow-peas, and pumpkins[1] is peculiar in that the weeds and grass are not turned in for green manure, as they are for all other crops (except rice), but are collected in heaps and burnt, just before the rains break at the end of the dry season. And the fire for this must be lighted ritually by the headman of the village. Using fire-sticks and 'medicine of plenty' (*unkota gwa ifugo*[2]) bought by the Kukwe from the Sangu people, he ignites a special fire in his own field and then, if a great wife of the chief lives in the village, he lights the heaps in her field. All the members of the village take fire from him, or from the field of the chief's wife. To take fire from a house is forbidden, because the owner of the house from which it is taken may be a witch, who will rot the heaps so that the millet does not grow, or will not ripen. Roasting food on a burning heap, or taking a brand to light tobacco is likewise forbidden, lest the person who does so has medicine which will rot the millet.

It is thought that if one breaks the rule, beginning a process before the headman, the fields of all the other villagers will suffer. 'If men hoe higgledy piggledy the food in their gardens does not grow, and if they reap higgledy piggledy the yield from all the

---

[1] Some Kukwe held that these rules about cultivation applied also to maize and to an old root crop, *umbogo*, but the most reliable informants were agreed that the rule was only strictly enforced with regard to the three crops planted 'at the break of the rains, in the new year'.

[2] 'A village headman, *ugwa ifugo*, is one who drives off witches and protects the food.'

gardens will be small.' And the crops of one who lags behind, when his fellows have planted together, are also said to suffer. For this reason, if one woman is delayed and unable to work along with them, her friends will plant a corner of her field when they plant their own, so that the fertility of her fields may not be lost.

An educated informant explained that 'those who have learnt agriculture may think that late planting is unsuccessful because it is not the right season—the weather is wrong—but others think the failure is due to not planting at the same time as their neighbours.' Christians living on mission land, with their gardens in a block by themselves, do not trouble about planting simultaneously, but many of those living in mixed villages with fields adjoining the fields of pagans conform 'because if they do not plant with them they do not have pleasant social relations'. In some chiefdoms, however, the custom is dying even among pagans. In Porokoto's country we were told: 'The custom is now dead, men just burn higgledy piggledy. A fire blazes up somewhere. We ask, "Whose is it?" "So and so's" comes the reply. "Oh! All right!" The custom has died because the Christians are many and the chiefs have turned to the Christians; their hearts are with the Christians even though they themselves are not baptized, and about this burning of the rubbish heaps for millet they say: "What is it for? Does it avail anything?" '

Among the people of Selya the rule was traditionally less elaborate than among the Kukwe. It is polite and customary for those whose fields adjoin to call one another so that they may begin each process together. 'We speak to each other saying: "Friends, let us hoe a millet field over there, all of us, hunger comes on us." ' And if a son hoes a field next to his father's his 'mothers' call their daughter-in-law to plant with them, since their fields adjoin. But the only sanctions for keeping in step in hoeing and planting are conventional; there is no suggestion that the laggard's crops will fail. If, however, a man *burns* his millet field before his neighbours have heaped their weeds, they have ground for complaint. They say: 'Why have you harmed our crops?'

Underlying the emphasis on neighbours cultivating simultaneously is the idea that the fertility of fields and crops in ear can be stolen by witchcraft and sorcery, and that if one man' crop is conspicuously better than that of his neighbours it is at their expense; he has illegally enticed the fertility or grain from their fields into his own; he has, in the Nyakyusa phrase 'overstepped' his neighbours.

Ideas as to what creates 'overstepping' vary slightly in the different local groups, but everywhere it is insisted that no man should get a start of his neighbours by burning his rubbish heaps with medicines before they are ready to do so. And not only does communal burning prevent individuals 'overstepping' their neighbours, but the medicine used is said to be a direct protection against witches and sorcerers. Dependence upon medicines and the elaboration of taboos are thus associated with a technique of cultivation—burning of weeds—in which fertility diminishes rapidly, much more rapidly than it does with the technique of green manuring practised for other crops.

The Nyakyusa have no elaborate communal ritual of the first-fruits, emphasizing precedence, such as plays a great part among many of the Southern Bantu. Significantly, their Ngonde relatives, with a more centralized political organization, forbade any man to eat of the new maize and pumpkin leaves until these had been offered ritually, first at the ancestral grove of their overlord, Kyungu, then at the groves of their chiefs, beginning with the senior, and then to the ancestors of each family. The Kukwe say that the headman of the village should be the first to eat certain of the new crops, just as he is the first to hoe, and plant, and reap, but the people of Selya do not trouble at all about precedence in this matter.

Among all the Nyakyusa, however, those who have been drinking the chief's *ifingela* medicine, or medicines for protection against sorcery which return the disease to the sender, must take special precautions when eating food grown on fields fertilized with ash. Now the medicine burnt with the rubbish is said to protect the crops from witches and sorcerers, and both the chief's *ifingela* medicine and retaliatory medicines border on sorcery. The underlying idea seems to be that since those who have been using these dangerous medicines partake in some measure of the nature of sorcerers, they are in danger from food nourished by the ash of that fire.[1] The important point here is that among the

---

[1] The associations made here will be developed in another book on Nyakyusa symbolism.

Nyakyusa generally it is kinship groups, not villages, which eat protective medicines with certain first-fruits.

Unlike many other cattle-keeping Bantu the Nyakyusa take great pride in cultivation, men boasting about their strength in hoeing, and praising those who are diligent. Significantly, the vocabulary relating to bananas matches in richness that relating to cattle: we recorded a dozen terms—and there were said to be many more—for varieties of bananas and plantains, which are distinguished by the form and flavour of the fruit, and thirteen terms for types of cattle, distinguished by colour and markings.

Not only does success in cultivation carry prestige in itself, but it provides the wherewithal for hospitality, on which status in a Nyakyusa community turns. To be respected a man must entertain his neighbours with food and millet-beer. Control of grain and vegetables to do this depends upon his own effort in hoeing, as well as upon having wives and sons to work with him. We have seen how the laggard among the Kukwe believes that the fertility of his gardens will be sapped by his neighbours being ahead. There is thus considerable social pressure compelling both men and women to cultivate diligently. At the same time, however, no individual should be too conspicuous. Each must keep in step in cultivation with his neighbours; and though his fields may be a little larger than the average, they must not be a great deal larger. The area cultivated (visible crops and stubble) by seven compound families on the Lake-shore plain in 1935 averaged 6·13 acres per family; which, divided by the number of members in each family, gave rather over half an acre per head (men, women, and children) or 1·3 acres per adult. The acreage ranged from 1·99 to 0·61 per adult.[1]

Cultivation thus involves co-operation primarily within elementary and compound families, but it also involves village co-operation, in that neighbours hold land together, help one another in some measure, and try to carry out each process simultaneously.

The pressure of neighbours still helps to keep laggards up to the mark, and also to keep the most energetic from getting far ahead. But the village control over cultivation is diminishing for, as we have seen, the custom of keeping in step is no longer strictly insisted upon even among the Kukwe, nor does it apply

---

[1] Monthly report of the Agricultural Officer, Tukuyu District, July 1933. Figures supplied by the courtesy of the Agricultural Officer, Tukuyu, 1935.

to those crops, production of which is now expanding—beans, groundnuts, coffee and rice—even though the latter is planted like millet in a seed-bed of ash. The cultivation of rice is on a commercial basis. A small number of men own ploughs which they hire out for preparing rice-fields, and the weeding and reaping is also often done by hired labour. For the hulling, grading, and marketing of coffee the Agricultural Department has established a coffee co-operative, to which all native-grown coffee is sold, but in this organization villages as such play no part.

d. Herding

In each village there are, as we have seen, several herd-groups, five to ten neighbours herding their cattle together. This association is voluntary, but it is usual for members of adjoining homesteads to co-operate—special friends in a village tend to build together—and the group is more or less stable. All the boys of appropriate age (six to eleven) go to herd, even though there is one son of their father already in the group, and when a man has cattle, but no sons of an age to herd, he may leave his cattle to be looked after by the sons of neighbours. As one old man put it: 'My cows are herded by other men's sons, but I give them neither milk nor payment, it is not done in this country. When I beget a son he will herd too.' There is thus considerable give-and-take between fellow members of the group. Among Christians, and those pagans who wish their sons to go to school, the herds take shifts, half attending the morning session of school, and half the afternoon session. Formerly, young men armed with spears herded the cattle for fear of raids, while boys herded the calves which grazed near the villages. The same young men used to herd and hoe, taking it in turn, or hoeing in the late afternoon when the cattle grazed near the villages and could be herded by the youngsters. The cattle were trained to follow the call of a herdsman and in case of danger were quickly led away and hidden.[1]

In the large villages of the plain an assistant headman, one of whose functions is the care of cattle, is connected with each herd-group. In his homestead, under the bananas, a smoky fire is kept going during the heat of the day, and there the cattle of the group

[1] D. Kerr-Cross, op. cit., p. 121; F. L. M. Moir, op. cit., p. 93.

stand protected from insects: hence his title 'he of the heap of hot ashes' (*ugwakyemo*, *vide supra*, p. 34). The protection of their cattle from raiders by day, and witches by night, was one of the main co-operative activities of the village, and each herd-group within the village was particularly concerned with the protection of its own cattle. For the boys of one herd-group the association is very close since they are together on the pasturage for the greater part of the day. Friendships then formed sometimes last a lifetime.

A few rich men choose to herd their cattle separately from those of their neighbours. 'They are the men who have many cattle! They want to show off their herd, so that men may say: "That's the herd of so and so." ' Sometimes their sons, against orders, foregather with other herd-boys on the pasturage, but they are careful to bring home the herds separately. We knew three men near Rungwe who were spoken of as herding their cattle separately, though in fact their sons often joined friends in the pasturage. To herd alone is regarded as somewhat ostentatious,[1] and only a few individuals do it.

Many rich men do not even keep all their cattle at their homesteads for fear of the jealous witchcraft of their neighbours. Instead, they disperse their herds among friends in other villages (of their own or neighbouring chiefdoms) believing that the cattle may in that way escape danger. Porokoto explained: 'We place cattle with friends (*ukufufya*) on account of sickness and death. Supposing I have three or four cows, and they all calf, but the calves die, then I place the cows with friends. People say: "The cows will escape in another village or chiefdom." If, when cattle die and are cut up, wounds are found in their stomachs,[2] then the owner places the others with friends.' Not all of them are sent to the same place.

The fear of witchcraft was traditionally, and is still, the main reason for placing out cattle, but nowadays they are sent away for other reasons also: Nyakyusa living around Rungwe often send cattle to friends on the other side of the mountains in Mbeya district, where grazing is particularly good, and wealthy Christians place out cattle because their wives, working single-handed,

---

[1] A beast which gores others may be herded apart without any imputation of pride to the owner.

[2] Taken as evidence that they have been killed by withcraft, *vide infra*, p. 116.

find the cleaning of byres in which many cattle are stalled, very
arduous. A pagan who has many cattle always has more than one
wife.

Thus, herding together was traditionally, and still is, one of
the main common activities of neighbours in a village; most cattle
are herded with those of neighbours, but there is a measure of
co-operation with relatives and personal friends of other villages.
It is likely that the practice of placing cattle with friends of other
villages is becoming more common.

e. Hunting and fishing

From the point of view of village co-operation, hunting and
fishing are relatively unimportant, for, in the first place, game and
fish provide the Nyakyusa with prized foods to eat as relish with
the staple bananas, roots, and cereals, rather than with main
items of diet; and secondly, hunting and fishing are not primarily
village enterprises.

Most fishing is done by men, individually, each keeping his
own catch; but groups of herd-boys or young men sometimes
co-operate to divert a branch of a stream temporarily, so that
they may tickle the fish stranded in the shallow pools. They
choose a place where a stream divides naturally, and block one
channel with stones; but such enterprises are on a small scale.
Periodically however, when fish were plentiful, communal fishing
was organized during the dry season. The seeds of a certain
legume, grown for the purpose, were thrown into the river to
stupefy the fish. Men, women, and children waited some way
down the stream with hand-nets, and when, an hour or two after
the poison had been put in, the fish began to float down stupefied,
they were easily netted. The poisoning was organized by the chief
and village headmen and all the villages of the chiefdom partici-
pated, as well as those from neighbouring chiefdoms, when their
chiefs were on good terms. Friends naturally went together, but
the various villages did not act as separate units as they do in a
communal hunt. Communal fishing never occurred regularly,
for if fish were scarce the chief might forbid it for a number of
years, and it is now rare, since poisoning the rivers has been forbidden by the Administration. We heard of only one such fishing
during our stay in Nyakyusa country.

Hunting for food, like most fishing, is an individual affair. A number of men have shot-guns with which they hunt buck (duiker, bushbuck, and waterbuck) which are scarce, and game birds (guinea fowl, partridge, and duck) which are plentiful. The limiting factor is ammunition, which is relatively expensive, and few men waste a cartridge on birds unless they are sure of getting at least two with one shot. They stalk the sitting birds and fire (at point-blank range) at several birds in a line. One or two chiefs employ men specially to shoot for them, but in the diet of the people as a whole game plays a very small part, and there is no tradition of it ever having been of great importance.

Hunting for the protection of life and property is, on the other hand, a communal concern, organized like war. The chief calls out his men who assemble by villages, each under its own head-man, and the chief disposes the groups. Attendance is compulsory and individuals or villages who fail to appear without good reason may be fined. Such communal hunts are still organized to kill wild pig, which devastate the gardens of some chiefdoms. We took part in one to which five village groups consisting of about 160 men and boys came. Formerly they were organized also if lion or leopard or other big game attacked men or cattle. The aim was to surround the animal and spear it, and here the importance of village relations became apparent, for the Nyakyusa argued that a man was less likely to be a coward if, in moments of danger, he stood with his relatives and village neighbours. 'We said that people of different age-villages should not stand together, every man should have his friends or relatives near him, so that if the leopard caught him the others would have to help and not shrink back! So people of the same age-village stood together, or relatives with relatives.'

Towards the end of last century Nyakyusa country abounded in big game.[1] Elephant were purposely shot out before 1935 because they were so destructive of crops, but lion, leopard, buffalo, hippo, and crocodile are still fairly common.

[1] Elton, op. cit., p. 319; D. Kerr-Cross, 'Geographical Notes on the Country between Lakes Nyassa, Rukwa, and Tanganyika', *The Scottish Geographical Magazine*, Vol. VI (1890), p. 282; 'Crater-lakes north of Lake Nyasa', *The Geographical Journal*, Vol. V (1895), p. 119; F. L. M. Moir, *After Livingstone* (1923), pp. 90–110,

f. Housekeeping

Every married woman has her own hearth and granary, and she works very largely alone when cooking and cleaning; but in one essential activity women who are neighbours in a village regularly co-operate, and that is in fetching firewood. We never saw a woman going alone; usually there is a group of three or four up to a dozen or more. Firewood must be fetched two or three times a week, and the journey and the collection of the wood takes from four to ten hours, depending upon the distance of the village from a patch of forest or bush. Thus the women spend up to thirty hours a week fetching wood, and it is with village neighbours that this time is spent, not with relatives from other villages. If a woman is ill her friends will help in bringing wood and cooked food for her. Some co-wives co-operate in this way, fetching wood together, and helping each other in sickness, but whether they do or not depends upon personal friendship. Often it is with an unrelated neighbour, rather than with a co-wife, that a woman works most closely. Only when co-wives are sisters, or aunt and niece, are they expected to work together regularly.

Village neighbours—women—also co-operate in the preparation of feasts, as we shall see in the following chapter.

g. Economic co-operation beyond the village

The economic relations of fellow villagers, and the changes taking place in these relations, cannot be understood without some reference to economic co-operation beyond the village boundaries. As we have already indicated, co-operation with relatives living in other villages is very important: cattle, the most prized possession of the Nyakyusa, circulate within kinship groups, between father and son, brother and brother, and between affines, and these same relatives assist one another in cultivation and building. But beyond the circle of kinsmen and village-mates there was formerly little economic co-operation. Each village and kinship group was largely self-sufficient, buying from outside little save iron spears and hoes, medicines, salt, cosmetics, and brass or copper wire for ornament.

Smiths were essential to the Nyakyusa economy for they

fashioned iron hoes for cultivation and spears for hunting and war; they also made the cow-bells with which rich men loved to decorate their cattle. Doctors were equally important, for the medicines supplied by them were believed to influence health, fertility, and success in every undertaking. Neither smiths nor doctors served only their own home villages—the number of smiths was much smaller than the number of villages—and doctors living at a distance were generally preferred to those living near by. The need for iron goods and for medicines therefore took men out of their own villages and made links with other villages, often in other chiefdoms. Some at least of the iron ore which the smiths smelted was obtained from the distant Kinga mountains outside the Nyakyusa area all together (*vide supra*, p. 7), and many medicines came from the Kinga or Sangu. *Umwafi* for the poison ordeal was bought from Ngonde. Three other commodities also came from far—these were salt, which Kinga bought from Bena country and sold to the Nyakyusa; a red root (*ikipimba*) used as a dye and cosmetic, bought by the Mahasi from the Sangu and sold to the Nyakyusa; and brass or copper wire for making body rings (*amanyeta*).[1] There was scarcely any cloth in the country when the Europeans first arrived.[2] Pots were sold throughout the Lake-shore plain by the Kisi—Thomson found the Kisi pot-market operating in 1879[3]—and in the hills by Penja specialists. The details of this trade will be discussed when we come to consider the wider relations of the Nyakyusa: here we are only concerned to show that though villagers were dependent on outsiders for a little iron and salt, together with some medicines and ornaments, the bulk of the trade remained very small—salt and iron were extremely scarce—and economic relations beyond the village and kinship group were tenuous.

[1] We do not know by what route the wire came in: it is possible that it was as scarce as cloth before the first contact with Europeans. Elton speaks of spear shafts 'beautifully inlaid with a delicate tracery of brass and copper wire' (op. cit., p. 323), but the first reference we have traced to *amanyeta* in Nyakyusa country is in D. Kerr-Cross 'Crater-lakes north of Lake Nyasa', *The Geographical Journal*, Vol. V (1895), p. 118, his observation having been made in 1893. At that time he says 'you could buy anything for brass wire'. c.f. Moir, op. cit., p. 89. Fotheringham (op. cit., p. 27) says that the brass wire used in Ngonde (before 1889) was imported from Britain.

[2] Elton, op. cit., pp. 316, 320, 322, 331; Thomson, op. cit., Vol. I, pp. 268, 274.

[3] Thomson, op. cit., Vol. I, p. 263. The market was at Pupanganda, at the N.E. corner of the Lake, on the narrow strip of land between the escarpment of the Livingstones and the water.

The modern position is quite different. Each village still produces almost all its own food, but very considerable quantities of clothing, metal utensils, and tools are imported, in addition to salt, medicines, and ornaments. All the men and some of the women wear cloth. Every man possesses at least one loin-cloth, a hoe, and an axe, and he must pay an annual tax of 12s. with an additional 2s. for every wife after the first. These essential expenses are met by the sale of produce and labour. Rungwe district is one of the main sources of food for the nearby Lupa gold-fields, while its native-grown coffee is sold on the London market. In 1936 produce to the value of some £24,000[1] was sold from Rungwe district to the outside world, and considerable quantities of produce were also sold within the district to Government officials, missionaries, traders, and their servants. At the same time an exchange of different types of produce, particularly of rice from the plains for ground-nuts from the hills, is developing, and markets flourish at several centres.

Trade is in the hands of Indians and Swahili settled in the Government station, Tukuyu, the military station, Masoko, and the Lake-shore port, Mwaya. These traders employ Nyakyusa agents on a commission basis, to sell their goods and bring in produce; and there are many small shops scattered through the district, where commercially-minded Nyakyusa sell cloth, salt, paraffin, matches, hoes, knives, tin dishes, padlocks, soap, and cigarettes; and buy produce. But the shop is not a village centre. In the first place, one shop usually serves several villages; in the second, dependence on trade-goods is not yet so great that shopping close at hand is a necessary convenience, and when a purchase is to be made the buyer often prefers to go to one of the three main trading centres where his choice is greater. There was no sign of a Nyakyusa shop serving as a meeting-place for a village or a group of villages, as does the trading store of the Transkei.[2] Tukuyu market is indeed a social centre but it attracts custom from all over Rungwe district, not merely from one village or group of villages. Trading thus draws men outside their village; it does not nourish relationships within the village.

Employment for wages is the second means of meeting essential expenses, and we estimated that in 1936 approximately

---

[1] *Vide supra*, p. 16.
[2] Monica Hunter, *Reaction to Conquest*, p. 356.

£25,500 was earned by Nyakyusa migrant labourers and those employed in the district.[1] Earnings from employment are thus probably about equal to the total earnings from the sale of produce.

Within the district Nyakyusa men are employed in Government service as clerks, hospital orderlies, agricultural inspectors, and as labourers on roads and buildings. They are employed also as house servants by Europeans, as labourers on the twelve European-owned estates in the district, and as shop assistants and servants by Indian traders. There is also a little employment of Nyakyusa by Nyakyusa in agricultural work. Traditionally chiefs, being responsible for hoeing the fields of many wives, sometimes employed poor men to hoe for them, rewarding them after two hoeing seasons with a heifer or bull, but the extent of such employment was, in the old days, small and confined to the chiefs. Nowadays it has been considerably extended, rich men employing others to hoe or, less commonly, to plough for them, and paying them in stock or cash. A few monogamists also employ young boys to assist their wives in fetching wood and water.

Most Nyakyusa men now take paid employment at one time or another. Of a small sample of seventy-nine men, seventy-six (94 per cent) had been in paid employment. There was, however, a marked difference between the work histories of young and old, and between pagan and Christian. Of the pagan men over middle age, the majority of those who worked had not done so willingly, but had been conscripted as carriers, and the total periods for which they had worked were short, averaging under six months per man. On the other hand, all the Christian men over middle age had worked willingly, and the total period for which each had worked averaged over twelve years. Of the young men, all who had worked had done so willingly, but as with the older men, there was a marked difference between the length of time pagans and Christians spent in employment. The profession of Christianity is, amongst the Nyakyusa, correlated with education, and Christian young men, more especially the sons of Christians, tend to secure the skilled or semi-skilled jobs. Those who have skilled work tend to stay longer in a job and return home less frequently because they fear lest they may not find an equally good job again, and because they have often travelled far to find skilled

[1] Based on the estimated number of men in employment, and an analysis of wage rates within and outside the district.

work. The unskilled can always get a job, and frequent moves make little difference to their pay. In the sample taken 81 per cent of the Christian sons of Christians, 40 per cent of the Christian sons of pagans, and 5 per cent of the pagan sons of pagans had had skilled or semi-skilled jobs. These cases are set out in a table on p. 193. Of twenty-eight individuals who remained over a year at a stretch in employment, twenty were in skilled or semi-skilled jobs, and eighteen had had some schooling.

It was very difficult to get adequate information on the proportion of time that young men spent away, for though the periods they spent at work might be accurately remembered, the periods at home were not easily recorded. Ten young Christians (other than those cited in the sample above), whose work histories were carefully investigated, had spent, on the average, eighteen and a half months, out of the twenty-five months preceding their return home, in employment outside Rungwe district. That is, they had spent less than a quarter of their time at home. They are certainly not typical of the whole district, but they are probably not unrepresentative of the young Christians.

Certain points emerge from this study. Firstly, the time spent away from their homes at work by middle-aged and elderly pagans is negligible. Secondly, the middle-aged Christians have all worked for long periods, but during most of that time they have lived with their families in Christian villages attached to missions in the district; they are not migrants in the sense that their sons are, though they move from one mission village to another following employment. Thirdly, the great bulk of the young men work outside the district at some time, and those in skilled jobs (mostly Christians) tend to stay away for much longer periods than the unskilled. The effects of this are noticed by Nyakyusa themselves, who remarked of Kabembe Christian village that: 'There were few nice houses, for so many of the young men are away at work.' Nevertheless, even in Christian villages, the effects of men's absence is much less marked than it is in Ngonde, where the percentage of absentees is estimated at over half the able-bodied men.[1]

---

[1] It was estimated in 1934 that the total male labour force of the district was approximately 10,000 and that, of these, 500 men were in Southern Rhodesia and the Union, and 5,000 on the Lupa goldfields. (Figures supplied by courtesy of the District Commissioner, Karonga, from District records.)

Economic co-operation beyond the village has therefore increased enormously, and this is correlated with a decrease in economic co-operation within the village. The change is most obvious in the case of migrant labourers who, while remaining members of their villages (for they are domiciled there) cease, during the period they are at labour centres, to co-operate with their village neighbours in building, herding, hoeing and hunting; and those of their wives who accompany them are also withdrawn from village activities.

Of the men in paid employment within the district, some, such as house servants, police, hospital orderlies, and clerks attached to the Government station, are very largely withdrawn from economic co-operation in their villages; and even labourers employed on European estates, who still cultivate for themselves, and those who meet essential expenses by growing cash crops on their own account, co-operate less with their village neighbours than was customary in the old days.

As we have seen there is no village co-operation in the production of the main cash crops—rice and coffee—such as there was in the cultivation of three of the main food crops; therefore those who grow cash crops spend a smaller proportion of their time working with their neighbours than their fathers did. Moreover, the cultivation of cash crops encourages the development of hired labour at the expense of work parties attended by neighbours. In effect, the cultivation of cash crops involves less village co-operation than did the traditional cultivation of food crops, and in so far as men's energies are directed into producing cash crops, village co-operation becomes relatively less important.

We argue that while traditionally there was considerable co-operation in production between fellow villagers, that co-operation is diminishing, and its diminution is correlated with employment for wages and the production of crops for sale. The more educated the individual the more time he is likely to spend working outside his village, and the less he co-operates in economic activities with his fellow villagers.

CHAPTER IV

VALUES

a. Good company

ONE of the values most constantly stressed by the Nyakyusa is that of *ukwangala* which, in its primary sense, means 'the enjoyment of good company' and, by extension, the mutual aid and sympathy which spring from personal friendship. It implies urbane manners and a friendliness which expresses itself in eating and drinking together; not only merry conversation, but also discussion between equals, which the Nyakyusa regard as the principal form of education. 'It is by conversing with our friends', said one of our witnesses, 'that we gain wisdom (*amahala*); it is bad to sit quite still in men's company. A man who does this is a fool; he learns no wisdom, he has only his own thoughts. Moreover, a man who does not spend time with other people is always dirty, he does not compare himself with any friends. For we learn cleanliness of body in company, those who are dirty learning from their more cleanly friends. Again, if a man is accused of some crime and brought before the chief and is unable to defend himself easily and with eloquence we mock at him and say: "What is the matter with you? Do you live all by yourself? How is it that you are so foolish?" Wisdom and cleanliness are the two great things to be learnt in company. It is bad to live alone far from other people, such a man learns nothing: he never learns to express himself well, to converse wittily with friends, or to argue a case with eloquence. It is better to live with other people.'

'To live with other people', says our informant, but he implies 'to live with contemporaries'. For *ukwangala*, in the sense of discussion and easy give-and-take, can never occur between men and women, and is made difficult between men of different generations by the respect required of sons for their fathers. Since men are held to acquire manners, eloquence, and wisdom only in company it is necessary, the Nyakyusa argue, that they should build in villages, rather than in scattered homesteads, and since

VII. A LITTLE GIRL PLANTING SWEET POTATOES IN HER MOTHER'S FIELD

ukwangala is only possible between contemporaries[1] they must build with contemporaries. The value set on *ukwangala* is thus related to the age-village; male contemporaries build together, and the company of, and good fellowship with, his age-mates is what creates a man of wisdom and character. Such is the Nyakyusa view of society.

For conversation to flow merrily and discussion to be profound there must be *ifyakwangalela*—'the wherewithal for good fellowship', that is, food and drink—and very great stress is laid on sharing these. Men and boys are expected to eat regularly with age-mates. Traditionally, fathers and sons never ate or drank together—to do so was held to be incompatible with the respect due from son to father—and men sought the company of equals at meals. From the time a small boy begins to herd he is encouraged to bring home two or three friends to eat with him, and in turn he visits each of them. Since boys have no fields of their own until they marry, but co-operate in cultivation with their parents, it is to their own mothers they go for food, and parents are proud of a son bringing many friends. 'Perhaps', said Angombwike, 'a son will come with his friends and cut a huge bunch of bananas, and take thick milk and eat with them. When the father comes back his wives will tell him: "Your son has eaten all the thick milk and cut a banana bunch!" Then he will ask: "How many men were with my son?" "Six!" "Ah, he's a chief!" the old man will say, smiling proudly.' 'And formerly if a young man came home often alone to eat, his father would beat him, or even take a spear and wound him, and when people asked why he would say: "This great fool comes *alone* to my place, again and again." It is good to eat with friends, for boys to go round in groups of four or five.'

After marriage each man is cooked for by his own wife, but he continues to eat with his friends, bringing them to his home or going to their's .The first wife to come to a young men's village is said to have a hard life. 'She has to draw water and cook for all the young men of the village—they come to drink, and to wash, and they beat her with a stick if she refuses them. No, the

---

[1] *Ukwangala* is sometimes used with reference to relatives as well as to village-mates, as in the phrase '*atikwangala kanunu nabakamu bake*', meaning 'he is not on good terms with his relatives'; but in its fullest sense it can only be used with reference to contemporaries.

husband will not be angry; if he were, he would be mocked at: "Did not your father provide marriage-cattle for this woman for you that she might be the wife (*unkasi*) of us all?" Sometimes, when the woman is cooking, her husband's friends come and take food out of the pot before she has finished cooking. When she protests, saying it is not yet cooked, the men say: "It is your work to cook, ours to eat." Then when her husband comes she tells him that so and so, and so and so, have eaten the food and there is only water left in the pot. . . . But when her husband's friends begin to get married they say to their wives: "That woman is really our wife! Listen to her!" And she has honour among the other women, and when they go to fetch firewood she walks with nothing, another carries her axe and head-pad.' This account cannot be taken literally—the first wife in the village does not provide *all* the food for her husband's friends, who still eat at their mothers' homes, nor do they have any sexual rights over her though they call her 'wife', but she must serve them as far as she can.

Sometimes, we were told, men's eating groups last a lifetime, but often friends quarrel or move, and the group breaks up. 'Perhaps one eats at midday and does not summon his friend, but only calls him to the evening meal, then the other, who always calls his friend to the midday meal also, is angry, saying: "He grudges me food", and they separate. They just stop calling each other to eat. Or sometimes one tries to seduce his friend's wife, and on that account they separate.'

Eating with contemporaries is still considered right and proper by Nyakyusa men, and it is generally practised by pagans, but the old men say that youths are less ready to share food than formerly. 'This custom of eating together is dying.' Certainly in Christian villages the practice has declined markedly. Many unmarried Christians eat with their friends, but the majority of the married men eat at home alone. Out of eight married men living in Rungwe, for example, only two ate together regularly, and the most educated group, the clerks, are notorious in the district for their eating habits. 'People are much shocked at the clerks for eating food alone. They say they are proud.'

Apart from eating regularly with certain close friends, well-to-do pagan men are expected to entertain generously, inviting fellow villagers to drink beer, or to a 'dinner party'—an ample meal with delicious dishes, very carefully served—from time to

time, and providing meat feasts at funerals and at the initiation
and marriage of daughters.

As it is proper for men to eat with their equals it is improper
for them to eat with their juniors, or with women. In the past
fathers and sons never ate or drank together. Nowadays they
sometimes do so, even though conservative pagans, especially if
the fathers and sons have been working together. Three reasons
are adduced for the change: first, the example of Europeans and
Swahili; secondly, the fact that the country is at peace and it is
safe for all the men to drink together, whereas formerly, when
there was constant danger of attack, the young men were forbidden to drink at all; and thirdly the fact that young men earn
money and buy beer for themselves which they may invite a
'father' to share (*vide* Document p. 194). When the Nyakyusa
drink beer they replenish the pot repeatedly with boiling water,
and men expect to have the water boiled for them by a woman.
As Mwambuputa explained, 'Sometimes my son brings his pot
(of beer) to my place and calls his friends saying: "We will take
the pot to mother's house and she will pour in water for us."
Then they come to my place, and they invite me to drink, and I
accept, and we drink together. How can I grudge my son beer
when I have some? Did he and his friends not entertain me?' The
change turns on the fact that a young man can earn money and
buy beer for himself while yet unmarried. Formerly no unmarried
man commanded millet for brewing. Now, when he is drinking
in his father's homestead he cannot but invite his father to join
him.

Women commonly eat alone with their young children and unmarried daughters. Sometimes co-wives who are good friends
eat together, but they have no obligation to do so, and in a big
homestead perhaps only two wives will eat together and each of
the others eat alone. More usually a woman sends a dish of food
to each co-wife to eat in her own hut. For a woman to eat food
with a man is considered quite impossible. In those families in
which men no longer ate with neighbours one or two ate with
their young sons, but we heard of none who ate with their wives.
The example of Europeans did not influence them to this extent.

It is admitted that women also enjoy company and profit from
it, and it is considered good that they should get on with their
fellows, but there is no suggestion that it is a woman's duty to

cultivate her mind by conversation, or to eat regularly in company. In more formal hospitality there is the same difference; a woman never invites her friends to drink beer with her, or to a 'dinner party', as her husband must do if he is to have prestige with his neighbours. Women only share the ritual feasts at initiation and marriage, and at death.

There are local variations in Nyakyusa rituals, notably between the Kukwe and Nyakyusa proper. But everywhere there is an obligation to provide feasts at the funerals and marriages of dependants. When his wife or unmarried child dies, a man must kill cattle for his relatives and neighbours to feast at the burial,[1] while an heir provides a feast for his relatives, and the neighbours of the 'father' from whom he has inherited. At these feasts equal portions of meat are allotted to relatives and neighbours—or were so allotted until the rights of neighbours to meat at funerals were formally limited (*vide infra*, p. 93). An heir must also brew beer, or kill a bull, to feast the deceased's neighbours when he begins to cohabit with his widow, or moves the property from his village. At the initiation and marriage of a girl there is a series of feasts (five in Selya), the food for which is provided partly by the groom's family and partly by the bride's; and if, as is usual, the bride is still a virgin or has been deflowered by the groom himself, he must provide a bull in thanks for her virginity (*engambako jabusungu*), which is killed to feast the neighbours and relatives of her parents. The carcass is divided into three portions, one for the immediate neighbours of her father (men), one for 'those relatives with whom the father is on good terms and exchanges cattle', and one for the 'mothers' of the bride. Women as well as men eat meat and other fine food at all the marriage and funeral feasts.

The third occasion on which a feast for the village neighbours is thought to be essential is when a man or woman has offended his (or her) neighbours, or the neighbours of a 'father'. Thus a woman who has shirked her duty of advising on the division of her brother's inheritance, and is disapproved of by her neighbours on this account, begs pardon of them over a brewing of beer (*vide infra*, pp. 107, 236); a son, having insulted his father's neighbours

---

[1] For the circumstances under which other relatives must provide cattle for funeral feasts see Godfrey Wilson, 'Nyakyusa Conventions of Burial', *Bantu Studies*, Vol. XIII (1939), p. 18.

IX. NDIMBOMI, A CHRISTIAN WOMAN, STOOPING TO GREET A MAN

X. 'THE DIGNITY OF THE HOMESTEAD'—— OLD STYLE

by insulting his father, begs pardon of them by bringing a bull which his father may eat with them; or a daughter-in-law, having inadvertently caught sight of her father-in-law, brings beer for him to drink with his neighbours.

At all feasts food is allotted in terms of kinship and village affiliation, and this tends to enhance the solidarity of kin groups and villages. For example, funeral meat is first divided between relatives and non-relatives, and that allocated to non-relatives is subdivided by villages, each village headman present being given a share to divide between his people, men and women. When a relative of the chief has died, and the whole country has come to mourn, the chief allots a cow to each of his senior headmen, who then divide the carcasses between the villages in their respective halves of the chiefdom. The meat at a 'coming out' ceremony, and at the great feasts which were held after battle, was divided in the same way, and we saw a division of this kind when a senior headman who had been in exile was welcomed home (cf. pp. 273–4). Thus the right to share in a feast depends either on kinship with the provider, or on membership of a village.

The Christians' code of hospitality differs somewhat from that of the pagans: the latter stress feeding *neighbours*, whether it be in the daily eating together, or at informal beer and dinner parties, or at ceremonies, while the Christians stress feeding strangers, quoting the text 'I was a stranger and ye took me in'[1] and the parable of the Good Samaritan.[2] The pagans jibe at the Christians for being inhospitable because (as the Christians themselves admit) they entertain their neighbours less than pagans do; the Christians point to their wider obligations, and the fact that they do feed and house visitors from a distance, especially fellow Christians gathering for Church festivals. The Christians are very conscious also of the difficulties of hospitality in a mono-gamous household, for a wife must not only do all the cooking for visitors (and many Nyakyusa dishes require considerable labour to prepare), but she must also help to grow the food. The pagan who can afford to entertain much has several wives who share the work between them, whereas a Christian, no matter how rich, cannot have more than one wife and remain a member of his Church—unless it be one of the two small independent

---

[1] Matthew xxv. 35.
[2] Luke x. 29.

African churches which countenance polygyny. The difficulty is partially overcome in some well-to-do Christian families by hiring labour to work in their fields and to fetch water and wood, and by offering visitors coffee or tea, which are easily prepared, in place of home-brewed beer; nevertheless the conflict between the value of hospitality (to which pagan and Christian alike subscribe, though they define it rather differently) and the value of monogamy, is often acute.

The mutual obligations of neighbours are not confined to feeding one another, for neighbours share with relatives the obligation of giving sympathy and assistance at the various crises in Nyakyusa life; the concept of *ukwangala* includes keeping on good terms with people by being sympathetic and obliging.

All the members of a village (except young children) are obliged to attend every burial of an adolescent or adult in that village; they go to mourn the death of a neighbour or condole with one who is burying a 'son', for if a man dies while his father (or father's full brother, or his own senior brother) is yet alive, he is often buried in his 'father's' homestead.[1] Where a youth or man is buried by his 'father', his fellow villagers must attend the funeral also, but boys and young men need not go to a funeral in their fathers' village unless it is a village-mate of their own who is being buried.

Funerals are occasions for feasting and dancing, so the obligation 'to mourn one another' (*ukulelanela*) does not press hardly, and the Nyakyusa feeling is that no one would fail to come unless he were a witch, and fearful lest his victim rise from the grave and denounce him. 'If a man does not go to his neighbour's burial then at once people say: "It was you who bewitched him. Why else do you not come to bury him?" ' Failure to come is certain evidence that the truant is 'a harsh man who does not keep on good terms with people (*nkali, atikwangala kanunu nabandu*)'.

One neighbour, 'he who went about most with the dead man', is appointed by the headman of the village to help the relatives dig the grave, and village neighbours must also bring small gifts of food and firewood for the entertainment of the many guests.

---

[1] A married man whose 'fathers' are dead, or do not choose to exercise their right to bury him, is buried at his own home, and a woman who has borne a child is buried at her husband's home.

Food (other than meat) is provided on the day of the burial by the women of the home at which the burial takes place, on the succeeding day by visiting relatives, and on the third day by village neighbours. Women neighbours, like woman relatives, often bring gifts of bark-cloth belts (*amakiba*) with which to bind up the bellies of their bereaved friends, who are all atremble and full of fear, and so support them. These belts symbolize the sympathy of friends in the fearful grief of the mourners. 'If a woman wears many belts at a burial that means that she has many friends; her passionate grief is comforted by their friendship.'[1] And neighbours, like relatives and close friends from other chiefdoms, may bring cloths which are used to wrap the corpse and bind up the bellies of the chief mourners. But these gifts of food, firewood, belts, and cloth are the limit of a neighbour's obligations; very rarely does a neighbour bring a bull to kill for the funeral feast, whereas close kinsmen and affines are obliged to provide a bull or cow for this purpose if they have one. And neighbours take virtually no share in the elaborate ritual which follows for cleansing relatives from the contagion of death, driving the thought of the deceased out of their minds, and bringing back his spirit to bless the home. Their only part is to bring small gifts of millet from which to brew the beer drunk at the close of this ritual.

At an ordinary birth there is very little ceremony and the village as a group is not concerned, though close friends will help the mother during her confinement, fetching wood and water for her, and bringing occasional gifts of cooked food; but twin births are regarded as fearful and dangerous, and an elaborate ritual is performed to cleanse relatives from the contagion which, if left untreated, is believed to lead to serious swelling of the arms, legs, and stomachs, accompanied by diarrhoea. Relatives are treated with many medicines, while village neighbours are sprinkled with one only, but their cattle, especially the cattle herded with those of the man who has begotten twins, are thought to be in danger. At one twin ritual we watched there was some discussion whether all the cattle of the age-village should be treated, or only those of the herd-group to which the father of the twins belonged. Finally it was decided that on previous occasions all the cattle of the village had been treated, and a message was sent

[1] cf. Godfrey Wilson, 'Nyakyusa Conventions of Burial', *Bantu Studies*, Vol. XIII (1939), p. 12.

to bring all the herds of the village for treatment. The father of these twins explained that neighbours would suffer less than relatives, if left untreated, but 'their legs would ache a little *because we eat with them*'. And here we come to an idea which appears in many situations in Nyakyusa life, the idea that contagion is spread through eating together. Relatives of parents of twins are not thought to be in danger until they eat or drink with one of the parents: the ritual is performed so that they may eat together safely. Similarly a murderer and his relatives are thought to be in magical danger from the relatives of the murdered man only if they should eat or drink with them. So too, the bond between neighbours which puts them in danger from the impurity of one of them is the sharing of food.

At the initiation and marriage of a girl, neighbours again assist and identify themselves with the principals. When she reaches puberty a girl is secluded, and her companions in the village—the girls who are her immediate juniors, for the older ones will have joined their husbands—keep her company. Some are her own younger sisters and half-sisters, others are not related at all. Should one girl of the village not join them she is not accused of witchcraft, but it is unusual for one to stay away; to do so would show 'pride' (*amatingo*). These companions (*abapanji*) sleep and eat with the 'bride' (*unsungu*)[1] and share her tasks and lessons, fetching firewood, making mats, learning songs, and listening to the instruction of 'the mothers'. They and the 'bride' go about together as a group and, accompanied by one or two 'mothers', may visit a 'bride' and her maids in another village, the two groups competing in dancing and singing. So keen is the rivalry that formerly, we were told, the visits sometimes led to fighting between the maids and 'mothers' of each 'bride', particularly when the competing groups came from different chiefdoms. At the end of the ritual two of the maids accompany the bride to her husband's house, and spend a few days with her there, sharing the attentions of her husband at night (*vide infra*, p. 87).

During her seclusion the bride avoids her father, whom she refers to as 'father-in-law', and she avoids also all his contem-

---

[1] *Unsungu* means a girl who has reached puberty but has not yet borne a child. She is usually, though not invariably, betrothed, and her 'husband' has a part in the puberty ritual. There is no exact English translation, and we think that 'bride' is the least misleading in this context.

poraries, the men of the village. They are forbidden to enter her hut, and if she catches sight of one outside she turns away from him and shields her face with a mat. And at the end of the seclusion each 'village father', as well as her own father, must make her a small gift, before she will greet him. The co-wives and some of the village neighbours of the bride's mother form the group of 'mothers' who treat and instruct the bride, help to provide food for the feasts, and finally take her to her husband. Not all the village neighbours are expected to cook for the marriage feasts of a commoner's daughter, only immediate neighbours and special friends (together with relatives) who have been asked to do so; but if an immediate neighbour is not invited to help he will feel affronted. Twijulege explained that 'If the owner of the homestead overlooks someone who has built close to him, and does not say to him, "They are coming to bring the marriage-cattle for *your* child, please help us to cook", then that friend will be angry, and will think to himself, "Perhaps we are not on good terms (*tutikwangala kanunu*) though I had always thought we were", and he will say to the father of the bride: "Why did you not tell me that they were coming to bring the marriage-cattle for your child that I might help you with the food? I was startled by the rejoicing." ' An old man who had only called one friend, besides relatives and the 'best man', to help cook at the marriage of his daughter, was stigmatized as 'a surly fellow who does not care about being on good terms with people'.

The groom, on his part, is supported by his village-mates, who come in a crowd driving the marriage-cattle, and dancing the stamping marriage dance (*ukukanya nganya*). His mother, who has a share in the ritual and brings gifts of food, follows him, accompanied by some of her co-wives and village neighbours.

Village solidarity is thus exhibited at ceremonies, not only in the allocation of food, but by the manner in which village contemporaries of the same sex rally to each other's help, dance together and, if need be, fight together.

Besides offering sympathy and help when their fellow is in need, it is the duty of neighbours to give him advice, and persuade him to act wisely. If, for example, a man has delayed very long in providing marriage-cattle for his son, his neighbours take the son's part, and try to persuade him to give the cattle. 'Perhaps', said one informant, 'the son may elope with a girl, and then if the father says his son has done wrong his neighbours reply: "You have caused him to do wrong yourself. Did you suppose him to be a boy that you did not provide marriage-cattle for him?" Then the father becomes more ready to pay damages for his son.' And again, 'If a young man finds that his father objects to his marrying the girl he loves, he complains to his father's neighbours (*pamafumu abapalamani ba gwise*). Then they discuss the matter and say to the father: "Do you want him to teach you a lesson by taking a chief's wife or daughter, for whom many cattle must be given?" So the father agrees.'

Neighbours are concerned, too, to see a fair distribution of a deceased fellow's estate, and the fulfilment of the heir's obligations to his wards. 'It is not the relatives, but "the fathers of the village" who watch over a young boy's interests when his father is dead' (*vide infra*, p. 106). We listened to one discussion of a quarrel over inheritance which was believed to have led to kinsmen working sorcery against each other. At this discussion four village neighbours of the sick man (thought to be suffering from the sorcery of his father's brother's son), as well as ten relatives, attended.

The father's neighbours are also asked to mediate when a son has wronged his father and seeks forgiveness. For example, Mwangobola's son had committed adultery with his father's wife. He paid six head of cattle and then went off to the coast, where he remained a long time. When he returned he brought two cows and approached his father's neighbours, asking them to take the cows to his father. When they took the cows his father said: 'He must find a bull as well, and brew beer, because he is my eldest son.' So he got a bull and brewed beer, and the father also brewed. 'Then', said the old man who reported the case, 'the fathers of the village came together and the bull was killed and they ate the meat and drank the beer. . . . Thus the son made friends with his father.'

Here we have the ritual of reconciliation between relatives in which neighbours of the senior must participate, for their anger is held to be as dangerous to the junior as that of his senior relative. Informal giving of advice merges into the practice of arbitration, and of murmuring against a wrong-doer, and thus, it is thought, causing him misfortune. These latter practices are discussed in ensuing chapters.

b. Dignity

Though the Nyakyusa lay so much stress on geniality, and praise a man for being 'a good mixer', yet they greatly admire dignity (*ubusisya*). To be *nsisya* (dignified, impressive) is one of the attributes of chiefs and village headmen, sought, as we have seen, through medicines; but ordinary men may also aspire to it in their persons and homesteads. Indeed, *ubusisysa bwa nkaja*, the dignity of the homestead, is one of the legitimate channels of ambition to a Nyakyusa, and is something achieved largely through hard work.

Two styles of huts are traditional—one round, with the wall slanting outwards towards the top, and a conical roof; the other rectangular with perpendicular walls, a pitched roof, and curving gables (cf. Plates X and XI). For a homestead to be dignified the huts must be built of good bamboos, and the space between them packed with oval-shaped mud bricks, carefully worked in patterns. Special pains are taken with the ends of long huts (*ifibaga*) to get a good curve on the roof pole, and a pleasing design of bricks and criss-cross binding on the gable (cf. Plate XI). Inside, the walls are plastered smooth, and house-proud women mould a pattern in the mud with their fingers, which runs round the wall like a frieze. A long hut, showing that the owner has many cattle and young wives to house, adds dignity, but the homestead of a relatively poor man may be *nsisya* if the huts are well built, the open space between them weeded and swept, and the bananas pruned and heavy with fruit; while a shabby long hut and a dirty court are never dignified, no matter how rich the owner. The insistence on cleanliness both within the huts and in the court is very marked;[1] men themselves weed and sweep regularly around their homesteads, and their young sons must help them. The Nyakyusa jibe at their neighbours for being dirty in person, in cooking, and in their homesteads: indeed the dirty habits of the women is given as a main reason for not intermarrying with the Kinga or Poroto; and a Christian confided in

---

[1] Thomson, Kerr-Cross, and Lugard were all greatly impressed by Nyakyusa cleanliness; Thomson, op. cit., p. 271; Kerr-Cross, 'Geographical Notes on the Country between Lakes Nyassa, Rukwa, and Tanganyika', *The Scottish Geographical Magazine*, Vol. VI (1890), p. 283; Lugard, op. cit., Vol. I, p. 131.

us that it was a great effort to her to accept food from the Poroto when she went on preaching tours, because their huts and pots were so dirty.

Trees are felt to add to the dignity of a homestead as well as throwing a grateful shade; the beautiful *umwali* trees have long been valued for this purpose, and to-day exotics are much sought after. For example, the old chief Mwaipopo, noticing a fine cypress when he visited us at Isumba (a cottage that had once been a German mission hospital) inquired whether there were not some seedlings under the tree. He himself carefully dug up one and took it away to plant in his 'capital'. Some Nyakyusa even *steal* trees to adorn their homesteads. It is said that jacarandas planted out in an avenue at Tukuyu disappeared within a very short time.

The attributes of dignity in the homestead are changing perceptibly. Well-built huts in the old style, a long *ikibaga*, a well-swept court, fruitful bananas, and fine *umwali* trees are mentioned by the old men; but many of the younger ones prefer hip-roofed houses (a style introduced by Europeans and known, appropriately enough, as 'the partridge') with windows and door of European pattern, beds of flowers, roses, fine coffee and exotic trees. Yet they keep the court well swept; for lawns have not become fashionable.

A fine presence, a well-kept homestead rich in cattle and bananas and shaded with stately trees, are in themselves impressive, but the possessor of them only reaches his full dignity when he acts as host, and uses his fine food and fine home for lavish hospitality. Wealth and an impressive manner, without urbanity and hospitality, may well lead to accusations of witchcraft.

c. Display

Feasts provide opportunity for swaggering parades and dances in which the Nyakyusa delight to display themselves and their possessions; they are the great occasions for *ukumoga*, that is, display in approved forms. Dancing, exhibiting a beautiful body with only a narrow bark-cloth belt to hide it, showing off physical strength and the aggressiveness of a warrior, parading orna-

XI. A TRADITIONAL STYLE LONG HUT (IKIBAGA)

XII. 'THE DIGNITY OF THE HOMESTEAD'—— NEW STYLE

ments and fine clothes, or a splendid herd of cattle—all these are forms of *ukumoga*.

Traditionally Nyakyusa women wore only a bark-cloth belt tied around the waist and drawn between the legs to fall in streamers in front (cf. Plate XIII), and the pagan women cling to this dress, maintaining that it is only 'Swahili women with dirty diseases' who have to wear clothes to cover their sores, and if a pagan woman has a cloth she will probably wave it like a flag or hang it over one shoulder, when she dances. Except for the Christians, few Nyakyusa women regularly wear clothes. The Christians like a brightly coloured cloth tied under the armpits, and hanging to the knees (cf. Plate IX). Women make their own bark-cloths with great care, and decorate them with geometrical patterns in red and black, the red dye being imported from the Livingstone mountains; they mix this same dye with a fatty ointment made from the seeds of the *unsyunguti* tree, and rub it all over themselves. The most prized ornament (worn by both sexes) are body rings of coiled brass or copper wire (cf. Plate XIII). In the past men went naked except for these body rings[1] but, unlike the women, they have taken enthusiastically to clothes, and swagger around in brilliant loin-cloths or flowing white togas; or, if rather more sophisticated, in freshly pressed shorts and shirts, or lounge suits and topees.

The series of ceremonies at a girl's initiation and marriage, and at a funeral, are regular occasions for dancing, and the birth and death rates are so high that these occur very frequently within a chiefdom of 3,000 men. Once in a generation the eagerly anti-cipated 'coming out' ceremony offers an even greater opportunity for display. Skill in dancing is admired and the young people are encouraged to practise. A bride's mother does a great deal of the heavy work for her daughter, saying '*amoge tasi*', which means literally 'let her display herself first', and implies 'let her have a good time while she can'; and a father may use the same phrase of his son. Angombwike explained: 'The old men used to take great pride in their sons; often a man would say to his son: "Don't you hoe for me, I'll do the hoeing myself, you go and swagger about." Sometimes a man would sell a cow and buy a huge-bladed spear and give it to his son. Then, if he heard that his son

[1] cf. Elton, op. cit., p. 322; H. H. Johnston, *British Central Africa*, p. 18.

was a fierce man in war, and always quarrelling with and spearing his fellows, he would say with pride: "He is my son!" And if he heard people saying: "The son of so and so is a fierce man", he would rejoice. And if the son wished to marry young his father would refuse him cows, saying: "Swagger first." ' That truculence (*ubukali*) is a form of swaggering for men, is still evident in the funeral dance, when men charge up and down with spears, displaying their strength, and take umbrage at the slightest thing (*vide infra*, p. 151). And marriage was deliberately delayed partly because a bachelor was thought to be a fiercer warrior than a married man.

This admiration of truculence, as shown in the funeral dance, reveals a contradiction in Nyakyusa values. On the one hand urbanity and good temper are praised—they are intrinsic to *ukwangala*—on the other truculence. Is the opposition one between old and new values, or is the contradiction itself traditional? It is obvious that a readiness to fight was a quality valuable to the village in the days of inter-village warfare, and the Nyakyusa tell of murderers and even thieves being reprieved just because they were so useful in war. 'We did not drive away violent men (*abagasi*) in the old days; we said: "They will fight along with us in the future" '; whereas since the pacification of the country, quarrelsome men have become nothing but a liability, likely to get their fellows and their chief into trouble with the Administration. The Christian emphasis, also, is all on the virtue of peaceableness. There has probably been some change in values with the disappearance of war from the villages, but we think that a certain contradiction always existed: swaggering young men were admired, and children were warned not to be quarrelsome (*nkali*) towards their fellows, lest they be accused of practising witchcraft, or rouse the anger of a witch. The contradiction is not, of course, peculiar to Nyakyusa society, and it may be resolved by defining the groups within which fighting is excluded, and those in which it is approved. Most Nyakyusa would hold that in the old days quarrelsomeness within the village was bad, that towards members of another village of the same chiefdom it was allowable, and towards members of another chiefdom it was good. In the wider society of to-day the same distinctions are apparent: the war dance at funerals is limited lest it lead to fighting between villages (*vide infra*, p. 151) but admiring audiences watch their friends in the detachment of the King's African Rifles at bayonet drill in Masoko.[1]

Display is felt to be particularly appropriate to young people, and bachelors were held to be the fiercest warriors, but neither dancing nor fighting was confined to young men. The chief Mwaipopo (Plate V) was famous as a skilful and ardent dancer when over seventy, and the leader in war was the senior headman of the country, who, if not already married when he took office, had to marry almost immediately, since his wife shared in the ritual of establishing his house. Furthermore the villages of married men of the ruling generation fought, as well as the villages of their bachelor brothers and sons.

That the Nyakyusa had some skill in warfare is certain, for they defeated and drove off Ngoni raiders and warriors of the Sangu chief Merere,[2] but they never developed a military kingdom like that of the Bemba to the west, or the Hehe to the east, nor did they raid at large like the Masai and Ngoni. Their geographical position sheltered them very considerably from outside attack, and discouraged raiding abroad. They confined themselves mostly to lifting the cattle of neighbouring chiefdoms.

Cattle, whether they be spoils of war or inherited wealth, are displayed. Not only does a long byre add to the dignity of a homestead, but, when there is some ceremony at the home of a rich man, he shows off his herd by driving it round and round the homestead. At other times his sons gallop it along the village street, the iron bells with which the animals are adorned ringing merrily. Nyakyusa smiths make cow-bells in sets,[3] to chime in harmony, and the aim of a rich man is to own a set of bells which ring a full chime, and a herd large enough to carry them. Nowadays those who own bicycles display them in the same sort of way, riding round and round the homestead at a ceremony, and ringing the bells madly.

Unlike the enjoyment of good company (*ukwangala*), display

---

[1] This detachment was not supposed to include Nyakyusa who were recruited for a detachment stationed outside the district, but in fact Nyakyusa got in by posing as men from Ngonde, Nyasaland.

[2] D. Kerr-Cross, 'Crater-lakes north of Lake Nyasa', *The Geographical Journal*, Vol. V (1895), p. 119–20; Lugard, op. cit., Vol. I, p. 56, speaks of the Nyakyusa as 'brave in war'.

[3] We deposited a set in the Livingstone Memorial Museum, Livingstone, N. Rhodesia.

(*ukumoga*) is not confined to the company of contemporaries of the same sex. Indeed the liveliest dancing is before members of the opposite sex, and is often the preliminary to love-making; but full opportunity for display is thought to depend upon living in a village, rather than in scattered homesteads. Some Nyakyusa are colonists, cultivating and building out in unoccupied bush country five or six miles from a settled area; but living out in the bush is disliked by most people and is done, we were told, only for gain. Cattle are said to increase very much more quickly out in bush, where grazing is plentiful, than they do on the village pastures, and the yield of virgin fields made in the bush is high. Hence the Nyakyusa dictum: 'People live in the villages for display, in the bush for gain.' And individuals commonly display themselves as members of a group—a group of contemporaries of the same sex, that is, of village-mates.

d. Decency

The basis of Nyakyusa sexual morality is the separation of the sexual activities of successive generations, more particularly the separation of the sexual activities of mothers and sons, and the complete segregation of fathers-in-law and daughters-in-law.

Nyakyusa informants hold that boys are sent out of their parents' village to build apart so that their parents may have privacy. Mwaisumo explained: 'If a boy over ten years old stays at home to sleep, he is laughed at by his friends, and his own parents send him away. They say, "If he sleeps at home he will hear what his parents talk about at night"; the night is always full of lewd talk; and he may even see them undressing. He will grow up a fool, with little wisdom! You see at the boys' village', he went on to say, 'the older boys tell all sorts of stories, especially about women, they discuss love-making and women, and tell tales of their own conquests. The younger ones listen to these things and that's all right in the boys' village, that is how we learn, but we compare in our minds and think that if a boy stays at home it is as if he listened to all this from his parents, and people always do talk lewdly at night; and that is very bad, that is foolishness. But in the boys' village it is good for the young ones to listen, that is how children grow up.'

Another informant added: 'Boys usually move of their own accord; if they don't their fellows mock them saying: "Why do you sleep with your mother and see the evil things of your mother when she puts on her bark-cloth? . . . You sleep with your mother and see the evil things of your father and mother. Perhaps they think you are asleep, but you see them." '

Sons and mothers are separated at night, but the boys come to their mothers' houses for food; fathers-in-law and daughters-in-law are completely segregated from the time a girl is betrothed or, if she has been betrothed in infancy, from the time she is about eight years old. Her father-in-law is pointed out once to the newly betrothed girl, and after that she must never look at him. She never enters a house in which he is, and she leaves a path if she catches a glimpse of him, or is warned by her friends that he is approaching; she also avoids his name and anything associated with him, being particularly careful to avoid going near the bed in her mother-in-law's house, should she visit her mother-in-law during her father-in-law's absence. The avoidance is extended to a large group of kinsmen—her father-in-law's brothers and cousins, her mother-in-law's brothers, the husbands of her mother-in-law's sisters, and the fathers-in-law (direct and by extension) of each of her own sisters;[1] but it is *not* extended to the father-in-law's village-mates. In practice, the forms of avoidance vary with the actual relationship—the more distant the connection the less strictly are the rules observed—and with the locality, for the Nyakyusa proper avoid in-laws more carefully than the Kukwe do. A Nyakyusa wife, for example, should *never* enter her father-in-law's house, but a Kukwe wife may do so during his absence.

The Nyakyusa argue, cogently enough, that it would be quite impossible for father-in-law and daughter-in-law to live in the same village and avoid one another as they do; and indeed the difficulties of avoidance are apparent at ceremonies when members of different villages are congregated. Then the women are on the watch all the time, and one or another is constantly taking refuge in a hut, or in the bananas, as her friends warn her of the approach of a 'father-in-law'. The practical difficulties were obvious when we attended a funeral ceremony at Mwambelike's

---

[1] cf. Monica Wilson, 'Nyakyusa Kinship' in *African Systems of Kinship and Marriage*, edited by A. R. Radcliffe-Brown and Daryll Forde.

house, one pouring wet day, when sitting or cooking out of doors was impossible. Mwambelike's wife was cooking for us and other visitors. Suddenly there was a cry from her husband and others, 'Father-in-law!' She ran out of the room, leaving her cooking. The man who came in was a mother's brother's son (*untani*) of Mwambelike's father, and counted as a mother's brother (*umwipa*) to Mwambelike. Mwambelike explained to him that his wife was cooking and asked him to stay 'at the door', so he went out, and the woman came back. She cooked placidly for half an hour. Mwambelike said: 'Tell my daughter to come and help you with the cooking', then, looking round, he said: 'Oh no, she can't, her father-in-law is here too.' This was her betrothed husband's mother's brother. Mwambelike's daughter was about thirteen years old and had not yet reached puberty. Some time later the wife called to this girl to bring her some water. Nothing was said by the men and after three calls the girl scurried in giggling, put the water down, and scurried out. Then the men took notice, the 'father-in-law' said nothing, but Mwambelike said apologetically: 'It's all right; she did not look at him.' When the wife had finished cooking our food she went out, and the men called her 'father-in-law' in. He stayed about five minutes then, realizing that all the men were hungry, he said: 'I will go away. Let her get on with her cooking'; so he went out and she came back and cooked for the other guests.

The strength of the feeling against seeing one's father-in-law is apparent in the behaviour of Christian women. The missionaries have taught that avoidance is unnecessary and inconvenient, if not unchristian, and that a daughter-in-law should behave as a daughter to her husband's father. Various Christian women assured us that they 'did not avoid their fathers-in-law', though most admitted to 'avoiding a little'. One day S—, who had volunteered that she did not avoid her father-in-law, had come to tea with us, together with another Christian woman. S—'s father-in-law, a chief, came along the veranda on an unexpected visit. Before he was visible S— leapt up, gasped 'father-in-law!' and hid herself in the corner of the room behind the door, facing the wall with her face buried in her hands. She stood there a few seconds gasping, then came back to her place and pushing away her chair, sat down on the floor, whispering determinedly: 'I *won't* avoid him, I *won't* avoid him.' Her friend also slipped off her chair and sat on the floor. We said to Mwaipopo as he entered: 'There is a daughter-in-law here.' He said: 'That's all right, she is enjoying the company of Kagile (M.W.)', but he was obviously restive, and went outside as soon as food appeared. He said to G.W.: 'That's quite all right, let them go on enjoying each other's company. She (i.e. S—) does not avoid me because M— (a local missionary) brought her to me one day and I killed a bull for them, but let us stay outside now, for they would be ashamed to eat.' The women protested very much saying *they* would go out, but the chief would not agree. As soon as they had drunk their tea they hurried off, and crouching down with their backs towards the men they answered their farewell greetings.

In reply to queries as to why they insist that father-in-law and daughter-in-law avoid one another, the Nyakyusa relate a myth of incest between them: 'Long ago a chief's son married a very beautiful wife. The boy's father saw the girl and after one look desired her, for she was very beautiful, and he said: "She is fit to be a chief's wife (*umwehe*)." Men said this was a very bad thing and agreed that in future they would not look at their daughters-in-law. That is how avoidance began. It was for fear of fathers making love to their sons' wives.' This myth is related with some diffidence, and not everyone knows it, but it was told us, or referred to, repeatedly, and may be taken as current in the society. One informant, a very intelligent woman doctor, also associated seeing a father-in-law with seeing his sexual activities. 'We think that to see your husband's father is very rude, because it is as if you saw him sleeping with your husband's mother. You compare, you see, your husband's body and you see your husband's father's body. It is very bad.'

Age-villages are then associated with the feeling that fathers-in-law and daughters-in-law must be kept completely separate lest they should commit incest, and that adolescent youths should not have any glimpse of the sexual activities of their parents; but the separation of the generations is not complete, for marriage with the daughter of a village neighbour is approved, provided he is not an *immediate* neighbour. Mwakionde explained that in the old days people disliked marriage with the daughter of a next-door neighbour because she was 'like a daughter'—'the fathers ate *embalaga* (a dish made with bananas) together'—but marriage with the daughters of other village-mates was always approved.

Marriage with the daughter of a father's age-mate is also favoured, though she is called 'a village-sister' (*ulilumbu pa kipanga*), and such a marriage means that a girl has to avoid a father-in-law in her own father's village.

Adultery with the wife of a village neighbour is regarded as a heinous offence, much worse than ordinary adultery, and so also is the seduction of the wife of one's father, or of one of his village neighbours, even though a father's wives are eventually inherited by his son. 'It is bad,' Mwaisumo said, 'because they are friends of one's own mother.' That is to say, there is a direct extension of the incest taboo so long as the father is alive. A son who has committed adultery with his own father's wives is afraid to attend his father's funeral lest he fall dead.[1]

Since marriage between 'brothers and sisters of the village' is approved, courtship goes on between the youths of a boys' village and the girls of their fathers' village, with this limitation, that brothers and sisters, or cousins—the descendants of a common grandfather or great-grandfather—must not be present at a flirtation. Boys from the same age-village go about together, and they commonly flirt with any group of girls they meet, whether from their fathers' village or not. It is then that the incest taboos are learnt. If one of the boys is known to be related to one of the girls his companions send him away saying: 'Don't you see your sister is here? You cannot come.'

Formerly, we were told, girls of the same village lived together (until they were married) in a girls' house (*isaka*), where they were visited secretly by lovers, who had external relations with them. Such girls' houses no longer exist among the Nyakyusa, each daughter living in her father's homestead until she is married, and sleeping with her own mother, or with a stepmother when her father visits her mother, or with the other children in a separate division of the long house, if her mother is the only wife. Only when she is keeping an older companion company at the initiation ritual does she sleep with the other girls of the village in a hut provided by the 'bride's' father.[2] But permanent girls' houses still exist in Ngonde. There each family

[1] Occasionally an elderly man gives his son leave to sleep with his wives in secret, while he (the father) is still alive; then an elaborate ritual is performed on the father's death.

[2] This hut is referred to as *isaka* also, but only during the initiation; it is to be distinguished from a hut regularly reserved for girls.

usually has a separate hut for its girls, to which, we were told, their lovers come secretly by night.

Nyakyusa informants connected the existence of girls' houses with the marriage age. In Ngonde the marriage age of girls is much higher than it is among the Nyakyusa, partly because there are many more Christians (45 per cent as against 16 per cent) who do not allow polygyny, partly because even the girls from pagan families in Ngonde dislike marrying a polygynist, and partly because a much higher percentage of young men are away at work, than from Nyakyusa country. Formerly, they said, the marriage age was higher among the Nyakyusa also, and then the Nyakyusa had *isaka*. It is certain that among the Nyakyusa betrothal of a girl has long taken place before puberty, for the husband plays an essential part in the puberty ritual, and there were always some girls who were betrothed when quite tiny; but the evidence is fairly clear that the average age of betrothal among the pagans has been going down. The Nyakyusa view is that no man in his senses, who is able to marry, will engage a little girl of eight if he can find one approaching puberty; and it is the scarcity of wives that makes men 'marry' little girls. It is also clear that the number of cattle in the country, and their rate of circulation, has increased during the last two decades, so there are 'too many cattle chasing too few brides' with the result that the marriage age of girls has fallen, and the number of cattle given at marriage has increased.

Once she is betrothed, a girl's 'husband' has exclusive sexual rights over her, and she cannot entertain lovers in the *isaka*. The only two occasions on which she may flirt and have external relations with a man other than her husband, are during an initiation ceremony, when the girls of the village who have not yet reached puberty sleep with their fellow who is being initiated, and there entertain young men, and when she accompanies a bride to her husband's house. A bridegroom is expected to have external relations with his wife's two friends, as well as with his wife, on the night they bring her to his house. Love-making at the initiation-marriage ritual is held to be 'part of the ritual' and a means of sex education, and a husband can make no complaint about his 'wife' receiving lovers then, provided that penetration does not take place.

Homosexual practices are said to be very common in the boys' villages—they begin among boys of ten to fourteen herding cows, and continue among young men until marriage, but they are said never to continue after that, and are regarded simply as a substitute for heterosexual pleasure. 'A man never dreams of making love to another man'—only of making love to a woman. If a boy's own father, or a village father, finds a son with another youth he will beat him, but provided both parties were willing, there is no court case, and the older men treat the practice tolerantly as a manifestation of adolescence. To force a fellow to have homosexual intercourse against his will is a serious offence, comparable to witchcraft (*vide* Document, p. 196). Lesbian practices are said also to exist, but we have no certain evidence of this: if they do occur it is much more likely to be among the older wives of chiefs and other polygynists than among the girls, who have so much attention from young men.

It is in conversation and play with village contemporaries that some knowledge of sex is acquired. Girls learn about sex from their immediate seniors, and they get some sex experience, along with formal instruction on morals, at the puberty rituals of their seniors in the age-village and at their own initiation. Boys learn from the conversation of their older fellows at night, in the boys' village. Any suggestion that sex education should be given by parents or middle-aged teachers shocks the Nyakyusa profoundly, for they hold that discussion of sex is totally incompatible with the respect due from children to parents. The taboo on sex talk between members of different generations appears to be absolute among men, but is less emphasized among women, for formal instruction on morals is given to a girl by her mother's fellows during the initiation ritual, and a young wife of her father, or of her father's neighbour, may whisper advice on sex matters even although she is classed as a 'mother'.

As we have already indicated, there are profound differences between pagans and Christians in their sex code. The Christian dogma that sex relations should only take place between adult married persons excludes the freedom of girls to have external sex relations before betrothal, or in the 'bride's' hut; it excludes girls visiting their betrothed husbands before puberty; and it excludes homosexuality, which is regarded as a mortal sin. Segregation of successive generations is not a part of the Christian tradition, hence the modifications in the rules of avoidance among Nyakyusa Christians, and the tendency for fathers and sons to build fairly close to one another.

The forms of display approved among Christians are also changing with the change in the sex code. The nakedness of the Nyakyusa shocked the missionaries, and it is insisted that Christian women, as well as men, should wear at least one cloth; also many of the traditional dances and songs are felt by the Nyakyusa converts themselves to be incompatible with the profession of Christianity, consequently at funerals and weddings there is often a group of Christians dancing quite separately from pagans, and singing their own song, which, more often than not, is a hymn. A wedding dance to a hymn does not appear incongruous to Nyakyusa, as it does to European observers.

e. Wisdom

There is a very close connection between the values we have cited, and all save one are coherent with one another. The enjoyment of good company implies observance of the rules of decency; *ukwangala* is between equals, not between parents and children; it merges into neighbourliness, for one who does not help, or seek help from, a neighbour is unfriendly (*atikwangala kanunu*); and it is dependent upon that generous hospitality which is one of the manifestations of dignity (*ubusisya*).

The one value which is not wholly coherent with the others is the value of display (*ukumoga*). Certain forms of display are compatible with urbanity and friendliness between neighbours, but the swaggering truculence of the warrior is not—it is liable to breed quarrels between fellow villagers, as well as with outsiders; and display also ceases to be compatible with other values when it involves adultery. The friends of a woman who has eloped with a lover may greet her with the phrase: '*Ndaga, umogile!*' which literally translated means 'Thank you, you have displayed yourself', and implies, 'Congratulations! Had a good time?' But no Nyakyusa would maintain that to commit adultery was, in general, good.

The all-embracing virtue to the Nyakyusa is wisdom (*amahala*). It includes the enjoyment of company and the practice of hospitality, for no man is wise who is surly, or aloof, or stingy; it includes neighbourly behaviour, dignity, and respect for law and convention, but it does not include display. The wise may dance, but they do not need to dance in order to be wise, and those who commit adultery, or are boastful, or quarrelsome show foolishness (*ubukonyofu*) and sinful pride (*amatingo*), the opposite of wisdom. Wisdom is expressed in all relationships, not only in village relationships, but it is *learned* in the village; pagan Nyakyusa insist that 'it is by conversing with our friends that we gain wisdom'.

The Christian view is somewhat different. Urbanity, neighbourliness, hospitality, and dignity are components of wisdom for a Christian also, but he would add something further—'the knowledge of God'—and such knowledge is sought not in village relationships only. It is sought also in schools, in the religious teaching of the missionaries, in the scriptures, in worship, and in prayer.

Having considered some of the values[1] realized in age-villages, we now turn to the sanctions maintaining them.

---

[1] It may be asked why we have omitted fertility in our discussion of values realized in village relationships, when fertility in men, cattle, and fields is one of the ultimate values of Nyakyusa society. The reason is that fertility is realized in the relationships of kinship and of the chiefdom, rather than in village relationships. The village rituals in the fields, which we have described, are primarily defensive—to protect the crops against the attacks of witches and sorcerers—and the fertility of the soil is held to depend mainly on the chief, and the rituals he performs on behalf of his country.

CHAPTER V

MYSTICAL INTERDEPENDENCE

a. Witchcraft and 'the breath of men'

In the Nyakyusa view two of the main co-operative activities of a village are defence against witches, and the punishment of wrong-doers through sickness brought upon them by the murmuring of their fellows. Fellow villagers are 'members of one another' as much on account of this mystical interdependence as on account of their economic co-operation and enjoyment of each other's company. The village headmen are spoken of as the leaders in the 'war by night' against witches, as they are leaders in war by day, and it is they also who are foremost in bringing 'the breath of men' (*embepo sya bandu*) on a wrongdoer, so that his body becomes cold, and he falls ill. We must therefore examine the concept of witchcraft and of this 'breath of men' in order to understand village relationships.

i. The nature of witchcraft

The Nyakyusa believe that certain people have pythons (*isota*) in their bellies which give them power to harm men and cattle, by throttling, tramping, wounding, and kicking them. These are the witches (*abalosi*). They are said to fly by night on their pythons, or 'on the wind', either singly or in covens, to attack a chosen victim, and to leave on their beds their skins, which 'can feel nothing'. So closely are the witch and his pythons identified that if a python is killed the witch will die. The pythons are thought to be usually inherited from one or other parent, children of both sexes inheriting from either father or mother: children are 'born with witchcraft in their stomachs', and it is developed by accompanying a parent on his or her evil errands. However, not *all* children of a witch are necessarily witches. 'If a man witch marries a woman witch then the whole family are witches, but if the man is pure (*mwelu*), and the woman only a bit of a witch, then she may say to herself when she first bears a child:

"This time I will respect my husband and leave the child to him", but the next one she makes her own.' Occasionally, it is said, pythons may be acquired in childhood from a woman, or perhaps even a fellow herd-boy, who is a witch, and who transfers his or her witchcraft by giving the child some mysterious substance to eat, but it is the inherited character of witchcraft which is emphasized.

Witchcraft (*ubulosi*) is sharply distinguished from sorcery (*ubutege*), that is, the illegal use of destructive medicines, for it is a physiological condition, not merely the manipulation of certain materials. The pythons are believed to be visible in an autopsy, a 'swollen bowel' (*ubula*) in a corpse being the typical mark of a witch. 'When the bowel is swollen, they take it out and say: "It is a python, he was a witch".' Some educated Nyakyusa maintain that the 'swollen bowel' is, in some cases at least, acute tapeworm; however that may be, the condition of the bowel is taken as conclusive evidence. 'If', said Mwangwanda, 'a man is accused of witchcraft during his lifetime, and then at the autopsy his bowels are found not to be swollen, people admit his innocence, saying: "We accused him falsely, see, he was pure!" '

ii. The supposed activities of witches

The typical crime of the witch, in Nyakyusa belief, is to harm men and cattle, and the motive is greed. The pythons are thought to lust for meat and milk, hence witches go in dreams by night to 'eat people inside', and to milk the cows of their neighbours. 'It is said', explained one of our friends, 'that throttling (*ukupita*) is in order to eat delicious food. The witches say that human flesh is delicious, and the milk of cows is also delicious' (cf. Document, p. 218). Another friend elaborated further: 'People say that it is the pythons of a witch that cause him to go and bewitch (*ukuloga*) the milk, because they wish to drink milk. When he has throttled the cows they are satisfied. And they are satisfied with human flesh when "he of the pythons" has eaten a man. So I hear. I have heard too, that if the pythons smell meat (of an animal killed for eating) and if people grudge meat to him (or her) of the pythons, then the pythons will fly with him to throttle people and eat them. Similarly smelling milk leads to the throttling of cows.' The stock myth of witchcraft (cf. Document, p. 217) is about a woman who was once caught by her husband when she came home during the night with human flesh and began to cook it. Domestic fires are thought to become infected, because the witches are in the habit of roasting human flesh over them; sometimes, it is said, they use the victim's hearth, sometimes their own. Fear of such contamination by witches was one of the reasons for clearing out the ashes and lighting new fires, at the new year, and when an epidemic or other misfortune threatened (*vide infra*, p. 121).

The human flesh eaten is always spoken of as that of living victims, never that of corpses, as in some other areas, though the living die of the witches' attacks. Further, it is believed that witches kill people in order to feast on the beef of cows killed at the funeral. 'To what', said old Mwandesi, 'are the many deaths among us due? They are due to meat!' So strong was this feeling that at the end of 1935 the chiefs and village headmen of a number of chiefdoms stretching from Mwaya on the Lake to Mwakeleli in the hills (but not including the western Nyakyusa chiefdoms), decided to abandon the custom of killing many cows at a funeral. 'There is', they said, 'too much death in the country, the witches are killing people so as to have meat. Let us go back to the old custom and kill few cows. . . . If anyone complains that at a burial he was given no meat to eat, he is a witch, and we will turn him out of the country.' Formerly, we were told, two was the maximum number of cows killed at a funeral, and they were not killed until the witch had been discovered by the ordeal.

The theme of the witches' lust for meat is elaborated in various ways. It is said, for example, that the witches never use their own teeth when they go to eat a victim but like to borrow the victim's teeth, and that if startled, they may go off with the teeth altogether. One whose teeth have been used by the witches and then put back, knows about it in the morning because he finds his teeth rather loose. Most fearful of all, those who dream of being chased by witches hear them boasting to one another: 'We will *all* eat!'

It is meat and milk, the most prized foods of the Nyakyusa, which are commonly spoken of as exciting the greed of witches. Millet (from which beer is brewed), beans, and rice, are said to be subject to occasional attacks by witches, e.g. millet (or beans, or rice) ripening in the fields, or drying in the sun, is thought to get less when 'he (or she) of the pythons' has passed by. Mwaisumo explained: 'They say that if the owner of pythons or the owner of medicines passes when food has been spread out to dry, the food will disappear. He bewitches it (ukuloga). It is as if he hankers after the food in his heart, and it disappears and becomes less.' Nevertheless, of the thirty-eight accusations of witchcraft recorded, none actually turned on loss of grain or pulse. We heard also that a witch may spoil a brewing of beer, causing it to taste bitter, but again we could trace no case of this.

The lust of witches for good food is constantly emphasized by the Nyakyusa and, unlike some other Bantu people, they do not make a direct connection between witchcraft and sex: there is no suggestion of incubi or succubae such as play a great part in Pondo thought,[1] and sexual dreams are not taken as evidence of witchcraft. The facts that the witches are witches by virtue of 'pythons in the stomach', that they always go naked, and fly through the air riding their pythons when on their evil nocturnal errands, suggest sexual associations, but we cannot prove that the Nyakyusa are conscious of such symbolism. It is, however, significant that the word commonly used for working witchcraft, 'throttling' (ukupita), is also used as a polite word for sexual intercourse, and that the other word for working witchcraft ukuloga[2] (passive: ukulogigwa) is similar to ukulogwa, meaning to copulate. Bestiality and homosexuality between a grown man and a boy (but not between two youths) are spoken of as witchcraft (ubulosi), and sex play between girls, including stretching of the vaginal opening, is called ubugalagala, a word used for the cunning—the wicked cleverness—of witches.

An association is also made between witchcraft on the one hand and menstruation and pregnancy on the other. A woman who is a witch is said to pass on her witchcraft to her child by neglecting the menstruation taboos before the child is yet conceived. 'It starts when a woman is menstruating, then she begins to give the child her cunning (ubugalagala).' Some of the menstrual blood is

---

[1] cf. Monica Hunter, Reation to Conquest, pp. 275–89.

[2] Ukuloga and ubulosi are from the same root. For its meaning in other Bantu languages cf. H. A. Junod, The Life of a South African Tribe, Vol. II, pp. 505ff. Also E. J. and J. D. Krige, The Realm of a Rain Queen, p. 250; C. M. N. White in Africa, 1948 (Vol. XVIII), pp. 83 ff.; H. H. Johnston, A Comparative Study of Bantu and Semi-Bantu Languages, Vol. II, p. 416. The close similarity of meaning in a number of languages is striking.

believed to remain in a woman and, if she has neglected the taboos, this blood 'rots' the child later conceived (cf. Document, p. 219). This connection is insisted upon, though witchcraft inherited from the father is spoken of as being carried directly in his blood, which is thought to be transferred to his wife during intercourse.

Furthermore, a pregnant woman is believed to have some of the attributes of a witch. She, like a witch, causes grain and pulse to diminish if she passes near by when it is spread out to dry, or greets women who are stamping or grinding grain. If she speaks or comes too close 'the child inside catches hold of the food, and it disappears'. And if she should speak inadvertently, forgetting that she is pregnant, she must throw a stone or a piece of stick into the grain, or take a little of the flour in her hand, otherwise the women will say: 'She is proud, that girl, she is a witch, why is she talking?' and it is thought that she will have a miscarriage. A pregnant woman, like a witch, and one who has been using medicine, is spoken of as 'heavy' (*nsito*) in contrast with one who is 'empty' (*bwasi*), having nothing in the belly, and Mwaikambo explained that, 'When they speak of a pregnant woman being "heavy", they think that perhaps the foetus is witchcraft.' The foetus and the python of witchcraft are felt to be somewhat alike; but in most situations they are clearly distinguished, and indeed it is held that a woman may have both. If the afterbirth is delayed it is said that the woman is herself a witch, and her python is closing up the vaginal passage, so that the afterbirth cannot come away. A pregnant woman is not spoken of as a witch unless she harms someone by neglecting the taboos connected with her state, and her husband, who must keep the same taboos, may also be called a witch if he breaks them.

Sickness and death among men and cattle, and a diminution in the milk yield of cows, are held to be common results of witchcraft, and any 'unnatural' event, such as a case of bestiality, or of sodomy between a grown man and a boy (not between two youths), or of intercourse between a young man and an old woman, or of unusual behaviour among animals or birds, is taken as evidence that witches are at work. It is the 'unnatural' element that is emphasized (cf. Document, p. 225). An owl hooting on one's roof, and someone staring at one, are also taken as indications of witchcraft.

iii. 'The defenders' and 'the breath of men'

Proof of the activity and identity of witches is sought first in the dreams of victims and of 'the defenders' (*abamanga*) of his village who are believed to have power to see and to fight witches in dreams. As we have seen, the witches are believed to leave their bodies sleeping and to fly through the air to the house of the man against whom they have a grudge, and there to enter his body while he sleeps, and either 'throttle' (*ukupita*), 'trample' (*uku-kwanga*), or 'eat' (*ukulya*) his inside. In the morning, or during the night, the victim wakes up more or less conscious of what has happened to him. If they come often, many nights running, he falls sick and may die, unless he takes steps to defend himself. 'The defenders' (*abamanga*) are believed to be able to see and recognize the identity of the witches and to counter them in two ways. First by turning them back at night, saying: 'Where are you going to throttle your fellow? Go back!' and then driving them off with spears or striking a witch's python, so that the witch dies; and secondly, by reporting to neighbours and to the political authorities the names of the people they have seen engaged in witchcraft. An ordinary person can never recognize the witch who attacks him, even though he may be conscious that he is being throttled. And all these things happen in dreams: 'The witches go out in dreams to throttle people.' 'It is in dreams that "the defenders" recognize them.' Certain dreams, interpreted by a traditional symbolism, are taken as signs of being bewitched: 'If I dream that someone comes to fight me, perhaps he beats me with a stick, perhaps he overwhelms me and crushes me down to earth, perhaps he hits me with his fist; then I wake up and tell people: "Last night they came to throttle me." ' 'If I recognize people who come to fight me in my dreams that means I have myself the power of defence; if I do not recognize them then I have not.' 'If I dream that I am flying alone through the air high up at night, that means they have come to throttle me.' 'If I wake up suddenly at night in fear and sweating, even though I do not recollect the dream, I know they have come to throttle me.' 'Dreams of being chased, of being beaten, of the house burning, of one coming to the door and weeping for me as if I were dead, these are all signs of witchcraft.' Close friends tell one another their dreams—provided they have not dreamed of attacking one another—and when more than one of them has dreamed of X as an aggressor, then the presumption is very strong that X is a witch. Dreams to the Nyakyusa are the stuff of religious reality, and the very close association between witchcraft and dreams is apparent in the language—*injosi* meaning a dream, and *ubulosi* (the same root in the abstract noun class) meaning witchcraft. It is perhaps also significant, that *ukugoga* means to dream, and *ukugogwa* (in the passive form) means to be killed. Restless nights are taken as proof that either the witches or ancestors are troubling a man: 'We do not sleep' (*tukigona*) is the formal phrase in which village headmen or priests notify the chief that something is amiss in the country, and a ritual is required; and an ordinary person using the same phrase implies that he is harried either by the ancestors or by witches. 'You *may* sleep or you may not' (*uligona*) is the commonest form in which a threat of witchcraft is made.

The vision and power of 'the defenders' (*abamanga*) comes from the same source as the power of the witches,[1] from pythons in the belly, the essential difference between the witches and 'the defenders' being that the latter use their power in accordance with law and morality, while the witches act for selfish ends, and their activities are illegal. This close association of 'the defenders' with the power of witchcraft is apparent in language, *ukumanga* being sometimes used almost synonomously with *ukuloga* for 'to bewitch', while *abamanga* means 'the defenders'.[2] There are, moreover, certain differences between the pythons of witches, and those of 'defenders'. In the first place, the condition of 'the

---

[1] For similar concepts among the Thonga and Azande cf. H. A. Junod, *The Life of a South African Tribe*, Vol. II, p. 516; E. E. Evans-Pritchard, *Witchcraft, Oracles and Magic among the Azande*, pp. 224 ff.

[2] cf. the Bemba *bwanga* discussed by R. J. B. Moore in *Africa*, Vol. XIII, 1940, pp. 211 ff. and *Bantu Studies*, Vol. 15, 1941, pp. 37 ff.; the note on the use of this root in a number of languages in *Africa*, Vol. XVI, 1946, pp. 119–20; and C. M. N. White in *Africa*, Vol. XVIII, 1948, pp. 83–102.

I translate -*manga* in Nyakyusa as 'mystical power', *uku-manga* 'to exercise mystical power' (for good and evil), and *aba-manga* as 'those possessing mystical power', with the further implication that they use this power for defence. Writing in *Africa*, Vol. IX, 1936, pp. 85, and Vol. X, 1937, pp. 265 ff., we translated *aba-manga* as 'defender witches' and *aba-losi* as 'aggressor witches'. On further reflection, however, I have preferred to confine 'witch' and 'witchcraft' to those acting in a manner disapproved by their society, since this is common usage, and for want of a better term I call *aba-manga* 'the defenders'.

defenders' is not visible at an autopsy. Secondly, it is maintained that while a witch has several pythons, a defender has only one, and whereas witchcraft is always inherited or acquired in early childhood, a python of defence may be acquired later, through drinking medicine. Old Mwandesi, recognized by the Nyakyusa themselves as an authority on law and history, explained it to us thus: 'Some are born with pythons; they are those with many pythons, perhaps three. Some get them from medicine made of leaves which is given them to drink at the "coming out", they have only one, it is they who watch over the cattle, they are the village headmen (*amafumu*). He who has many pythons, who is born with them, having inherited them, suns them secretly at his home. He takes them out and suns them, then swallows them again, they are his intestines. Such a man is a great witch; he is the kind who is convicted of witchcraft. But the village headman who has got his python through medicine has only one, he does not sun it, he is not convicted of witchcraft, he only detects the witches in dreams. When he begets a child the latter will have one python only. If his son or daughter goes about throttling people, then his father says: "Where did you get *many* pythons? See! I have only one. It is you woman! (accusing his wife)." So they submit themselves to the poison ordeal. The man vomits and the ordeal catches the woman.' Mwandesi contradicted himself in this statement, first suggesting that the power of defence was only acquired through drinking medicines, and then that the child of a village headman inherited one python from his father. Most Nyakyusa maintain that the power of defence can be acquired in either fashion. The medicines drunk at the 'coming out' develop it even in an 'empty' man, but many men, including assistant headmen and ordinary citizens who are not specially treated at the 'coming out', are believed to have it. It is asserted that no women have it, though many of them are spoken of as witches, and in particular instances informants implied that some women 'saw' the witches (cf. Document, pp. 252–3).

Mbukile confirmed Mwandesi's main point, saying: 'Some of us are empty, pure (*bwelu*), we have no pythons, not one; some are 'defenders' and pure, they are those who watch over the country; such a man has only one python to watch over his country. The ruler of the country, the chief, also has one python; for both village headman and chief watch over the country. Some are witches, they have two or three pythons, it is they who are caught by the poison ordeal.' 'Watching over the country' implies detecting the witches and turning them back, and also reporting them the next morning to the authorities. Particularly 'the defenders' watch over the cows, and they are said actually to increase the milk yield by sucking the milk from the teats and spitting it out again. Mbukile explained this also: ' "The defender" watches over the cows. He takes milk in his mouth and squirts it on the ground; he does not swallow it in his dream. The next day the milk will be plentiful.' A village headman we knew enlarged further on the point: 'If a man is the son of a true village headman and goes to drink the milk of cows, he drinks from the teats, but his python vomits the milk and the next day the owner of the cow will find much milk and say: "He who came last night was the child of a village headman (*ulifumu*). He was good, he was not a witch, no, but a benefactor."[1] So they say. But if a real witch goes to bewitch the cows then the milk dries up altogether for a time. The owners of the cows will milk none for many days. He is a witch indeed.' Similarly, it is held that if witches can be compelled to vomit the human flesh they have eaten, 'to put back the meat', the patient will recover.

'Emptiness' and 'innocence' are associated in several contexts; and vomiting, spitting, and confession (*ukusosya*) are all taken as expressions of good will and repentance. *Ukuswa*, for example, means both 'to spit' and 'to forgive', the symbolism being interpreted in this way: 'If a father is angry with his son or daughter he may say some day, "I forgive you now" and spit on the ground: all the anger that is in him comes out like spit.' Blowing water from the mouth is an essential element in prayers to the ancestors, and the close association between them is apparent in the language: *ukuputa* meaning to 'blow out water' and *ukwiputa* (the reflexive form) meaning 'to pray',[2] with the implication of confessing whatever anger or grudge a man may have in his heart. Kasitile, the rainmaker, explained: 'This prayer with water is to confess *everything*. If I do not pray with water then something is left within.'

---

[1] For a similar concept among the Thonga cf. Junod, *The Life of a South African Tribe*, Vol. II, p. 515.
[2] The Zande symbolism is very similar: cf. E. E. Evans-Pritchard, 'Zande Theology' in *Sudan Notes and Records*, Vol. XIX (1936), pp. 11–12.

In Nyakyusa society it is senior relatives who formally blow out water to express their good will, not suspected witches, as among the Azande. But the admission of anger by the supposed witch or justly shocked neighbours, and their wishes for the patient's good health, are anxiously sought (*vide infra*, p. 101), for such good wishes are thought to lead directly to his recovery.

The reverse of this emphasis on the value of confessing anger is the belief that the man who nurses a grudge in secret without ever admitting it is the most dangerous enemy, whether he be a senior relative muttering to the shades, or a neighbour using witchcraft, or a rival who has turned to sorcery. Mwambuputa, a conservative village headman without any school education, was very explicit on the point: 'The root of witchcraft is this—when two people have a quarrel in their hearts and do not let it out. Maybe I have a neighbour who hates me, but he never lets it out, he says nothing and we seem to be on friendly terms—these are the quarrels that are pregnant with witchcraft. But if he lets it out and tells me that I have wronged him in some way then the quarrel has no menace in it. It is when he lets nothing out and stays silent, though angry in his heart, that he comes in dreams to throttle me. That is the root of witchcraft.' Hence the insistence on one accused of witchcraft admitting guilt (*vide* infra, p. 112).

'The defenders' are powerful, but it is believed that witches are occasionally able in dreams to get past them, and throttle men against whom they have a grudge, or their cows. ' "The defenders" do not go out in dreams to fight the aggressors every night. A witch wanting to throttle a man comes night after night.' 'Nowadays it is much worse than it used to be, since the Europeans prevent us reporting them, and getting them stopped; "the defenders" work hard, but some nights they sleep without dreaming and the witches get past.'

Although the primary function of 'the defenders' is to see and drive off witches, nevertheless they are also thought to use their power to punish a wrong-doer. In doing so they are assisted by the witches, but, the Nyakyusa argue, the village headman who leads this night attack in dreams is no more breaking the law than he is when he fines a thief in court. In both cases he is exerting power to maintain the law. The Nyakyusa have a lively fear of shocking their neighbours, for it is held that the shocked astonishment of fellow villagers (*bikuswiga*) or their angry murmuring (*bikwibunesya*) will bring on wrong-doers 'the breath of men' (*embepo sya bandu*) causing them, or their children, or cattle, to fall ill, and this breath is the power of the pythons exerted by 'defenders' and witches acting together. We asked Mbukile whether 'the defenders' really came to choke a proud, quarrelsome person. 'Mother! They come. "The defenders" and the witches all call one another. They all go. "The defender" is not angry (at the attack), he says, "The man killed himself, he was a quarrelsome fellow!" ' And another friend explained: 'If a woman witch wishes to choke her husband, perhaps the first night "the defenders" will turn her back, but then she will plead with them and explain that her husband is a bad man and ill-treats her, then perhaps on the second night they will change their minds and come and help her. Yes, "the defenders" turn round sometimes and throttle people.'

'The breath of men' is thought to cause prolonged illness but not death, and should a death occur then a charge of witchcraft may be brought, and the suspects be required to drink the poison ordeal. 'We said, it is forbidden to kill a man. We others were afraid, although we had disliked the victim ourselves, we feared at some later time the witch would kill us.' All our informants accepted this view in theory, but in practice several cases in which the supposed victims died were cited as instances of 'the breath of men' (see table, pp. 206–8).

The effect of 'the breath of men' is spoken of as 'the curse' (*ikigune*)[1] and its typical symptom is sterility, or a paralysis of the legs, which, it is thought, can only be cured when the sinner repents and reforms his behaviour, providing at the same time a feast of beer and meat for men of his village or, if it be against his father that he has sinned, of his father's village. At the feast it is essential that the men of the village should *admit their responsibility* for the sickness, and express hopes for the recovery of the patient. 'Formerly, they would pray and pray, they would let out all their anger, saying: "Certainly we were angry, it was us, but now it is all over." Then life would come back to the sick man and he recovered' (cf. Document, p. 240).

We see then, that a clear distinction is made by the Nyakyusa

---

[1] *Ikigune* is not used in the Kukwe dialect, but is common usage in Selya, on the Lake-shore plain, and in Ngonde.

between the legal and illegal use of power derived from pythons. 'The breath of men' is the general public opinion of a whole group—of an age-village or chiefdom—acting through the 'python power' of those of its members who happen to be possessed of it, led by one or more village headmen and directed against a single person. On the other hand, individuals proved to be witches are those believed to have acted by themselves, either against the public opinion of their age-village or chiefdom, or at any rate without securing its support. No pagan Nyakyusa doubts that witchcraft is bad, or that 'the breath of men' is used to bring legitimate punishment on evil-doers, but the classification of particular cases varies somewhat with the point of view of the individual. The victim of 'the breath of men' may speak indignantly about the attacks of 'the witches'.[1]

'The defenders' are regarded as pillars of society, and their exercise of python power as right and proper, yet no one readily admits to the possession of such power; it is a proud and boastful thing to do, and not good manners. Informants, when discussing it, rarely spoke as if they had direct knowledge of the power, usually prefacing their remarks with: 'It is said that', or 'I hear that'. This was true even of village headmen who are all believed to have the power. One such man, to whom a direct question was put, replied: 'I would not go so far as to boast of it myself, but other people in my village have it.' In villages of mature and old men, others besides the headmen are often known by name as having it; and besides this there is the general belief that in each such age-village 'some people', not specified, have it as well.

iv. Witchcraft, 'the breath of men' and morality

Now the power of witchcraft and 'the breath of men' is held to operate primarily within one age-village, and it is denied that it can ever extend beyond the chiefdom. 'How could the people of another chiefdom "eat" a man?' said the village headman, Mwafula, 'It is those *here*'. The typical accusations are against neighbours and wives or co-wives and, nowadays, against fellow workers living in the same camp (cf. table, p. 198). The fact that it is within the village that witchcraft is thought to operate is

---

[1] cf. Godfrey Wilson, 'An African Morality' in *Africa*, Vol. IX (1936), pp. 87-8, for such a case.

shown by the way in which one fearing witchcraft, or accused of practising it, moves to another village. Sometimes he goes to another chiefdom, but often he only moves to another village in the same chiefdom—the chief himself may feel safe in one village of his country and not in another (*vide* Document, p. 190). It is on his fellow villagers that the good man depends for protection, and it is they whom the evil-doer fears.

Accusations within the lineage are rare. At first we were told that they did not occur at all; later a number of elderly informants agreed that this was not true—'the young men have misled you', they said; but careful inquiry only elicited three concrete cases[1] of witchcraft within the lineage (cf. table, p. 204). As we have seen, fellow members of a lineage normally live in different villages, and just how the idea of attacks by kinsmen is reconciled with the theory of village defence is not clear. Possibly it is argued that the witch attacks while visiting his kinsman, for it is in terms of visiting that the effect of 'the breath of men' on erring sons or younger brothers is explained. Where 'the breath of men' is thought to have affected someone of another village, it is argued that he or she came frequently to visit in the village of the attackers (cf. Document, p. 237), and the heir who neglects his elder brother's or father's funeral rites, and who is thought to suffer from 'the breath' of the deceased's justly indignant neighbours, is supposed to fall ill when he comes to their village to enter into his inheritance, or to make arrangements for the disposal of his property.

Even within the village it is the immediate neighbours that are primarily concerned in a case of suspected witchcraft. In the large villages of the plains the leader of a section, 'he of the heap of hot ashes', has the specific duty of protecting the herd which stands in the smoke of his fire against witches; and in smaller villages, also, a witchcraft case commonly begins with murmuring among a few next-door neighbours. Suspicion of witchcraft falls first on a member of the same village-section, then on a fellow villager; only rarely, and in peculiar circumstances, does it fall on a member of another village, and never on someone outside the chiefdom.

Differences of rank are relatively slight in Nyakyusa society

---

[1] A possible fourth is quoted on p. 246, but the exact relationship of the accused to the victim was not known to our informant.

and scarcely affect accusations of practising witchcraft, save that the chief himself is never accused, though he is often thought to suffer from the witchcraft, or 'the breath', of his men. The commoners, 'the black people' (*abatitu*), are said to be the real witches, but a study of cases shows that junior brothers and sons of the chiefs are, in fact, sometimes accused. Village headmen may be accused just like the humblest of their followers, and men are accused at least as often as women (cf. table p. 198). Thus though witchcraft is held to be hereditary, and is particularly associated with menstrual blood, it is individual behaviour, not birth, or sex, that determines accusations.

What sort of behaviour, then, leads to accusations of witchcraft, and what sort of behaviour is thought to provoke attack by a witch, or bring upon one the chilling breath of men? We found that some quite specific teaching was given to Nyakyusa children on this point.

The type most usually described as a witch is the person whose character makes him (or her) to some extent isolated and unpopular—a proud man who treats his neighbours with disdain; a retiring man who always keeps silent in public; a glum wife, or one who fails to greet the other women she meets and to inquire after their children. Such people are treated by their neighbours with less courtesy and hospitality than the traditional ideals of good manners demand. 'Perhaps we do not summon him to drink beer, or to eat with us: and then when our cows fail to give milk we think, "doubtless it is he who is throttling them".'

One who fails to show sympathy with a neighbour in bereavement, neglecting to attend a funeral in the village, or one who does not try to persuade a neighbour to remain, when that neighbour is preparing to move for fear of witchcraft, is immediately suspect. The chief characteristic of witches is always said to be pride (*amatingo*), which includes a cold aloofness, as well as boastfulness and irascibility.

And what sort of people are thought to be attacked by witches? Informants agree that, though they act without public support, witches seldom act without provocation. It is argued on the one hand that they act from greed, and on the other that suppressed hatred drives them to attack (*vide supra*, pp. 92–4 and table, pp. 198–205). The Nyakyusa see no contradiction in this, for they believe that the witches, lusting after food, choose as victims those against whom they have a grudge. The exception is the witch who, having eaten with his fellow witches, fails to provide a victim in his turn and is compelled to offer a kinsman of his own. Mwamunda, talking of witchcraft between relatives, explained: 'Throttling of relatives is of two kinds: firstly, when kinsmen quarrel over something, perhaps cattle, and one throttles the child of his relative; secondly, when there is no quarrel, but a witch has gone with his fellow witches to eat of their food in his dreams, then they come to him and say: "You have eaten our food with us, give us your food. If you don't we shall eat your wife." Then he points out the child of his kinsman to them' (vide infra, p. 114). Far more often, however, the witches' attack is attributed to a quarrel, or to envy roused by conspicuous success. Men are said to excite the envy of witches by acquiring many cattle, hoeing a much larger garden than others, earning more at work, or by boasting about the importance of the position they hold in government or other employment. A woman excites envy by becoming the favourite wife of her husband, or by carrying a heavier load than her fellows when she goes with them to fetch firewood (cf. Document, p. 229). Our friends constantly referred to the danger of rousing envy; it is in fact believed to be the motive behind witchcraft in a large proportion of cases.

Good food rouses the envy of witches also, and the man who eats alone is felt to be in danger, but not only from the witches. It is said: 'If you have grudged your neighbours meat . . . those who watch over the village by night, "the defenders", will be angry, and call the witches to help; they will eat you.' Here we come to the legitimate use of python power, 'the breath of men'. Greed at a feast; failure to share whatever meat, or beer, or other fine food one has, whether it be prepared in the village, or brought as a gift from affines; failure to send the customary cut of an animal killed as a gift to the chief; and failure to provide a feast on certain occasions, are all regarded as sins liable to bring on the wrong-doer the 'curse' or 'breath' of his aggrieved neighbours. The feasts specially mentioned as being necessary are those at death and at marriage (vide supra, p. 70, and Document, p. 206). As Mwakwelebeja, an old commoner, put it: 'If I did not kill at a funeral, the neighbours, those who eat the meat, would be angry. As they scattered from the funeral they would say:"He is

hard, he has not killed a cow for the death of his child." When
they go round telling other people like this, they bring down the
"breath of men".'

But it is not thought that neighbours are concerned only with
enforcing hospitality within the village; they are also shocked
(*bikuswiga*) by disrespectful behaviour towards parents and
parents-in-law; by a wife swearing at her husband or hitting him;
by incest; by a woman 'soiling' her lover, i.e. by running off with
him repeatedly, and so enraging her husband that he forces him
to eat filth; by a woman continuing to bear children after her son
has married a girl who has reached puberty; and by any other
manifestation of 'pride' (*amatingo*). Their shocked astonishment
is held to bring on the wrong-doer their chilling 'breath' which
causes sterility, paralysis, or some other lingering illness, or
makes the child of a woman who has insulted her mother-in-law,
or peeped at her father-in-law, thin and sickly.

'If a woman should look at her father-in-law on purpose her
friends shout at her and say: "You are proud (*namatingo*) you
look on your father-in-law." Then she won't get children or her
child falls ill. It is true also that if she says the name or looks on a
father-in-law she will have difficulty when she comes to die. . . .
She might die slowly and in pain or she might be old and weary
and wish to die, and not be able to do so. . . . It is "the breath of
men" that causes her child to be ill. If the father-in-law on whom
she looked said nothing about it nothing would happen, but if he
told his friends then the woman's child would be made ill by
"the breath of men"—the child the woman was carrying when
she saw the man, or her first-born child, would suffer' (cf.
Document, p. 236).

Another informant said: 'Suppose that a man dies leaving a
young son, and his brother, the heir, refuses to give this boy a
cow for milk or, later, cows for marriage, then the dead man
comes in a dream to the heir and reproaches him. Then he, the
heir, fetches his wife and tells her: "We must give him (the
ward) a cow, my brother came to me by night and reproached
me," and so he will give the boy a cow. If he still refuses to do so,
his fellows in the village, fellows of his elder brother (the heir
having taken over the elder brother's homestead) will pass judgement on him and there will be much "breath". And if he refuses
to provide marriage-cattle for his brother's son and provides them

for his own son whom he begot saying: "He is my own flesh and blood", then the men of the village will pass judgement.'

This 'breath' is thought also to fall on a chief who is harsh towards his people, or who acts unconstitutionally, as in refusing to make a 'coming out' ceremony for his sons when his village headmen advise him; and it falls on a village headman who treats a junior in office unfairly, or is overbearing to his men. Both pagan and Christian informants insisted that fear of 'the breath of men' was a powerful sanction in the traditional system against arbitrary rule. Asagene, a Christian deacon, himself raised the subject one day and said: 'Headmen and chiefs— pagans—would be hard on their people and seize their goods if they (the headmen and chiefs) did not fear witchcraft. Witchcraft is like God to them.'

At every point the solidarity of the village is emphasized; the neighbours themselves are held to be insulted by the bad behaviour of a son—'their son'—to one of their fellows, or by a woman 'soiling their son', or by an heir failing to recognize their concern in the inheritance of a deceased fellow. For example, Mwakanyamale had begotten no child for ten years, and this was attributed to the fact that, after quarrelling with his elder brother and refusing to attend his funeral, he had not admitted his fault to the men of the village when he came back and killed a cow. His impotence was attributed to their curse.

As we have seen, recovery is thought to depend (i) upon the wrong-doer reforming and providing the men of the village, which is angry, with a bull or beer for a feast, acknowledging guilt as he does so; and (ii) upon the men of the village admitting their anger and responsibility for his illness, and expressing good will. 'If a daughter-in-law should have looked on her father-in-law by mistake she makes beer and sends it to her father-in-law. He calls his friends and admits: "Indeed I was angry with her for she looked at me", and the others say: "Yes, indeed, let her child get fat".' (*vide* pp. 235-6).

It may well be asked, is there any objective reality at the root of this belief in 'the breath of men'? Does the wrong-doer, fearing his neighbours, really become paralysed or impotent? It is possible that a sinner may sometimes develop these symptoms as the result of fear. We do not know, what is certain is that impotence, sterility, lingering illnesses including paralysis, and sickly children, are not uncommon; that the penalty of sin is believed often to be delayed, and an illness may be attributed to a wrong committed many years previously; and lastly, that the victim of retribution may be one of several individuals. Parents are thought to be punished by the sickness of their children as well as in their own persons; in a case of sexual transgression it may be either partner who suffers; in the case of a neglected death ritual it may be either the heir or the widow on whose behalf it should have been performed (cf. Document, pp. 206, 236–7). When a woman bears a child after her son is married to a girl who has reached puberty, it is thought that she may fall ill herself, or her husband may be cursed 'because he had agreed to his son marrying a grown girl before the son's mother had grown old'; or the son may have no children because he eloped with his wife, or has 'married a grown girl when his father had only agreed that he should be betrothed to a little girl'.

A lively fear of witchcraft and of the 'breath of men' is inculcated in Nyakyusa children when quite young; Mwaikambo, a Christian, explained that boys learn about witchcraft from their senior play-mates when they are out herding, and in the hut at night in the boys' village, when tales are told. 'Then one fears in one's stomach and thinks: "Father! perhaps I, also, will be eaten by witches." ' Ambilikile, another Christian informant, confirmed this, saying: 'We learn about witches from comments on cases of sickness, and from tales. When someone has died people say: "He was a witch, we found a python." Or perhaps of another it is said that "the witches had eaten him". In these tales the witches are said to have eaten people, or speared them, by means of witchcraft, so that the victim dies. We are also told how the witches fight in the power of witchcraft with their fellows from other villages, and how they fly on their pythons. What we hear always makes witchcraft awe-inspiring. I feared it very much.'

We had ample evidence that for most Nyakyusa the fear of witchcraft and of 'the breath of men' continues throughout life, and that it directly affects behaviour. It is, perhaps, the main sanction for moral behaviour within the village.

v. Procedure in witchcraft cases

Whenever someone is very ill there is anxious speculation among relatives and neighbours as to the cause of the illness. If witchcraft is suspected—and witchcraft is thought to be by far the commonest cause of sickness and death—people begin to whisper (*ukuheha*) that so and so is responsible. Even if the trouble is only a sudden fall in the milk supply there are whispers about witchcraft and the identity of the witch. Then the neighbours meet and complain (*ukwijaja*), or else the leader of the village-section, or even the headman of the village, takes the initiative and, summoning his people, admonishes them. The object of such complaint and exhortation is to warn off the witch. 'People speak very angrily, then the witches are ashamed within themselves, and stop their witchcraft, because they die of shame.' If the warning is effective—that is if the patient or the cows recover —the case will be dropped; but if the trouble continues then the village proceeds to the discovery of the witch. Mwaisumo explained: 'If sickness occurs, the village headman will call his people round him and say: "This village is not right, disease is killing the people, there must be someone who is bewitching them. We warn him to stop!" Then, if he does not stop he will call the people round him again and say: "Well, we must drive him away." Then they discuss their dreams with the headman, it is always by their dreams that they find out the witch, no other way.' A case was quoted in which the milk yield of a village had diminished and the villagers had 'called one another' to come together to complain. While they were complaining a 'defender' called out: 'I have seen the one who is throttling the cows; come together again to-morrow, and no one must stay behind.' When they met the next day one man called the names of each villager in turn, and 'the defender' responded to each with 'Yes', until 'Mwasalutaba' was called. Then he was silent. The name was called three times, and at the third time the whole company groaned. Mwasalutaba got up and, denying the accusation, appealed to the ordeal. He was found guilty by it and was driven from the village (cf. Document, pp. 241–3).

Mwakwelebeja, himself a commoner credited with the power of discovering witches in dreams, made a revealing comment on the discovery of witches. He said: 'The witches betray themselves. When we are sitting discussing the witches throttling people, we may notice one looking nervous and glancing sidelong at his friends, then we, who are innocent, know that he is the man.' Certainly a suspect is closely watched, and if he shows anxiety, or fails to join in the condemnation of witches and the expression of good will, this is brought up against him, as the following case shows.

'A certain man called Mwakagugu had a guest staying with him, a soldier on leave. Now this soldier was in the habit of calling in the neighbours to eat when his wife cooked a meal, and M. was always angry in his heart, wishing to eat alone with his guest. When the soldier invited in other people M. would refuse to join them. (The soldier was correct, according to Nyakyusa custom, in what he did. It is good to call in friends to eat.) On one occasion the soldier bought some beer and a crowd of men were drinking it, in another house, not M.'s; but they took a dry bamboo from M.'s place as firewood, to heat the water for the beer. Then M. was very angry indeed and asked: "What do you mean by taking my bamboo?" And his neighbours silently criticized him, thinking "Our friend here has not even bought this beer, and then he gets angry when we take his bamboo!" Another day when the soldier killed a bullock and gave a leg of the meat to some guests of his who were present his child fell ill, its ear swelled up and burst, and it screamed with pain. Later, a neighbour's wife cooked some porridge for her husband without any relish so when she brought the porridge to where the men were sitting, the soldier called to his own wife to bring a chicken she had cooked, as relish, and he offered it to the other men, eating none himself. Again, on yet another occasion, when his wife brought him his porridge she called M. to join him; but M. laughed and said: "Let them (the soldier and his other friends), eat it by themselves." This was the woman's story. And then straight away they were startled by the child screaming and refusing to lie down.

'So then all the neighbours gathered together and gave expression to their anger (ukwijaja), asking themselves the cause of the sickness, and why it was that it always became apparent when they were eating. "If the man in question" they said, naming no one, "does it again, we will expel him from the country!" As soon as this was over M. at once began to whisper to a friend: "Why do they ask about this sickness, and all the other sicknesses we have they say nothing about? When we are ill is that not an illness?" His friend answered: "It is taboo to speak like this, they will hear you!" And when M. went on whispering he said: "Get out of my house." When the others heard of this they drove M. away, saying that it was he who was making the child sick. And that night the child's illness reached its height, and was worse than ever before.'

(In reply to question): 'At first when they met to express their anger they knew it was M. but feared to accuse him openly. When, however, he began to whisper they feared no longer and said openly: "You are a witch!" The headmen have forbidden all private whispering about witchcraft, as distinct from a formal public gathering to express anger; so that when his friend said to M.: "It is forbidden to speak like this", this was what he referred to. What he meant was: "Why did you not say this openly if it pains your heart? Now you seem to be making the illness worse!" In other words, the object of the open expression of anger was to warn M. off, but by continuing to whisper himself he showed that he had not repented. He was still angry. If he had said nothing they would not have expelled him.

'After M.'s neighbours had driven him from his home (by word of mouth only) he moved, but the village headman, Mwambuputa, brought him back to a different part of his village, not to the section of it (*akapanga*) where M. had previously built; he put him in the house of one of his men. Then his neighbours grew angry asking why Mwambuputa, who himself had forbidden murmuring, had brought back one whom they had convicted of witchcraft! So they went to Mwambuputa's place and expressed their anger to him. Then he agreed to go and expel him. I who recount the case, went with them.

'When we reached the house where M. was staying the assistant headman of M.'s old section, Mwakyandwike, stood out and said: "I have a word to say to my father Mwambuputa. I am astonished that you received back M. after I had driven him away because he is an evil man who does not like to have friendly dealings with us his neighbours." Then Mwambuputa replied: "When I fetched him back I did not know you had convicted him of witchcraft, I thought he was simply moving." "Yes," replied the other, "that is why I have followed him, for your house is my home! If you love M. you too will be expelled!" And the others said: "Had you known about the case, we should have expelled you both!" "Let us tell him then", said Mwambuputa. But M. was not in the house and had to be fetched. When he came Mwambuputa said: "Your neighbours have followed you saying that they have expelled you. You have done some evil, have you not? I, when I received you, did not know of this, I thought you were just moving." "What is their reason for driving me away?" asked M. "That I've not yet asked them, we will ask them together." Then one man said: "You M., when you moved, why did you move?" M.: "The reason was this, our child (*sic*) at home was sick and we met to express our anger; after this I said to a friend, 'Why do they express their anger and say some one of us has eaten the child for there is a great deal of fever about and many children are sick?' This I said, and then found my friends said I was the witch. 'We expel you' they said, so I moved." "Yes," they said, "you knew yourself to be a witch, why else did you not show indignation and surprise and take your friends to Mwambuputa to be tried? Now you've given them power, and they have followed you here!" Another said: "If your friends drive you from the village will you be obstinate?" Then Mwambuputa said: "No more words, leave the village, your fellows tell you to go!" '

M. condemned himself in the eyes of his neighbours by suggesting that their hinted accusation was false, after they had gathered to express indignation; and here we come to one of the essential points in the Nyakyusa concept of witchcraft. A witch may repent; if he does repent he is no longer a danger to the village, but an asset, since as a witch he has the power to defend the village as well as to attack; and *admission of guilt is taken as a sign of repentance*. The Nyakyusa hold that a witch is always conscious of his evil activity and they have no ritual expressions of good will such as the Zande blowing on chicken wings, but they stress the obligation of a suspect to admit guilt, either directly or by implication. It is said that in the past, if a suspect admitted guilt, he was not driven out. Very few people, however, do admit guilt; the only case we traced was that of a labourer on the Lupa gold-fields who was accused by his fellows of harming the eyes of one of the gang, who had just discovered a large nugget of gold. This 'witch' was actually expelled from the camp by his fellows, but Nyakyusa, commenting on the case, remarked that had it occurred in one of the home villages, he would only have been fined.

Sometimes a case begins with the startling shout of 'a defender' in the night, who claims to have seen in his dreams that a witch is attacking either himself or a fellow villager. 'A man who dreams of fighting, or being beaten, will sometimes wake up in the middle of the night and go out of his house and shout: "You, so and so, why do you come and fight with me?" But often he will not mention the name then, but waits till the morning when his friends will come and ask him: "Why were you shouting last night?" Then he tells them the name of the man he dreamed of, and if another man dreams of him in the same way the next night or later, then they say he is a witch.' Such a case was described by Mwaikambo: 'A certain man, Kololo, dreamed of his fellow, and in the morning he called out on the road, "I dreamed of so and so, we fought with him in the night, he was throttling me." So his fellows came to his help and said to the accused man: "You, Moses, we have caught you, move elsewhere!" So Moses [who was a pagan, despite his name] moved to another village in the same chiefdom, that of Korosso.'

Occasionally a witch reveals himself by threatening a neighbour with whom he has quarrelled, using the stereotyped phrases: 'You *may* sleep or you may not' (*Uligona*), or 'What are you?' (*Uligwaki*), or 'Something may happen!' Here is an actual case as reported to us: 'Mwantibe once ordered a boy, the son of a village neighbour, to go on a message for him, but the boy refused, though it is customary for men to send their neighbours' sons on messages. Then Mwantibe got angry with him and snatched his cloth away, saying in anger: "You, boy, something may happen!" implying that the boy would fall ill. The boy fell ill that very evening, and died shortly afterwards. Mwantibe hurried to return the cloth, but the boy's people drove him away with it saying: "What sort of sorrow have you? Are you pretending, so that we shall not suspect you?" For they said it was he who had "eaten" the boy.'

The cases quoted so far all involve a direct accusation of witchcraft against the suspect, but sometimes he is compelled to move without ever being accused face to face. Mwaisumo explained: 'The men of the village cut a banana stem and wrap banana leaves round it, and go at night and put it in front of his door; they also pull some of the thatching off the roof and put it with the banana stem. They do this without ever accusing him to his face of being a witch. Then, in the morning, when others pass by, they notice and say to each other: "See, he has been caught, he is a witch!" In the fields men will call out to one another, saying: "Have you heard? So and so has been caught as a witch?" They will call out where he can hear them, and he cannot stand it. He will go away to another chief.'

Instead of using a banana stem his neighbours may barricade his doorway with thorns while he is out. 'This symbolizes', Mwaikambo said, 'that we (your neighbours) wish to spear you; because, if you try to pass, the thorns will spear you. But we have left you, get out!' Or, as another informant explained: 'The thorns are the hearts of men, symbolizing that the men are all angry.' Occasionally, it is said, a brave man will clear away the thorns and remain, but his neighbours whisper about it and later on they will barricade his doorway again, and he will move. Placing the banana stem, or the thorns, is a joint action by the neighbours—should an individual do it on his own his neighbours will bring a charge against him. One informant suggested that the procedure is a new one developed to avoid making a direct accusation of witchcraft, which is a punishable offence under European administration; but this is doubtful.

The following case illustrates not only the practice of barricading the doorway of a supposed witch, but also the responsibility of headmen for the defence of the village, together with the belief that a witch may throttle his own child. 'Nsekela was an assistant headman in the village of Mwambuputa, appointed by Mwambuputa himself. Nsekela's child cried by night and Mwambuputa was angry with him because he did not report the matter. "Why did you not tell me that your child was ill here? Why do you hide it? Indeed you are bad, it is you who are making the child ill, get out of our country!" Nsekela watched over a village-section, he was Mwambuputa's assistant, therefore it was that Mwambuputa said: "Why do you hide the fact that your child is ill here, you my assistant? Indeed you have bewitched it yourself." Nsekela denied the charge saying: "It is not I. No!" Then he went away to Selika about a case. While he was away his neighbours barricaded his doorway with thorns. On his return he found them, and he moved to Mwaihojo's country (the adjoining chiefdom).'

Often an accusation of witchcraft is made without resort to divination at all: the behaviour of the accused (as in the cases quoted on pp. 110–13) or the word of 'the defender', is taken as evidence. But if there is doubt as to the identity of the witch, the patient or his family may consult a diviner (*undagusi*),[1] putting before him the names of persons they suspect. Whatever the grounds of accusation, however, it was normally confirmed by the *umwafi* ordeal, if the accused did not admit guilt. The chief might order a suspect to go to the ordeal, or a man or woman accused by his neighbours would appeal to the ordeal, when denying the charge. In such a case the accuser and accused first went to the chief to report and get official witnesses, then, accompanied by these witnesses and other friends, they went to a doctor who had a store of a certain medicine, *umwafi*, and there, at his homestead, they drank the *umwafi* together. Those who failed to vomit were judged guilty. The procedure was described by a number of witnesses (*vide* Documents, pp. 241–6). The accuser and the accused, each accompanied by supporters, go to the doctor, who warns them not to drink if what they have said is false. The doctor sprinkles powder into tepid water and gives the accuser and the accused the infusion to drink. He addresses the *umwafi*, and the supporters address each their own friend. Then, when one vomits his (or her) supporters applaud trilling,[2] and they go home, the man who vomited paying the doctor. Mwandesi described how after one of the two had vomited the other would sit tense and miserable, quite still. He would be left alone awhile, but later the doctor would try to make him bring up the poison: 'Should a man die?' they said. Only rarely, it seems, did anyone die of drinking *umwafi*.

If the accuser failed to vomit he was judged guilty of witchcraft himself; if neither vomited both were judged guilty; if both vomited the accuser was fined, paying two or more cows to the accused in compensation for slander. If he had no cows he might give a girl in marriage.

[1] For the methods of divination see Godfrey Wilson 'An African Morality', *Africa*, Vol. IX (1936), p. 80.
[2] A high-pitched *ulu-ulu-ulu* expressing praise and triumph.

Sometimes the individuals concerned did not actually take the ordeal themselves, but each was represented by one of his or her children, as when Mwaisumo's mother was accused of bewitching the village cows, and one of her younger sons drank the *umwafi* representing her (cf. Document, p. 241). Very often the ordeal was used to discover which *group* was responsible for the trouble, whether it was the father's people or the mother's, or perhaps the village, and a child was chosen to represent each group and given the poison. Mwaisumo himself had drunk *umwafi* as a child, representing his father's people (cf. Document, p. 244). And a sceptic explained that each family chose a member who vomited readily—his family was always represented by a certain daughter who vomited *umwafi* immediately.

The ordeal is only administered nowadays in the greatest secrecy, and probably very rarely, for informants who had no hesitation in discussing with us witchcraft accusations and trials of supposed witches, though these were well known to be illegal, denied that the ordeal was administered. The most recent example we traced occurred in 1932.

So far we have only dealt with cases in which witchcraft is suspected as the cause of illness among men, or of a decrease in the milk supply. The matter is more serious if someone has actually died. If there is any doubt as to the cause of death, an autopsy is performed, and a diagnosis made from the condition of the stomach and intestines. 'Wounds' or scars in the stomach are taken as evidence of attacks by witches, and a black oily substance in the bowel, or red streaked with black and white, is a mark of sorcery; if the bowel is swollen, or if the entrails burst out of the incision, it is proof that the deceased was himself a witch, and was probably killed in a quarrel with fellow witches. Death due to a relative having been bound with ropes (cf. Document, p. 249), or a disease of the bowels (*ikitasya*) attributed to natural causes, is also thought to be apparent at an autopsy. Some maintain too, that the source of witchcraft can be discovered from the examination, wounds on the right side of the stomach indicating that the witch is a member of the father's family, or of the age-village; wounds on the left indicating that he is a member of the mother's family (cf. Document p. 246).

At the autopsy the crowd is kept at a distance and usually only one or two senior relatives or neighbours, the headman of the village, and the doctor who operates are present. Occasionally their judgement is challenged.

'Once an old pagan woman, whose husband was reputed to have been a witch, demanded an autopsy. When they opened the stomach the entrails (*elitondobeli*) jumped out. [When the entrails jump out this way they say "the python is fighting".] The observers looked, and said to the doctor, "All right, all right, bind him up again!" But the widow objected, saying, "No, come near all of you." She called all the people and went to the corpse, and tore open the stomach. All cried out, saying: "Alas! do not do that. It is forbidden." Then she turned to the old people and said: "Is there anything here? Nothing! He is only a witch by hearsay. Yes, indeed, just because the entrails jumped out you convicted him." ' For detailed accounts of two of the autopsies observed see the Document on pp. 247–50.

In the past the source of witchcraft was always confirmed through the ordeal; nowadays divination with the rubbing-board is sometimes used instead. Mwamunda described the procedure: 'The custom of drinking *umwafi* has ceased, but some, when a person has died, perhaps a child, make an autopsy. . . . Then, if they find wounds of witchcraft (*efilonda efya manga*) the father and the mother of the child go to a doctor to divine, but they do not drink *umwafi*, they divine with the rubbing-board. Perhaps the divination indicates the mother. She then goes to her father, and he goes to divine with his wife, the grandmother of the dead child. If he (the grandfather) is then indicated he next takes his kinsmen with him, and when the divination indicates one of them the man will say: "This divination is nonsense; it always deceives." But others will think him guilty and say: "A kinsman was caught, he had eaten his grandchild." Or perhaps the divination indicates the father of the dead child. If so he divines again asking: "Is it relatives, or is it the country?" (For a man has a country, not a woman.) Then perhaps the divination will show that it is not relatives, but the "breath of God" (*Kyala*), that is to say other people, non-relatives. Or perhaps the divination indicates the father of the dead child and his relatives; and if so the father goes with his kinsmen and one of them is indicated. Then the father goes again with the man indicated by the previous divination, to confirm the verdict. Before going to court he asks himself: "How shall I bring a case which depends for evidence on divination?

Will the Europeans allow it?" And so (instead of bringing a charge of witchcraft) he sues his kinsman for a shilling. Later he sues him for a cow, and some even get a court order to collect the cow. Another man in such a position may claim a legal separation from his kinsman and their reciprocal debts in cattle are repaid.[1] It's a case indeed, that!'

Mwamunda came from Rungwe, not far from the administrative centre, Tukuyu, hence perhaps his hesitation in preferring a charge of witchcraft; in more remote parts cases concerning witchcraft are taken to the courts. Nsusa explained: 'We judge cases concerning witchcraft openly, but we do not have them written in the court book. When "a defender" has seen his fellow throttling someone he tells us, and we judge that witch. It is "the defenders" who see the witches. Perhaps "the defender" comes out of his house by night and calls out: "I see so and so throttling so and so! Listen to-morrow!" Yes, that happens nowadays. When someone tells us this we agree, the witch is convicted, even though he denies it. We say: "You are a witch, a thief, even though you do not admit it, get out of the country." Formerly when the accused denied he was a witch they went to the ordeal, and the ordeal caught the witch; now, since the Europeans have forbidden the use of umwafi, we accept the word of "the defenders". For you know the defenders see the witches! In dreams!' 'What about the man who accused the wife of Mwakobela?' we asked. 'He denied it; he said: "I did not see her". So on that account we said: "Since you have slandered her you must pay thirty shillings." If he had really seen her. and told us properly we should have decided against the woman and divorced her from her husband, but he denied it, saying: "I did not see her", and we all said: "The woman is not a witch, who has seen her?" And if a man is fined because he has accused his fellow of witchcraft without seeing him really, we do not write that in the book either.'

Formerly, when a man was convicted of witchcraft, and did not admit it, he was compelled to move from his village, and often to leave the chiefdom altogether. Often his cattle and crops were taken by the chief, who killed one or more for 'the innocent' to eat. No compensation was paid to relatives as in an ordinary

[1] cf. Monica Wilson, 'Nyakyusa Kinship' in *African Systems of Kinship and Marriage.*

homicide. 'Was he speared by *day*?' say the Nyakyusa. On the other hand, if relatives themselves brought the accusation, the chief could not take the accused's property. Since kinsmen them-themselves were driving the man out, whose property should the chief take? Everything went to the kinsmen, save one cow, which they gave the man they were driving out, that he might start a herd in his new home. A wife convicted of witchcraft was commonly divorced, being sent back to her father, who had then to return the marriage-cattle given for her. Rarely was a supposed witch killed.

As we have seen, supposed witches are still often banished if men, or divorced if women, but property is no longer seized, the practice having been effectively stopped by the British Administration. There is considerable variation in the actual treatment of supposed witches at the present time. Some husbands do not divorce their wives when they are convicted of witchcraft, others do so immediately; some chiefs drive supposed witches out of their country, and others allow them to settle in another village of the chiefdom. We have no evidence that those who are supposed to have killed others by witchcraft are usually treated more severely than those whose crime is causing sickness or a decrease in the milk supply. The punishment seems to vary, and to have varied formerly, rather with the status and personal popularity of the accused in his village, or with the affection a man has for his wife, than with the nature of the crime.

Those who have been convicted of witchcraft are not ostracized. A wife divorced on account of her witchcraft commonly re-marries soon after; a man driven out for witchcraft is admitted to another village. The attitude is: 'Perhaps he bewitched his fellows there, we do not know, but he has not bewitched us.' Often a man who has been driven away by neighbours is fetched back again, a year or more later. Such was the case with the village headman Mwamila, who went to his chief and said: 'People are eating your child'—one of the chief's children had a disease of the eyes which blinded him. 'The chief ordered his people (i.e. their representatives) to take the ordeal. Then all were angry at Mwamila for going to the chief, because he went alone to whisper about them. Had he gone with others they would have been satisfied, but to go alone was not right. The ordeal indicated Mwamila himself, and the chief took all his four cows. No, they did not take his food and mats, was he not a village headman? He moved; but, after one year only, they went to fetch him back.'

Here, in the accusation against a village headman, who, by virtue of his office has the power of defence and of bringing 'the breath' on wrong-doers, we come to the root of the ambivalence towards those accused of witchcraft. Witches are dangerous, but the very power which makes them dangerous also makes them valuable as 'defenders', for no distinction between the power of attack and defence is consistently maintained. The essential difference lies in the use of the power. Hence, Mwaisumo declared, people actually like it when a man who has admitted witchcraft builds among them. 'They say he has the power of defence, and they think that a man who has once admitted witchcraft will not throttle them.' A parallel attitude towards homicides and cattle-thieves existed in the traditional culture, when chiefs were sometimes urged to rescue a homicide from the vengeance of a dead man's kin, or a cattle-thief from enraged victims, on the grounds that one who had proved himself such a fierce warrior (by killing another) or so skilful in lifting cattle, was too useful in war to be lost to the chiefdom.

Nevertheless, if a person who has once been accused of witchcraft makes himself (or herself) unpopular again, the old case is raked up against him or her; and there are men who have been driven from one chiefdom to another, each time accused by their neighbours, and wives who have been divorced for witchcraft by one husband after another. This is the terrible fate held up before 'proud' children.

And what of the slur on the family when a member is convicted of witchcraft? We have seen that witchcraft is considered hereditary in all but a few exceptional cases, and the stock reaction to an accusation is: 'We are astounded! No one in *our* family has ever been convicted of witchcraft!' In practice, parents are loath to allow a son or daughter to marry into a family in which either parent has a reputation of witchcraft; two or three cases were cited in which parents had opposed a marriage for this reason (*vide* Document, p. 252). But such arguments are private within the family, and the family feared by one group of neighbours need not be considered dangerous by people from another village. Since practically every adult marries at least once, the objection to marrying the child of one who has been convicted is clearly not pushed to its logical conclusion. No slur is cast on any one lineage when an individual is convicted of witchcraft, for he may have inherited it from either parent, or even got it from a friend; conversely no lineage is cleared by an autopsy, for not all the children of a witch are necessarily witches. Thus a man may have a father or brother or son who is 'pure', yet be a witch himself. As we have seen, even persons belonging to the same lineage may occasionally accuse each other. Nevertheless, when an individual who is reputed to be a witch dies, the close relatives do sometimes insist on an autopsy, in order to clear the deceased of suspicion, and possibly themselves also (*vide supra*, p. 117). In one case we recorded it was a daughter who insisted on the autopsy being performed on her mother, a reputed witch. No witchcraft was found.

So far we have dealt with cases of misfortune befalling an individual, followed by action against a fellow villager who is suspected of being responsible. This type of case is far the commonest within the field of witchcraft. When a general misfortune, such as a plague or epidemic, threatens, the chiefdom acts as a whole, not the villages separately, and the ritual is directed primarily to securing the blessing of the shades. There is some suggestion of ridding the chiefdom of witchcraft at the same time, but the emphasis is on appeasing the ancestors. The traditional new year cleansing (*ukutag' ikikungu*), now rarely performed, was also the concern of chiefdoms not separate villages, and it involved prayer to the ancestors.

b. The age-village and the ancestors

We have dwelt at length on witchcraft and 'the breath of men , for, in Nyakyusa belief, the defence of the village against witches and the punishment of wrong-doers by 'the breath' of their fellows is the main corporate activity of the village in the religious sphere. There are no village rituals directed to the ancestors comparable to those performed on behalf of lineages and chiefdoms. Indeed, belief in the power of shades operates only in situations where social position is determined by descent, as it is in lineages and in the succession to chieftainship. The office of village headman is not hereditary. The son of a village headman

cannot be appointed as headman in any village of his own generation, and villages of past generations disappear. When a headman
dies, his village still being in existence, his place is taken by his
heir who may be a son, but this office is only temporary. The
village ceases to exist when its original members die off. Moreover,
there is no suggestion that the shade of a headman's father broods
over the village as the shade of a chief is thought to brood over
the land he ruled.

The Nyakyusa have a lively belief in the power of shades, a
belief closely connected with the dependence of the members of
a lineage upon one another for cattle,[1] and with the office of
'divine king', but such belief scarcely affects village relationships,
for the shades are not thought to be concerned with behaviour
between neighbours, as distinct from relatives.

It is true that the proper performance of family rituals includes
feasting neighbours, but the implication always is that the shades
are concerned only in enforcing obligations towards themselves
and fellow kinsmen, not towards non-relatives. On the other
hand, neighbours are concerned in the enforcement of kinship
obligations. When a son insults his father, the father's neighbours
are insulted also; when a daughter-in-law peeps at her father-in-
law the shocked astonishment of the neighbours may cause her
children to pine. And so, when an erring son begs pardon of his
father, he must provide a feast for the neighbours, 'that they may
see that his father is satisfied'.

A situation often arises in which both the shades and 'the breath
of men' operate, sometimes 'the breath' of shocked neighbours
supporting the shades, and sometimes shades and men each
exacting their due. One illustration of this was given us by
Kalunda: 'If you do not carry out the burial rites for your father,
people are angry, they throttle you, and the shade is angry also,
he comes on your body. No, the witches do not call the ancestors
to help; both are angry on their own account. To-day the black
ones, the witches, come and throttle you; to-morrow the ancestors
come. People are angry because they do not eat meat; the shade
is angry because you did not perform the burial rites for him. He
says: "See, I left much property, why did you not bury me
properly?" ' And in discussing the obligation of a daughter-in-

---

[1] cf. Godfrey Wilson, 'An African Morality', *Africa*, Vol. IX (1936); Monica
Wilson, 'Nyakyusa Kinship' in *African Systems of Kinship and Marriage*.

law to avoid her father-in-law, another informant said: 'It is forbidden to look at fathers-in-law. If we do look then we shall not die well, we shall long to die and not be able to do so, because both those below (the dead) and those above (the living) are angry. Yes, it is the witches we mean when we say "those above".'

c. *The age-village and medicines*

Unlike the belief in witchcraft and 'the breath of men', which mainly affects relationships within a village, or the ancestor cult which is confined to the relations between kinsmen, and between chief and people, the use of medicines (*imikota*)[1] enters into every type of relationship in Nyakyusa society. Medicines are employed to win success in almost every undertaking: cultivating, herding, hunting, love-making, war. They are regarded as one of the main props of authority; the impressiveness (*ubusisya*) of a chief, and the power of a village headman to command, being directly related to the medicines with which they are treated (*vide supra*, pp. 24–5). They are resorted to for the promotion of fertility, for the treatment of the sick, and for protection and retaliation generally, as well as the means of directly harming an enemy. Medicines are believed to operate along with other mystical powers. For example, they are an essential element in rituals directed to the ancestors, and they are used for the discovery of witchcraft (in the ordeal) as well as for protection against it, and for the treatment of patients thought to have been 'eaten' by the witches or chilled by 'the breath of men'. Used alone, medicines are held to be ineffective against witchcraft or 'the breath of men', but they are regarded as a useful complement to other action, such as the banishment of the witch or the repentance of the sinner.

The power of witchcraft or of defence against witches (*amanga*) is connected with medicines, for it is thought often to be acquired for defensive purposes (and more rarely for aggressive purposes) through drinking medicines (*vide* pp. 25, 221). But the powers of witchcraft, or witch defence, and of medicines are quite distinct; the one implies a peculiar physical condition, the presence of one or more pythons in the belly, whereas the other may be bought from a doctor and used by anyone, and its

---

[1] The root -*kota* implies something derived from a plant. cf. *iki-kota*, a wooden stool.

efficacy neither depends upon nor affects the user's anatomy. The creation and control of wild animals, for example, is thought to turn on knowing the right medicines, not on any innate power, and is not therefore classed as witchcraft.

The Nyakyusa hold that just as 'python power' may be put to good or evil use, so also medicines may be employed legally or illegally. Particular techniques are not in themselves either good or bad; their morality turns on the purpose which they serve. Thus our friend and neighbour, Mwakionde, who was believed to have created four lions, which were roaming the neighbourhood, by placing certain bundles of twigs in the long grass, was regarded as a benefactor; for the lions had attacked neither men nor cattle, and besides adding dignity (*ubusisya*) to the country were killing the wild pig, which had been destroying the gardens. But a certain X— was driven out of Mwaijande's country because he was alleged to have created leopards which had killed children and cows. 'In 1926 X— was notorious for making leopards. It was said that he got a medicine from Misuku to make them. His neighbours feared to quarrel with him for in that year leopards infested the whole of Selya, especially the country of Mwaijande. It was said that if one quarrelled with this man one's child would be killed by leopards the following day. He was notorious. Once he quarrelled with a neighbour, saying: "Your cattle are eating my food." Then the following day the child of that man was taken by a leopard. The chief drove X— out. When they questioned him he denied having familiars ("animals") but the chief said: "Move from my country, for your animals are destroying this country." He said: "Chief, give me the ordeal." The chief refused, saying: "No! get out of my country." So he moved. Now he is back in the country of Mwaijande. He returned to the place from which he had moved.'[1]

Not all medicines believed to cause sickness and death are illegal; there are many retaliatory medicines which are believed only to harm the evil-doer, e.g. the thief, the adulterer, or the eater of stolen food; and the use of these 'medicines of ownership' (*ifilembeko*) is considered quite legitimate. A man gives his wives medicines to drink (without their knowledge) and then any lover who may sleep with them will, it is said, contract disease in

[1] In another context this man was spoken of as a witch (*undosi*), cf. Document, p. 252.

consequence, though the wives themselves are free. Further the adulterer will pass the disease on to any women he subsequently sleeps with, including his own wives. Gonorrhoea is one of the diseases attributed to this type of medicine. Medicines are also put on houses or fields, for the purpose of bringing upon thieves, or eaters of stolen food, the itch, swollen genitals, dislocation of the knee-cap and thigh, and other ills. One doctor proudly told us of a medicine he possessed which would prevent a thief leaving the field in which he was stealing 'and make him go round and round till daylight, when he is discovered and admits his theft'. Certain protective medicines are thought to cause sorcery to recoil on the sender. But their use is legal; so also is the use of a vengeance magic called 'the horn', *ulupembe* (cf. Document, p. 212), and another type, *ilyepa*, which is held to work only between relatives. These medicines are resorted to when one party to a dispute is dissatisfied with the judgement given in court, and occasionally in cases which have never been taken to court. They are held to harm the person against whom they are directed only if he be guilty. If he is innocent, they recoil on the user. What is illegal is the direct use of medicines to harm an enemy, without any safeguard to ensure that the medicine should only harm the guilty. This is *ubutege*, 'the snaring of men', which we translate here as sorcery.[1] The common techniques of sorcery are said to be putting medicine in an enemy's path, pricking it into his footprints, or putting it into his food and drink.

In theory the distinction between the legal and illegal use of destructive medicines is clear, but the classification of a particular case depends upon the standpoint of the informant. Just as the supposed victims of 'the breath of men' referred angrily to the attacks of 'witches', so informants whose families were alleged to have suffered from 'the horn', referred to it as 'sorcery' (*ubutege*).

The belief in sorcery and in retaliatory magic is directly parallel to the belief in witchcraft and the 'breath of men', while the belief in protective medicines is parallel to the belief in the power of 'the defenders'. The distinction between the two sets of beliefs turns, however, not only on the difference between the manipulation of medicines, and the exercise of an innate power,

---

[1] In 'An African Morality', *Africa*, Vol. IX (1936) 'sorcery' was used for all destructive magic; I now confine it to the illegal use of destructive medicine.

but also on the relationships to which they apply. While witchcraft, 'the breath of men', and the power of 'the defenders' are thought to operate primarily within the village and never beyond the chiefdom, sorcery, retaliatory and protective medicines may operate beyond the village and chiefdom as well as within them. Moreover, while the whole village, led by the headman, joins in defence against witchcraft, protective and retaliatory medicines are used primarily by individuals and families. Medicines of vengeance ('the horn' and *ilyepa*) are directed against kinship groups—members of an agnatic lineage, their spouses, and the children of daughters, are all held to be in danger—not local groups. The next-door neighbours of a man attacked will be safe so long as they are not kinsmen or affines.

The one occasion on which the village or village-section, acting as a group, uses medicines, is at the burning of rubbish heaps in the fields, before planting millet and certain other crops (*vide supra*, pp. 51–4). As we have shown, these medicines are supposed to protect the grain from witches and sorcerers, as well as to increase the yield. The Kukwe argue that the headman who lit the medicated fires must also be the first to taste the food grown on the fields, and he takes it with medicines, but this is not insisted upon by all the Nyakyusa; most commonly it is family groups that are careful to eat protective medicines with the first-fruits from their fields.

Envy is what makes men take to sorcery, the Nyakyusa say, envy of another's riches, or power, or employment. As we have seen, envy is cited as a motive for witchcraft also. But it is not the sole motive. Greed is the primary cause (*vide supra*, p. 92). And while witchcraft can only be used to work off a grudge against a village neighbour, sorcery can be used against anyone. Like witchcraft, the effects of 'the breath of men' are said to be confined to the village. Moreover 'the breath' can only operate against a known sinner—it is the murmuring of neighbours about an individual which causes him to sicken; whereas most retaliatory medicines work against unknown persons, discovering the thief, adulterer, or sorcerer, as well as punishing him. As elsewhere in Africa, the use of sorcery and retaliatory medicines is said to be almost entirely confined to men, though women are often named as witches. In short, the situations in which sorcery and medicines of retaliation are used overlap at one or two points with those in which witchcraft and 'the breath of men' operate, but their supposed fields of action are relatively distinct.

In the past, the punishment for sorcery was death with torture by impaling, not merely confiscation of property and banishment. Proof of the practice of sorcery depended upon the evidence of the doctor who had supplied the medicine (who was not regarded as implicated in the crime) and upon the *umwafi* ordeal. The Nyakyusa insist that the practice of sorcery was formerly rare, and that it has increased enormously, much more than the practice of witchcraft. This belief is to be related to two facts. First, Nyakyusa co-operate much more than they formerly did with people who live in different villages. The clerks who work together in Government offices, and who have a fearsome reputation as sorcerers, do not necessarily live in the same village; and being apart at night when the witches fly, they cannot be supposed to bewitch one another. But there is frequent occasion for friction between them and therefore a standing temptation to employ sorcery. So also in other types of employment, in trade and on journeys, individuals are frequently in contact with men of different villages. Secondly, belief in sorcery is felt to be compatible with the acceptance of a scientific explanation of causes of disease in a way that belief in witchcraft is not. *Ubutege* is commonly translated as 'poisoning' by those who speak English, whether the medicine is or is not put into food or drink, or whether it is supposed to affect all who eat it or only the individual against whom it is directed. All types of sorcery tend to be rationalized as 'poisoning'; and many educated Nyakyusa who deny the reality of witchcraft admit to a lively fear of sorcerers.

As the table on pp. 198–213 shows, however, accusations of witchcraft are still much more common than accusations of sorcery in the community as a whole. We heard of thirty-eight cases of supposed witchcraft to eleven of sorcery, and there was no reason to think that our friends were more likely to mention the one type of case than the other.

d. The age-village and Christianity

Since common action against witches, and to punish transgressors through 'the breath of men', is one of the primary functions of an age-village, what happens in a Christian village, or

when members of a pagan village embrace Christianity? Orthodox Nyakyusa Christians, that is, those accepting the teaching of
the European missionaries of any of the four denominations at
work in the area, deny the reality of witchcraft and of 'the breath
of men'; they deny the power of any individual to harm another
by virtue of 'a python' in the stomach, or to bring illness to his
erring neighbour by murmuring with others about him.

As we have already seen, the profession of Christianity and school
education tend to coincide among the Nyakyusa, and the educated tend to be sceptical of witchcraft, while believing in sorcery.
Such scepticism is directly related to the dogmatic teaching of
missionaries, to instruction in physiology in schools, and to the
challenge of certain missionaries and Nyakyusa Christians that
pagans should prove the existence of witchcraft at autopsies (*vide*
Document, p. 254). The suggestion that 'pythons' are really
acute tape-worm (*vide supra* p. 92) or an enlarged kidney
is typical of the critical attitude of educated Christians to pagan
dogma. We have no doubt that belief in witchcraft is weakening, and that this weakening is directly due to mission teaching.

Nevertheless most Christians continue to have some belief in a
mystical power exerted by individuals or groups to the harm of
others. For a few the contradiction between the traditional and
the Christian dogma involves acute mental conflict; for many the
conflict is resolved through the concept of 'the curse' (*ikigune*) of
the congregation, led by the priest or pastor and elders, and
through emphasis on sorcery rather than on witchcraft. Most
Christians believe that the just wrath of those set in authority,
and of the faithful members of a congregation, may bring misfortune on a sinner. They argue that the power which punishes the
wrong-doer comes from God, not from ancestors or from pythons
in men's bellies, but that it is brought upon an individual by the
anger and murmuring of men.[1] Further, it is believed that

---

[1] The phrase 'the breath of men' (*embepo sya bandu*) is never used with reference to the punishment of sinners in the Christian congregation, but always 'the
curse' (*ikigune*), a word which is used to translate certain phrases in the Gospels,
and which conveys an idea felt to be compatible with Christian dogma. As
already noted (p. 101) the pagans of the plain and of Selya use 'the curse'
(*ikigune*) more or less synonomously with 'the breath of men' (*embepo sya
bandu*). For details of cases of misfortune attributed to the curse of Christians see
Monica Hunter, 'An African Christian Morality', *Africa*, Vol. X (1937), pp.
265–91.

Christians are only affected by the shocked astonishment of fellow Christians, not by the disapproval of pagans, and the unit within which 'the curse' is commonly spoken of as operating is the congregation In two of the cases we recorded (*vide* Document, p. 209) it was suggested that illness was due to the anger of neighbours, fellow Christians, over stinginess and greed, but in the other cases it was not village neighbours who were primarily concerned, but the Christian congregation, a group embracing members from many villages.

The type of behaviour believed to be punishable by 'the curse' of fellow Christ ans also differs somewhat from that thought to be punished by 'the breath of men'. The virtue Christians emphasize most is chastity, and 'the curse' is often said to be a punishment for fornication or adultery. The other sin commonly spoken of as bringing down a curse is disobedience, or disrespectful behaviour to the minister (or priest) or elder of the congregation. Among pagans 'the breath of men' serves also to sanction sexual morals and to sustain respect for those in authority, but their sex code is different. It is incest, or familiarity between father- and daughter-in-law, which they regard as really evil, not sex relations outside marriage. And they emphasize respect to senior relatives and fathers' neighbours rather than to the leaders of any wider group.

Christians lay much less stress on hospitality to neighbours than pagans, and it is generally agreed that they eat alone more than pagans would dare to do. As one Christian put it, a pagan would *always* call his neighbours to share meat or beer when he had it, but a Christian might eat a sheep, or a goat, or even a calf, alone with his family. It is good, the Christians say, to call friends to share a feast, but not an inescapable obligation. Nor do Christians regularly send the saddle and ribs of any animal they kill to the chief, as pagans do; 'for', they say, 'we do not fear "the breath of men".' But hospitality towards strangers is felt to be a condition of salvation. One informant explained that 'If a man is stingy towards his neighbours it does not matter; but if he is stingy towards a stranger from a distance, he might die from lack of food; and that would be the fault of the stingy one. Such a fault would prevent him from entering Heaven.' This statement points to the most striking difference between Christian and pagan morality—the range of moral obligations. A pagan's duties are primarily to his kinsmen and fellow villagers, and secondarily to fellow members of his chiefdom; beyond the chiefdom and circle of kinsmen he had, traditionally, no obligations. The Christian definition of 'neighbour' is a much wider one. It is emphasized by the missionaries that the Christian Church is universal, and Nyakyusa Christians themselves are conscious of their unity with, and obligations to, members of other chiefdoms, other cultural groups, and other races. The new sanctions for behaviour operating within the Christian group—the emphasis on Christian duty; the hope of that 'peace which passeth all understanding' and of eternal life; and the fear of suspension or expulsion from the communion of the faithful, and of hell-fire[1]—all these apply to relations beyond, as well as within, the village, the chiefdom, and the circle of kin.

Two other points were mentioned by Christian informants when discussing the differences between pagan and Christian morality: they said that Christian children growing up were liable to be 'proud' (*namatingo*) in their bearing and manner of greeting, because they do not fear 'the breath of men'; and also that Christian men were not afraid to ask many cattle for their daughters at marriage, again because they do not fear their neighbours' disapproval in the way pagans fear it. The implication is that there is less insistence upon conformity to a given code among Christians than among pagans; a greater tolerance of diversity of behaviour.

These differences between pagan and Christian dogma are matched by differences between their ritual. There are no Christian rituals in which the village as a group, distinct from other groups, is concerned. The congregation—the group worshipping in one church—is drawn from many villages, and though devout Christians living in the same neighbourhood often gather for morning and evening prayer, such rituals never include a whole village. Even in a Christian village on mission land only a small proportion of the villagers attend daily prayer regularly. As we have seen, the members of a pagan village meet from time to time to warn off witches, or to bless a repentant wrong-doer (*vide supra*, pp. 101, 109 ff.), but since belief in witchcraft or in 'the curse' is not orthodox among Christians, there is no ritual con-

---

[1] cf. Monica Hunter, 'An African Christian Morality', *Africa*, Vol. X (1937), p. 265–91.

XIII. DISPLAY—THE *UKUMOGA* DANCE AT A MARRIAGE FEAST

A woman in the foreground is wearing the traditional brass body-rings

XIV A MEN'S *UKUMOG* A DANCE AT A FUNERAL

nected with it in a Christian village or village-section. The nearest parallel to the pagan ritual of reconciliation is the formal re-admission of a repentant sinner to the congregation.

The change in belief and ritual tends to weaken village solidarity; for the Christian village is neither a defensive unit, nor is it the group from within which retribution and forgiveness come. A Christian does not feel himself dependent upon village neighbours to the same degree as does a pagan. We argue that the extension of the range of interdependence reduces its intensity in the narrower circles of relationship, and this is evident in the religious as in the economic aspect.[1]

Since the authority of a village headman is largely dependent upon his supposed mystical power, Christians are rarely appointed to this office by the Nyakyusa. We heard of only one Christian headman and he was in the country of a Christian chief. Christians cannot go through the full 'coming out' ceremony which involves treatment with medicines to give *amanga*, and a Christian headman cannot fulfil the traditional ritual functions in relation to the chief and his ancestors. But in Ngonde, where the percentage of Christians is high (46 per cent as opposed to 15 per cent among the Nyakyusa) and the 'coming out' ceremony has been dropped, there are a number of Christian headmen who simply abstain from the performance of any pagan rituals (as does the Kyungu himself) leaving them to those headmen who are pagan and feel the ritual to be important. And pagan informants whom we asked about defence against witchcraft in a village in which the headman was a Christian, replied: 'Others will protect the country from witchcraft,' implying that there are always other 'defenders' in a village besides its leader.

In Christian village-sections the same difficulties do not arise, for assistant headmen are never treated at the 'coming out', nor have they ritual functions, other than the formal reproof of supposed witches (*vide supra*, p. 109). Hence the recognized leader of any group of Christians living in a pagan village is normally a Christian. In Christian villages on mission land the leaders are, of course, always Christian. These villages do not participate in any 'coming out' ceremony and the leaders are appointed by the missionary in consultation with the 'session' (i.e. representatives of the congregation), not by the old chief and

[1] cf. G. and M. Wilson, *The Analysis of Social Change*, pp. 25-41.

his village headmen. In some villages the 'elder' is both a religious leader and a secular authority, but there is a tendency to separate the two offices and to appoint a 'peacemaker' whose duty it is to settle disputes, collect taxes, and represent the village in its relationships with the chief and the administration, while the 'elder' confines himself to watching over the spiritual welfare of his people. Such division of authority is symptomatic of the growing differentiation of Nyakyusa society.

e. Witchcraft, medicines, and the British administration

Under British administration the use of the *umwafi* ordeal, imputation of witchcraft, intimidation or obtaining goods under false pretences by threats of witchcraft or sorcery, or offers of protection against them, are punishable offences. As we have seen, the ordeal is now administered only in the greatest secrecy, and probably very seldom, but accusations of witchcraft are frequent, and are even heard before the Native Courts, though not recorded (*vide* Document, p. 257). In the villages near the Government station more caution is observed in making accusations than in more remote parts of the district: very often the identity of the witch is only hinted at, or thorns are piled at his door by persons who remain anonymous (*vide supra*, p. 114) so that no individual can be convicted of imputing witchcraft. As one man put it: ' "The defenders" see the witches, but cannot name them to anyone.' Autopsies continue in conservative villages but they are no longer performed on every corpse, as is said to have been customary in the old days. The chief Porokoto, himself a sceptic, argued that it was no use performing an autopsy when a charge could not be laid. If the members of a village are all convinced that a particular fellow is a witch he is forced to move, since his unpopularity becomes intolerable to him (*supra*, pp. 110–5). As Mwambuputa put it: 'We don't like him, and he doesn't like us either: he does not enjoy our company (*atikwangala na nuswe*), so he moves.' But if the friction is only between two individuals, the supposed witch may brazen it out, for without resort to the *umwafi* ordeal there is no sure means of deciding between the accuser and the accused.

The prohibition of witch-finding is not accepted as right and just: the common view is that the Europeans 'protect the witches', and they are condemned for doing so. One old man argued in this way: 'Where you Europeans are wrong is in forbidding witchcraft in word only and not in spirit. It does no good to say that witchcraft does not exist; but if you had driven witchcraft out of our hearts that would have been good.' And again: ' "The defenders" still fight the witches, they make great efforts, but they may no longer speak about it. In the old days when a witch went to choke his fellow "the defenders" would see him and turn him back, and then on the morrow they would tell people that he was a witch, and he would have to go to the chief and take the ordeal which would convict him. But now "the defenders" have to be silent because of you Europeans who say there is no witchcraft, so that though the witch is perhaps turned back the first night, the next night he goes again and throttles his fellow.' Many Nyakyusa think that Europeans are hypocrites when they deny belief in witchcraft. One friend, the Christian wife of a chief, said to us: 'You are dissembling like all Europeans, you don't want to admit the reality of witchcraft. You are just dissembling.' Nor are Europeans thought to be immune from witchcraft: the attacks of malaria from which we ourselves suffered were immediately interpreted by our servants and friends as due to witches.

Since most people are sure that evil desires manifesting themselves as witchcraft or sorcery exist, movements of witch-finders partake of the nature of religious revivals. The *Muchapi* movement, described by Dr. Richards for the Bemba[1] appeared among the Nyakyusa in 1932, and had a brief popularity, dying out again before 1934. The professed aim of the leader was to rid the country of witchcraft and sorcery, and the attitude of most Nyakyusa was expressed in the comment of a Christian friend who said to us: 'He (the witch-finder) did very well because he brought to light all those that killed people and made them hand over the medicines which they had used.'

The sense of insecurity created by a continuing belief in witchcraft along with the prohibition of the traditional means of discovering witches, finds expression in the frequent movement of individuals from village to village. Such movement occurred in the past, and it was often linked with suspicion of witchcraft, but whereas in the old days it was always the individual convicted in

[1] A. I. Richards, 'A Modern Movement of Witch-finders', *Africa*, Vol. VIII (1935). pp. 448–61.

the *umwafi* ordeal who moved, now it is often the man who supposes himself a victim of witchcraft who flies for his life (*vide infra*, pp. 153 ff.); and it is probable that circulation between villages has in this way increased very considerably.

Denying the reality of witchcraft, the British administration ignores the belief in the legitimate use of 'python power' to enforce law and morality, any disputes arising out of this being classed as 'witchcraft'. One case turning on the belief in 'the breath of men' was heard by the District Officer of Tukuyu while we were in the district. The facts, as given us by the District Officer concerned, and by Nyakyusa informants, were as follows:

Mwankuga, a chief, fell sick and one of his sons-in-law, a clerk, advised him to get treatment from the European doctor then investigating tuberculosis in the district. When Mwankuga's junior half-brother heard this he came to Mwankuga, along with others, advised him not to go to a European doctor, and offered to cure him himself. He said that *he* had made Mwankuga ill—'had closed his stomach'—because Mwankuga had refused to make the 'coming out' ceremony for his sons when pressed by his village headmen to do so. Mwankuga's half-brother said 'the country was angry' because of the delay in the 'coming out' ceremony. He insisted that Mwankuga's illness was due to 'the breath' of the whole country, not to the sorcery (*ubutege*) of an individual. Mwankuga acknowledged that he had done wrong in refusing to hold the ceremony, and handed over two cows which his half-brother demanded, receiving in turn medicine, which he drank. Five days later Mwankuga gave his half-brother three more cows which were killed at Mwankuga's homestead and eaten by his people. Then, later on, since he did not recover, and one of his sons for whom the 'coming out' should have been held died, Mwankuga reported the matter to a senior chief, Mwakatumbula, president of the court district in which he lived. Mwakatumbula referred the case to the District Officer, and Mwankuga's half-brother was tried for 'obtaining goods by false pretences', under Section 287 of the Penal Code. The accused denied that he had ever said that he was the cause of Mwankuga's illness, and though the latter brought witnesses, the District Officer found that their testimony was 'not sufficiently reliable to substantiate the charge', and 'that there was no reason to suppose that the accused had acted in bad faith'. He referred the case back to Mwakatumbula's court 'for investigation for an offence under Native Law and Custom'. Two points which came out in the examination before the District Officer are significant. First, Mwankuga readily admitted that he had done wrong in delaying the 'coming out' ceremony. He said to the court: 'I did wrong in refusing to hold the *ubusoka*, I did wrong.' Secondly, the court (i.e. the Nyakyusa assessors) specifically inquired whether or not Mwankuga's half-brother had got his share of the meat provided by Mwankuga. It emerged that he had eaten some meat, but the witnesses were not clear as to how much he had got.

When the case came up again before the Native Court the general opinion was: 'The son of the chief has died. They (i.e. the witches) have "eaten" him. The chief himself has been ill because he refused to hold the "coming out" ceremony.'

Two other so-called 'witchcraft' cases came before the District Officer while we were in Tukuyu District. One turned on the use of vengeance magic to collect a debt, the doctor who had supplied the medicines being the accused (see Document, p. 213). The Nyakyusa view that only the individual who has commissioned a doctor to work sorcery on his behalf, and not the doctor himself, is guilty, if death from sorcery (or poisoning) has been proved, is not, of course, accepted by the Administration. In the other case a Sangu doctor told two individuals that they were threatened with 'witchcraft' and got cattle from them in return for his supposed protection. He was expelled from the district (see Document, pp. 258–61).

The difficulties of administration in this field are obvious. No one with a background of western science can admit the reality of witchcraft or 'the breath of men', as defined by the Nyakyusa, or the possibility of discovering truth through the *umwafi* ordeal. Yet prohibition of the ordeal, when belief in witchcraft is so strong, breeds a sense of insecurity. The only solution is to kill the belief in witchcraft. As we have shown, it is somewhat weakened by elementary education and Christian teaching; and we believe that its disappearance turns on increasing technical control, particularly in the field of disease, on scientific education, and on the development of impersonal relationships.[1]

---

[1] cf. G. and M. Wilson, *The Analysis of Social Change*, pp. 88–95, 102–4.

CHAPTER VI

THE MAINTENANCE OF ORDER

VARIOUS forms of social pressure which serve to maintain order in the village have already been discussed: economic reciprocity, the need to be approved, and a supposed mystical interdependence are the foundation of order. We have shown that neighbours depend upon each other for help in many undertakings, that prestige accrues to affability and generosity, that men fear to shock their neighbours lest sickness fall on them, and that they admonish their children not to be proud and quarrelsome lest they be accused of practising witchcraft. The desire for prestige and the fear of sickness, or of gaining the reputation of being a witch, directly modify behaviour towards neighbours. Nevertheless, disputes between fellow villagers occur, and there is a regular legal mechanism for dealing with them.

a. Arbitration

The Nyakyusa set great store on arbitration by a friend. It is common practice for individuals who have quarrelled to state their dispute before a respected friend and ask for his opinion on the case. The statement is made in public and any man who happens to be present may offer an opinion. There is no attempt to hush up a quarrel—rather it is held that the expression of it paves the way for reconciliation—and the emphasis is laid on arriving at a settlement which is agreed to by both parties. Arbitration of this sort begins in the herd-group when two small boys will take their dispute to a fellow, the leader of their group, and the practice continues throughout their lives in the villages of youths, mature men, and elders. The respected friend to whom the case is first submitted is most often the leader of the village-section to which one or both parties to the dispute belong. But he need not necessarily be an appointed leader; any respected man may be asked to arbitrate. If his decision is not accepted by both parties, or if he declares the case too difficult and refuses to give an opinion, then it is taken to the headman of the village. Should the headman fail to settle the dispute, it goes to the senior headman of his side of the chiefdom, thence to the chief sitting with his headmen, and nowadays it may go on through the Native Court, and the Native Appeal Court, to the District Officer sitting with native assessors, the Provincial Commissioner, and the High Court of Tanganyika.

Village headmen neither have, nor had, power to enforce their decisions; such power lay with the chief alone in the old days—he would send some of his junior kinsmen and men from his capital (*ikitangalala*) to execute judgement—and he alone could order the parties to a dispute to drink the poison ordeal, from which verdict there was no appeal. Nor is a village headman or other arbitrator paid a fee—a pot of beer or a hoe from the plaintiff to 'open the case', and beer (or occasionally a bull) as a thank-offering from the party for whom judgement was given, were the perquisites of a chief alone. The arbitrator's reward is prestige—the honour and respect of his fellows. As we have said, a case may be submitted to anyone for arbitration and no slight to the existing authorities is thereby implied; but if cases are constantly taken to some individual in the section other than himself, a section leader may grow jealous. We heard of one who was reputed to have tried to poison a new-comer to his section, a Christian, who was hospitable and became so popular as an arbitrator that the appointed leader feared lest he might lose all his authority. The hospitable man is respected and his fellows often ask for his opinion on a case as they sit together over a pot of beer.

But though village headmen cannot enforce their decisions, they are not to be ignored. An individual does not take a case direct to the chief; usually his village headman takes it to the senior headman of the side,[1] and the latter then takes it to the chief. Both will have heard something of the case and, if it is not regarded as 'too difficult', will have attempted to reconcile the

[1] It appears that a village headman *should* proceed though the senior headman of his side, but in Porokoto's chiefdom procedure was modified by the fact that there had been no 'coming out' ceremony. There Mwafula, the headman of a junior village, brought cases direct to the chief (*vide infra*, p. 146). It was modified also in Mwaipopo's country by the absence of Mwansambe, one of his two senior headmen (cf. Document, p. 181).

parties before referring the matter to the chief. And any decisions they may have reached are reported to the chief.

Disputes between members of a boys' village may be settled by the leader of their village, but more serious cases go to the headman of their fathers' village, and may proceed through him to the senior headman of the side. Old men go to their own headmen, but there is an appeal to the senior headman of the ruling generation, on the side in which they live, except in inheritance cases. In these the old men are the ultimate authority. Christians living in sections of pagan villages take their cases to their section leader—himself a Christian, whose position is comparable to that of a pagan assistant headman. Thence a civil case goes to the village headman, but where an offence against the Christian code is involved (as in theft, or adultery, or wife-beating) the case also comes before the court of the congregation, consisting of the minister, elders, and deacons. Disputes between members of Christian villages established on mission land come before the 'elder' or 'peacemaker' of the village, appointed by the Church, and if they are not settled by him they usually go directly to the chief. They also come before the court of the congregation if they involve an offence against Church law (cf. Document, pp. 262–3).

Disputes between pagan women are settled in the same way as disputes between men. There is neither the leadership and authority of a senior woman of the homestead as among the Nguni and Bemba,[1] nor that of a senior age-set or women's council as among the Meru[2]. The first woman to be settled as a wife in a young men's village is, as we have seen, entitled to the deference of the wives who follow her, but she has no authority over them. In the same way, though a man's senior wife takes precedence in family rituals, and the wife of a headman may lead in a village ritual, or the wife of a chief in one made on behalf of the country, such precedence in ritual does not carry authority over other women. Certain women versed in the rituals performed at puberty, marriage, birth, and death, and knowing the proper medicines to use, are called in on these occasions, but such

[1] Monica Hunter, Reaction to Conquest, pp. 18, 35–41; H. Kuper, An African Aristocracy, pp. 38–9; A. I. Richards, Bemba Marriage and Present Economic Conditions, Rhodes-Livingstone Papers No. 4, pp. 67–9.

[2] E. M. Holding, 'Women's Institutions and the African Church', International Review of Missions, July 1942, pp. 290–300,

abanyago have no more general authority than the doctors who divine or treat the sick. Their parallels among men are the priests (also called *abanyago*) who perform the rain ritual and the sacrifices to dead chiefs.

The one position which endows a woman with legal authority is that of father's sister. A senior sister has a joint responsibility, along with the headman of the village, for the distribution of her dead brother's property, and her brother's children may appeal to her to arbitrate if they have a dispute with their father while he is yet alive: this is particularly important in the families of chiefs, since a chief's son cannot bring his father before commoners for arbitration. The authority of a father's sister is, however, exercised only within the lineage and does not extend even to wives of lineage members. Co-wives may take a dispute for arbitration to their husband, but if, as often happens, he is thought to be prejudiced, they go to a male neighbour, or to the headman of the village, in the same way as when the dispute is with an unrelated person (cf. p. 140).

Only in the group of unmarried girls in a village does there appear to be the germ of control by seniors of the same sex. We traced one case in which a quarrel between two girls nearing the age of puberty was settled by the slightly older girls of the same village, who punished one who had beaten her fellow without justification, and then lied to them when they inquired into the case, by scratching her with their nails. As they reach puberty the girls, who have grown up together in one village and formed a closely knit group, become scattered among the different age-villages of their husbands and there leadership among women is not developed (*vide infra*, pp. 171–2). This does not mean, however, that women are excluded from arbitration; they can, and frequently do, bring cases on their own account, not necessarily acting through husband or father. Unlike the pagans, Christian women who have quarrelled do sometimes ask a leading woman of their congregation to arbitrate. At Rungwe the women leaders were the sister of the chief and the wife of a teacher, both personalities; and it was to them that their fellows went to relate their troubles and ask for an opinion. We traced two such cases. Very often, however, Christian women go to a man, the Christian leader of the village, as their husbands do.

The Administration has not attempted to suppress arbitration among the Nyakyusa, though the villagers say they have been told to 'bring all cases to Court and write them in the book', and a District Officer, in fining a man 5s. for accepting a fee of 2s. for adjudicating in a case concerning marriage-cattle, commented: 'I am afraid that arbitration is a common offence.' He went on to say, however, that 'preclusion of headman and elders from hearing cases is repugnant to the native sense of justice', and pointed out that he fined the accused only because he had accepted a fee. Nevertheless the Nyakyusa maintain that individuals submit less readily than formerly to the judgement of village headmen and are anxious to bring cases to the Native Court 'that they may be paid quickly'. European officers are constantly pressing that fines or payments ordered should be handed over quickly, whereas in cases of arbitration payment is often long deferred, even though its justice has been accepted by both parties. Again and again the report of a case before a village headman ended with 'So and so was ordered to pay such and such, but he has not yet done so'. It was suggested that disputants are less ready to reach an amicable settlement, and more prone to press for their pound of flesh than formerly (*vide infra*, p. 147).

The cases settled by friends and village headmen are mainly disputes over the ownership, destruction, or sale of property; often such minor property as a bunch of bananas, a hen, a few cents, or a pot of beer. For example, a certain woman, A, took a hen belonging to her co-wife, B, while the latter was away, and cooked it for their husband. On her return B asked her husband about her hen, but he denied any knowledge of what had happened to it. B's friends, however, told her that A had cooked the hen for their husband while B was away, and B actually asked her husband where the hen he had eaten had come from. He replied that he did not know—possibly it came from A's father. So B brought her co-wife to the headman of the village, who ruled that A and the husband must each pay B a hen. The husband's fault lay in his not asking whence the hen he ate came.

Another woman was carrying a pot of beer to a smith to pay for an axe which her husband had bought. Three young men stopped her on the way and begged her to sell it to them instead, promising the regular price of 1s.; but though they drank the beer they delayed payment, and after some time she sued for it before the headman of their village. The young men admitted their debt, but when the case was recorded 45 c. was still outstanding, one man having paid 30 c., another 25 c., and the third nothing.

Another dispute brought for arbitration to a male neighbour was between two women who had together brewed beer for sale. The beer went sour and they quarrelled over the division of the 1s. 10 c. they got for it; they had expended 1s. on millet with which to brew so there was only 10 c. to divide.

Cases involving property of greater value are brought in exactly the same way. For example, one man, A, accused another B, of stealing the cow-bell off one of his cows, when A's herd was grazing near B's homestead. The case was first brought before B's immediate neighbours who thought him guilty, and ordered him to produce the bell. He refused and the case went to the village headman, who also found B guilty and ordered him to pay 10s. fine. B accepted this judgement but had not yet paid the fine when the case was reported.

Very often a claim on a kinsman or an affine to hand over cattle due is also pressed before a friend or village headman, as when a young man, Y, brought his father before one of his father's most respected friends, Kasitile the rain-maker, demanding that his father somehow 'find' a cow which he owed him. The case was as follows: A, the father, had two sons, X and Y. When X's full sister married, one cow from the marriage-cattle was given to Y. When Y's full sister married one cow was duly given in return to X. Then X's sister left her husband and the marriage-cattle had to be returned, plus two for the adultery fine. Y not only lost the cow he had received for her, but A took from him also a cow for the fine. This cow Y had got as an adultery fine for his own wife. Y was therefore demanding one cow back from A, and wanted him to 'look for it among his sons-in-law'. People commenting on this case said that it was perfectly proper for Y to bring his father before a friend, but he should not take the case to Court as he was threatening to do.

Besides the many disputes over property a smaller number of accusations of assault or insulting behaviour are settled by arbitration. In one case a woman complained that her husband had beaten her unjustly. His defence was that he suspected her of adultery. A certain man who had bought a bunch of bananas from his wife had asked for a calabash ladle (for drinking), and when he asked for it they were close together. The husband saw them. Next morning the wife took the bananas to the purchaser. In the evening the husband went off to visit his friends so his wife 'left the hearth empty'. He came home late, and finding no food prepared, accused her of adultery and beat her. The village headman argued that had the husband really suspected adultery he would have 'caught' his wife when she was talking with the man who bought the bananas, and the husband was ordered to pay 2s. to his wife. Accepting the decision he offered her a cloth worth 2s. but she asked for cash which he had not yet found when the case was recorded.

In another case a herd-boy, X, supported by his father, accused a fellow herd-boy, Y, of insulting and beating him. Y had called X a witch and accused him of 'throttling the cattle'. X and his father took the case first to Y's father who ordered Y to pay X 1s. When Y refused, X and his father proceeded to the village headman who ordered Y to pay 2s. which he eventually did.

Accusations of practising witchcraft are also aired in village-section and village, and may be settled there without ever going to the chief. This procedure we have already described.

As is evident from the examples cited, friends and village headmen arbitrate not only in cases between neighbours, but also in those between members of different villages; the plaintiff always applying to the friends or headman of the defendant for an opinion on the case. Very often the disputants are relatives who may choose to apply to another relative to arbitrate, but who have no obligation to do so;[1] fathers and sons, husband and wife bring their disputes as readily before friends and village headmen as before relatives. There is, however, a strong feeling that they should settle by arbitration and not proceed to the chief's court. Indeed it is felt that all cases should be settled amicably by agreement before arbitrators, and not by order of the court; the obligation to reach agreement is all the greater when the disputants are relatives.

We quote a final case in some detail as it exemplifies the emphasis laid on agreement as well as illustrating procedure. The case, which we followed throughout ourselves, was one between two comparative new-comers to the village, a young man almost a boy, called Kenani, and L. a man of forty or more.

[1] cf. Godfrey Wilson, 'An Introduction to Nyakyusa Law', *Africa*, Vol. IX, 1936.

Kenani first came to the chief Porokoto, saying: 'Someone has burnt my maize-field.' The chief replied: 'Is the village headman not there? He takes cases; only if there are hard words does it come up to me.' So Kenani went to the village headman, Mwafula. He arrived about 4.15 p.m. and the man he accused came about 5 p.m. Mwafula sent for four or five neighbours to help him try the case. The two disputants stood up with one of the neighbours between them, as if they were at court. Kenani stated his case, L (the accused) intervening with comments.

K.: 'On Thursday last week [eight days previously] L. was burning the grass and my maize was burnt too.'

L.: 'I was burning to get fresh pasture for my cattle.'

K.: 'But I am not a stranger in this country. The cattle ought not to graze in the village; it's within the village there; sheep ought to graze there, not cattle. That part has never been fired before. I was ill when my food was burnt, but I sent my sister to say to L.: "See, you burn the grass and my maize is destroyed." But he said: "I burnt for fresh pasture only, did I deliberately kindle the rubbish in your field in order to spread the fire to it?"'

Here the arbitrators[1] expressed surprise to each other that L. should insult a man after burning his maize. They asked L.:'Did the woman, his sister, come to ask you about the matter?'

L.: 'Yes, she came, but she said [speaking in her brother's name] "You have burnt my maize and you burnt it deliberately, give me two plots (imbaka) of maize." To which I replied: "What! Two plots indeed! Did I kindle the rubbish on your field? I didn't know there was any maize where the fire scorched the field."'

K.: 'It is this which especially hurts me, this talk about "not kindling the rubbish in my field". If he had come to me and said, "Friend, I was burning a patch for fresh pasture, but the fire spread into your field, I am sorry, I am indeed very much to blame." Had he said this, I should not have come here. You see that L. is my senior. I should have said: "Since you, my senior, have admitted that you are at fault I am satisfied. That's all right." But when he began talking about not kindling the rubbish

---

[1] The same word abalongi is used for members of a court of arbitration, and the chief's court, and Native Court. We translate it as 'arbitrator' in the first context and 'judge' in the other two.

in my field, I thought to myself, "He did indeed burn arrogantly and deliberately." And so I have come for a judgement.'

The arbitrators, speaking partly to one another and partly to L.: 'When somebody's crop has been burnt, who would you expect to take offence? Surely the owner of the food, not he who burnt it? It is for the latter to abase himself and say, "I am at fault". The owner of the food is naturally sore at the thought of his burnt food.'

To L. direct: 'Had you spoken to your fellow saying: "It is true, friend, I was burning for fresh pasture and the fire spread," we should have pressed Kenani to forgive you, saying: "Friend, your senior has admitted his fault, forgive him." What have you to say to this?'

L.: 'Do you mean I deny that I did the burning? I was certainly burning, for fresh pasture. If you say, "Pay!" I will pay for the land I burned, but for the maize I will not pay. How should I know its whereabouts?'

Arbitrators: 'For the land you don't pay, it is not his, and it's not yours. There is an owner from whom we always seek land. And you are both new-comers. But you have burned somebody's crop.'

L.: 'I was burning to get fresh pasture for cattle. I did not burn crops.'

K.: 'But cattle should not graze there. It's part of the village.'

Mwafula: 'It is certainly part of the village—I went to see.'

Here the discussion was interrupted by one of the arbitrators, Jacobu, who protested that this was a breach of procedure. Mwafula should not have gone beforehand with only one of the disputants to see about a disputed point, but two arbitrators should have risen now and gone with the disputants to see. He shouted a lot; and so did Mwafula, who explained that when the chief had told Kenani to lay the case before him, he had ordered him to go with Kenani to see the burnt maize. At last they calmed down and Jacobu was rebuked by one of the other judges who said in a quiet voice: 'Perhaps you have been drinking beer —or haven't you?' After this they continued the case, but as it was getting late and both Kenani and L. showed signs of rising temper and began shouting again, the case was deferred to the next morning.

During the proceedings Mwafula was referred to by all parties as 'father', and he addressed the parties singly by name and collectively as 'countrymen' (*mwe ba kisu*). Sometimes the procedure was formal, sometimes not. Sometimes one of the arbitrators addressed the man standing between the disputants who repeated the question to them, and they conveyed the answer in the same way; but sometimes this procedure was omitted and conversation, with even two or three speaking and shouting at once, took its place. There were many repetitions which we have omitted, and the whole case was recapitulated at one point for the benefit of a late-comer.

When the case was resumed the next morning Nsajigwa, a next-door neighbour of Mwafula who had not attended the first sitting, was present, and the case was explained to him. L. was less aggressive than previously and agreed to pay 'for burning for fresh pasturage', in the same words as before, but he did not press the point that he thereby implicitly renounced responsibility for the maize, though he clearly did so. The arbitrators attempted again to get him to make some apology to K. and so have the whole thing settled amicably, but this he would not do.

K.: 'Had L. said, "I am sorry it spread from the pasturage", I should not have come here; but since he only admits to burning rubbish in my field, and offers to pay for the land, refusing to pay anything for the crop, I say he does not care at all that he has destroyed someone's food. He thinks, "The maize was small and the owner is small; the maize was not full grown and the owner is not full grown either." But just as even a hen has a house to enter (for refuge) so I have a shelter, the Law (*ubulongi*), which is a refuge for us all.' Kenani then went on to relate how L. had beaten him with a stick and had had to pay a fine of 7s. for it; and that this was why L. still hated him. But Jacobu told him not to bring up a case already settled.

All the arbitrators were agreed that L. was in the wrong. Some wished to 'cut the case' and name a fine, but Nsajigwa, before they had well begun to discuss the amount, said: 'Since it has come to fining and they do not agree, let the case go up to the chief, we cannot finish it.' He spoke with authority, and the sitting broke up.

Lingering behind we asked Mwafula why they did not give a

judgement. He replied: 'Because in the villages we only arbitrate, we do not compel people to submit to a decision. If hard words are spoken and the disputants do not agree, then we take the case to the chief. But (turning to another man) we were wrong not to decide on a fine, we ought to have named so many shillings. Then if L. had refused to pay it we should have taken the case to the chief.'

When we arrived at the chief's place he at once sent off two men with the two disputants to count the burnt maize stalks. They found eighty-seven stalks burnt irretrievably and sixty-eight scorched but recovering.

Chief to K., through Mwafula, who acted as spokesman: 'What have you to say? The maize is really burnt.'

K.: 'I say he must pay. Had he expressed regret I should not have come here, but even at Mwafula's he did not apologize, he said: "I will pay for the land, but the maize has not been burnt, I will not pay for that." Though the arbitrators, Mwafula and the others, pressed him to admit his liability, saying: "The fire spread from the pasture", he would not admit it. And even when we went there with witnesses to see the maize he called to some young men, "If the mother or sister of Kenani comes to fetch firewood here tell them I shall imprison them, I have bought this land. I have paid Kenani." (Laughter in court.) And he said to some women who were gathering firewood near by: "Why do you gather firewood on my land?" (More laughter.) It seems that he does not regret at all that my food is burnt. Had we two been alone when he was questioned he would have speared me. He has long sought to injure me and now he is destroying my food. Therefore I have to run to the Law to escape from him.'

Timothy Mwanjesi, who had not heard the case, now arrived and started speaking, saying: 'It always happens when a man has fired the pasture and burnt another's field that he goes to his fellow and says: "Friend, it has spread . . ." and nothing more is done about it.' The judges explained the case to him; after which K. continued: 'If you say he should not pay, then I wish to have a letter to show the European Administration, saying, "L. has burnt the food of K., and has not paid", so that if I should burn your food, Timothy, and you say "Pay", I shall refuse, supported by this letter which proves there is no payment for such things.'

XV. SETTLEMENT OF A DISPUTE

The anthropologist (Godfrey Wilson) is sitting with the court. On his right is the chief Mwaihojo, on his left Kasitile the rain-maker. Behind him (in a topee) is Mwaisumo the clerk, and Mwakionde, famous as a doctor and maker of lions. In the background is a half-built hut

XVI. THE FAVOURITE WIFE OF A CHIEF

One of the other judges: 'How does he seek to injure you?'

K.: 'No, that is another matter, we are only concerned with the case of the maize.'

Porokoto: 'Answer the judge's questions. Tell him.'

K. explained that his sister had run off with a man and that the lovers had hidden in L.'s home. The court messengers searched for them for many days but could not find them, and K. joined in the search, for his sister's husband was pressing him to return the cattle given for her. At last one day K. and a friend called at L.'s home, not searching, just calling, and were startled to find his sister's seducer. The latter seized a stick and fought K, who fled to the chief. The chief sent messengers to fetch the wanted man and L., in whose house he was hiding. They were some time in coming, so the chief sent K. to the top of the hill to bid them hurry up. He did so, and L., coming up first, said: 'Were you calling me?' 'No', said K., 'I was calling the messenger', but L., being an older man, felt insulted, thinking he had been shouted for by a boy, and took a stick and beat K. savagely. He was summoned for this and fined 7s.

Porokoto: 'Oh, it is this you mean when you say he sought to injure you, and now he seeks to destroy your food?'

K.: 'Yes.'

Porokoto: 'You, L., have done wrong in one thing; you insulted K. by saying "Did I kindle the the rubbish on your field?" As it is a fining matter, come to the Court on Monday."

Men at the chief's place, commenting on this case, said it should have been settled amicably. 'The country has decayed, we have turned ourselves into bees instead of men. European times (*ikisungu*) have come, constantly we pay one another. People fear to come and build with us, saying: "See, there they pay, I have cattle, and children" (implying, I am a prosperous man and do not wish to grow poor by going there).'

We asked Porokoto how the case would have been settled in the old days. He replied: 'In the old days L. would have given K. seed to plant again; but a new way has come now, we have discarded our own way; now we pay shillings. When millet was burned in the past they paid a bull, because a basket of millet was sold for a bull.' Turning to an old man, Mwambege, who was there, he asked: 'Was it not so, Mwambege?' 'Yes—perhaps an iron hoe was paid. When I came here from Lugulu country I burnt some pasturage and the fire destroyed two plots of millet. I gave the owner an iron hoe.'

The ideal is settlement by agreement; in practice (at the present time) a large number of cases go (like this one) to the chief, and then on to the Nat ve Court. Thence there are many appeals to the Native Appeal Court, the District and Provincial Officers' Courts, and even to the High Court of Tanganyika. As we have indicated, it is likely that fewer cases are settled by arbitration than formerly; but before the coming of the Europeans, chiefs' courts with power to enforce judgement existed, and were used. There was no 'golden age' in which all cases were settled by agreement.

The decision of arbitrators is essentially the judgement of public opinion in the village, or the respective villages, of the disputants. Cases are heard in public, neighbours drop in and join in the discussion, and a decision cannot be given contrary to their expressed opinions.

b. *Witness to contracts*

Not only do fellow villagers play a part in settling disputes, they also act as official witnesses in various types of legal transaction. The village headman is an essential witness at an autopsy (*vide supra*, p. 116) and at the distribution of the estate of one of his men. Whenever marriage-cattle are handed over, two or more non-relatives are called upon to serve as witnesses,[1] and those chosen are commonly village neighbours of either the groom or his father-in-law. We heard one man censured by his friends because he had neglected to take a village neighbour with him as witness when he went to summon his son-in-law to his daughter's puberty ritual. He had visited his son-in-law's 'best man' (*umfusya*) as was correct, but had omitted to take a friend with him to witness the conversation that took place. Even in matters that are kept very secret at least one official witness may be summoned. For example, an old man occasionally gives his heir permission to sleep with his wives while he is yet alive, and he does so in the presence of a neighbour or senior relative, for though the affair is very private it is absolutely necessary to have a witness to prove that the right was granted.

[1] cf. Godfrey Wilson, 'An Introduction to Nyakyusa Law', *Africa*, Vol. X (1937).

This practice of having official witnesses to every contract, and summoning them to give evidence should a dispute later arise, is one of the most important means of maintaining order in Nyakyusa society, and village neighbours are the usual witnesses.

c. Communal responsibility of the age-village

Formerly, in Nyakyusa law two forms of group responsibility were emphasized: the mutual responsibility of kinsmen, and the mutual responsibility of fellow villagers. A case of murder or manslaughter was primarily the concern of the agnatic lineage if the victim was a male or an unmarried girl, and of the lineages of both husband and father if the victim was a married woman. The kinsmen either killed the murderer, or brought him before the chief, who imposed a fine which went to the injured relatives. The Nyakyusa make a distinction between 'spearing by day' (direct physical injury) and 'spearing by night' (witchcraft); and only in the latter type of case did the fine go to the chief. Witchcraft was thus treated as an offence against the state—the chiefdom—while murder or manslaughter was an offence against the kinsmen of the dead. The concern of the state in witchcraft, and the joint responsibility of kinsmen on the one hand, and of fellow villagers on the other, was evident when, as sometimes happened, both groups were required by the chief to clear themselves of suspicion of witchcraft by each providing a representative to take the poison ordeal. Should the representative of either group fail to vomit then the responsible individual within that group was sought out by means of divination and the ordeal (vide supra, p. 116).

In a case of adultery the injured husband, together with his kinsmen, pursued and attempted to kill, or torture and kill, the adulterer: self-help was not only permitted but expected in this situation,[1] and a man's near kinsmen were obliged to assist him. Neighbours were not obliged to assist in executing vengeance, but they might be victims of it, for if the injured husband did not find the adulterer he might kill any village-mate of his enemy. Such an attack commonly led to war between the two villages;

[1] D. R. MacKenzie, The Spirit-Ridden Konde (1925), p. 61, says: 'The injured husband has the right to inflict death on the paramour. This is no mere tale of the past but a grim fact to-day . . . cases of this nature are very numerous.'

and some informants suggested that it only occurred between the villages of different chiefs, though others insisted that it did occur between villages of the same chiefdom. Indeed any seduction of a woman of another village was liable to lead to war. A man of Bulindanajo seduced the wife of the headman of Bujege, Mwansambe. The men of Bulindanajo returned the woman to her husband, saying to their fellow: 'The men of Bujege are fearsome (*basisya*), it's a village of fathers, she's your mother' (cf. Document p. 181). But Mwansambe was angry and made war. The men of Bulindanajo protested, saying: 'We brought the woman back!' but he took no notice and attacked them. He was defeated, and fled.

A thief or an obstinate debtor was also a danger to his neighbours. For a victim or creditor living in another chiefdom, and so unable to obtain satisfaction in a chief's court—since a chief paid little attention to a complainant who was not his own man—might seize the wife of any village-mate of the man who had his property. Hence, the old men say, thieves and adulterers were liable to be banished from a village[1] just like witches and sorcerers, for they too brought misfortune on their fellows.

War between villages was apparently the usual upshot of an attack on the village neighbour of an enemy, but occasionally a settlement was arranged between the two villages concerned, and the adulterer or thief was held responsible for compensating his injured neighbour, or the latter's kinsmen. Kalunda and Mwalubunju explained: 'In the old days if a man ran off with my wife I should go and kill a village-mate of his. That meant, "Go, you villagers and look for my wife." Yes, this happened even in a village of my own chief. Then the villagers would go and look for my wife and when they found her with their neighbour they would bring her back to me with a spear or hoe as compensation. The man they would accuse, saying: "It was you who killed your fellow", so that he would have to make peace with the family of the dead man, not I. He would give them a daughter of his own to wife, or else pay ten cows, and they would be relatives then. Yes, ten cows they paid for a man's death, though only two for a woman in marriage.' Here the differing responsibilities of kinsmen and fellow villagers are evident.

The village was a fighting unit taking up quarrels on its own

[1] A cattle thief caught in the act was speared. . . . MacKenzie, op. cit., p. 86.

account with other villages of the same chiefdom, and forming a detachment under its own headman in the army of the chiefdom. Before an attack each village was harangued by its headman who urged: 'Keep all your spears together. If you abandon your fellow you have a case against you! All return together!' And, as we have seen, it was held that men of the same village should stand shoulder to shoulder in war and in a hunt, that they might be brave.

Cattle raids and adultery cases were the prime causes of war— fighting commonly began with a dispute over a woman, or lust for meat. Less frequently it was a quarrel between two villages or two chiefdoms over a boundary that led to war. Hostilities often flared up at a funeral when men danced the war dance with spears (*ukukina*). The Nyakyusa interpret this dancing at funerals as an expression of anger at death, a protest against death.[1] 'Formerly we protested against death, we said: "Our fellow has died, *aje!* Let us put our friend to rest!" We protested with war, we protested with spears, and people died.' Or as another inform- ant put it, 'The war dance is a way of weeping. We dance the war dance because war is in our hearts.' But the anger at death very easily merged into anger against human enemies. 'If the men of two chiefdoms or two villages were present at a burial they would quarrel and fight. The fight began when one hurled his spear into the ground and thus spewed the earth over someone else. Perhaps there would be only a few dancing at first and many sitting down, but when a neighbouring chief was seen approaching with his men, and the sound of the trumpets was heard, those already there would say: "If we sit still they will say there are no men but only women at this funeral. Let us dance too." So they would all get up and dance, and if the others did anything there would be war. Now the custom of the war dance is dying out. We chiefs control it, and when another chief comes to a funeral we tell all our men to sit down while he and his men dance at the grave, because if we do not, the war of old times is liable to break out.'

In fact peace has been effectively enforced among the Nyak- yusa.[2] We neither saw nor heard of a fight in the three years we were there. Thus mutual dependence in war is no longer a strong sanction for village unity. The joint responsibility for certain

---

[1] cf. Godfrey Wilson, 'Nyakyusa Conventions of Burial', *Bantu Studies*, Vol. XIII (1939.)

[2] A contrast to Pondoland or Zululand.

torts committed by its members has also disappeared. Instead, there is both a great increase in the number of cases treated as offences against the state; murder, manslaughter and grievous bodily injury being no longer treated as offences against a group of kin, but as crimes against the state; and a great extension in the *range* of law. A modern Nyakyusa has no difficulty in suing a debtor, or the seducer of his wife, living in another chiefdom.

Nevertheless neighbours still feel a certain obligation for the maintenance of each other's rights. For example, a certain young man eloped with a very young girl, who, though betrothed, had not yet reached puberty. On their way out of the district they were seen by a 'village father' of the girl, who brought them back to her father, and then joined with him and other neighbours in beating the young man and taking him to the chief. The youth admitted his fault in seducing so young a girl and asked the chief to summon his father-in-law (for he was already married) that he might borrow from his father-in-law the cattle with which to pay the fine for seduction. But his father-in-law was a neighbour of the father of the girl he had seduced, and he refused to lend any cattle, saying, 'You have run off with the daughter of my neighbour in the village: that means you have wronged *me*.'

And a group of herd-boys are still liable to be treated by their fathers as responsible for one another. One informant, discussing a case of bestiality committed by a herd-boy, remarked that the leader of the group forbade the others to mention it at home on the ground that 'if our fathers know they will say that we all (in this herd group) do it.'

d. Social separation

One of the mechanisms for maintaining good relations in Nyakyusa villages (as in all groups) is the separation of the dissident individual from the group.[1] This separation may be compulsory or voluntary. As we have seen, witches, thieves, adulterers, and obstinate debtors were formerly banished from Nyakyusa villages because they were regarded as a danger to their neighbours, liable to harm them directly or to bring retribution upon them. The village, being held responsible for certain actions of its members, and forming a defensive unit against the sup-

[1] cf. G. and M. Wilson, *The Analysis of Social Change*, pp. 60-1.

posed action of witches, exercised the right of expelling members thought to be dangerous to it. Nowadays, since a village is no longer held responsible for the torts of its members, men are not often banished for theft or adultery, but supposed witches and sorcerers are still frequently compelled to move.

There is also a great deal of voluntary movement to escape friction in the village. This is commonly expressed in terms of witchcraft—a family moves to avoid the witchcraft of its neighbours; but neighbours are not feared unless there has been a quarrel. It is when the parties to some dispute have *not* been reconciled that fear of witchcraft germinates, and illness precipitates a move.

Among ordinary commoners only their immediate neighbours are believed to be dangerous and such men therefore sometimes move only from one village to another of the same chiefdom; but very many move right outside to another chiefdom altogether, preferring to make assurance doubly sure and to put a long distance between themselves and their spiritual persecutors. And in the case of certain men of high social status, such as senior village headmen who are the advisers of the chief, and priests, for whom a wider circle is dangerous, it is held to be essential to leave the chiefdom.

We have argued (*vide supra*, p. 36) that movement from village to village has always occurred among the Nyakyusa but that it is increasing. The change is almost certainly a symptom of increasing friction within the village. One traditional mechanism of settling disputes—the ordeal—has lapsed, while fear of one's neighbours' witchcraft continues. It is possible also that the incidence of disease, and hence of suspected witchcraft and sorcery, has increased among the Nyakyusa—tuberculosis and venereal diseases are said to have spread greatly since 1914[1] and, in the opinion of the German missionaries, malaria is much more prevalent at the higher altitudes than it was before 1914; but there

---

[1] The incidence of tuberculosis in Rungwe district is now thought to be about sixteen per thousand (C. Wilcocks, *Tuberculosis in Tanganyika Territory*, Government Printer, Dar-es-salaam, 1938). Dr. D. Kerr-Cross, in a list of diseases encountered during ten years' practice in north Nyasaland before 1897 reports that he only saw one case of 'pulmonary tubercular phthisis', but syphilis (which the natives called 'the disease of the Arabs'), was very prevalent. Dr. Kerr-Cross was a missionary doctor who travelled extensively in Nyakyusa country. (See his articles already cited and H. H. Johnston, *British Central Africa*, pp. 473-7.)

is another reason also for increasing movement. Formerly, to move to a strange chiefdom was hazardous—a refugee might be killed, or his wife or cattle seized by the chief; nowadays it is safe. Even to-day a man's status is lower in the village in which he is a stranger than in his home village. The old families of a village, 'the owners of the soil' (*abilema*), are spoken of as *amafumu*, which, in its restricted sense, means village headmen who have 'come out' with the chief, but which is also used more widely for commoners of importance. And in the past, we were told, an individual's security of life and property depended upon the support of his neighbours, the *amafumu*, and a stranger was much less likely to receive this than an 'owner of the soil'. If a chief seized a stranger's wife no one would protest, but if he dared to touch the wife of an 'owner of the soil' the village would rise as one man. Hence the incentive to overcome friction by submission, rather than by moving, was stronger in the old society than it is to-day.[1] It may well become stronger again soon. The present circulation from village to village is possible because men are still scarcer than land in Nyakyusa country, but as the population increases, and the production of crops for sale expands, it is probable that strangers will be less welcome and movement more difficult.

To lose a member who has not been expelled is a slur on a village, for the implication is that the man who has moved has suffered from the witchcraft of his neighbours. A good neighbour should persuade a fellow contemplating a voluntary move to stay (*vide infra*, p. 243), and when someone has moved of his own accord (and sometimes even when he has been expelled) his fellows go, after the lapse of a little time, to fetch him back.

'When a man moves from his home chiefdom, his village neighbours there, in the majority of cases, follow him within two months and ceremonially invite him back with a show of force by seizing his belongings and carrying them off home to his old village. They may really like and respect him and if, as is usually the case, he has moved because of sickness, they are most anxious to prove to him that his tacit suspicions are unfounded, they wish to rid themselves of the slur of witchcraft. To invite him back is to express affection for him and so to demonstrate that he could

---

[1] cf. the modern tendency for Pondo homesteads to break up. Hunter, op. cit., pp. 15, 59.

not have been bewitched, for see, everyone likes him! Such an invitation is often, but by no means always, accepted. If a man refuses the first time then the villagers may or may not go again later to ask him back; but if he was an important member of the village—the headman, a noted doctor, the son of an old family— the invitation may go on being repeated for years; and he will then almost certainly return in the end. Whether or not he accepts a particular invitation depends again largely on his own health and that of his family and upon his relations with his new neighbours at the time it is made. Sickness and suspected witchcraft, or quarrels and insults in the new village will incline him to go home (see Document, p. 267). And a man can always return, even without an invitation, unless he was originally expelled for being himself a witch.'[1]

If an important or popular man is slow to return 'home' his former friends not only go to fetch him, again and again, during the course of years but, if he dies before his return, his corpse may be fetched back to be buried in his original village. He is also summoned to feasts there. The village was a fighting unit, and its strength, like that of the chiefdom, depended upon its numbers; hence the reluctance to lose a man and the readiness to welcome new-comers.

Men who have moved voluntarily usually return 'home' to their original village in the end. As a Selya man explained: 'The majority do come back, only a few stay permanently away. Some move for better food, the great majority because they fall sick and wish to recollect themselves in the tranquillity of another chiefdom—this is the main reason for moving, but they come back in the end. Whenever a man is slighted in the country to which he has gone, whenever he falls sick there—back he goes home. A man does not lose his affection for home, for there is his sacred grove, his fathers' graves. But the real reason for returning is that in every other place a man is less respected than at home, he is made light of; but in his own country he is known to belong to an old family and is treated with great respect, his neighbours call to mind the days when he and they herded cows together as boys, and the fact that his father is buried among them. That is why people go home again.'

[1] Godfrey Wilson, *The Land Rights of Individuals among the Nyakyusa*, pp. 32-3.

A man who has been driven out and then fetched back provides a feast for his friends on his return. This feast is essentially the same as the 'ritual of reconciliation' that takes place when a wrong-doer begs pardon of his own village or that of his father (*vide supra*, p. 101). For a private individual only his own village is concerned, but if the exile happens to be a senior headman then all the villages of the chiefdom participate. A detailed account of such a feast, which we attended, is given on pp. 271–4.

In a civilized society social separation overcomes friction in two ways: first, it separates individuals who are personally incompatible, and secondly, it provides the individual who is a misfit in one group with a choice of groups whose values may be more compatible with his own than those of the group from which he came.[1] In Nyakyusa society villages were formerly all of the same type, with virtually identical group values, therefore the individual only escaped from personal incompatibilities by moving. In the modern society, however, there is a variation of type as between pagan and Christian villages and, among the Christians, as between the several denominations. The convert in a pagan village often moves to a Christian village finding that more compatible, and the son of a Christian, having abandoned Christianity and perhaps married several wives, leaves the Christian village in which he grew up and joins a pagan one with whose members he has more in common.

The Nyakyusa, in their rationalizations about witchcraft, recognize the fact that friction is often personal and may be overcome by moving. Constantly villages receive individuals who have been driven out of some other village for practising witchcraft, and when we inquired whether a man who had once been accused was not feared as a neighbour, the reply was always in the same tenor as that of Mwamunda: 'Perhaps he has bewitched his fellows there, we do not know, but he has not bewitched us.' There is also the implication that quarrels may be forgotten after a temporary separation, since those who have moved because they feared witchcraft, and even some who have been accused of practising witchcraft, are welcomed back.

When our informants discussed moving and returning to the home village they always emphasized friction with one's fellows (*abanine*) as providing the chief impetus to move, and the desire

[1] cf. G. and M. Wilson, op. cit., pp. 60–1.

to rejoin the group in which he is 'known', in which he has 'friends with whom he herded cattle as a boy', as that which provides the chief impetus to return. Never once did an informant suggest friction with the village headman as the reason for moving[1] or loyalty to a former headman as the reason for returning. The Nyakyusa village is in no way the personal following of a headman, as the villages of some other central African peoples (such as the Bemba,[2] Yao, and Ngoni[3]) appear to be. It is essentially a group of equals, established before adolescence, whose stability and continuity turn on friendship and co-operation between its members. It is already a corporate group, with very close bonds forged through years between its members, before the permanent leader is chosen, and it continues as a group though its leader dies or moves.

We do not deny that the personality of the village headman—particularly his generosity and his skill in settling disputes between his men—affects the stability and growth of the village; some villages increase noticeably in size after the 'coming out', while others shrink, and headmen (like chiefs) use medicines to attract men to them; but the Nyakyusa themselves imply that it is the character of the villagers rather than the character of the headman which determines movement to and from the village.

The headman, like any private individual in the village, must remain on good terms with the other members lest *he* be driven out. A number of cases were cited in which headmen had moved because they had become unpopular with their men and feared their 'breath' or witchcraft (*vide* pp. 204–8; 268–70) but most of them had returned after the lapse of a little time.

What private individuals and headmen alike fear is not a quarrel with one individual, but the disapproval of the village or village-section as a whole; for 'the breath of men' is but the crystallization of adverse public opinion. The man who has the support of his fellows in a dispute with one neighbour is shielded in 'the war by night'.

---

[1] Personal friction with a chief occurs (*vide* pp. 191–2).

[2] A. I. Richards, *Land, Labour and Diet in Northern Rhodesia*, pp. 110 ff.

[3] M. Gluckman, J. C. Mitchell, and J. A. Barnes, 'The Village Headman in British Central Africa', *Africa*, Vol. XIX (1949), pp. 91, 98, 100.

CHAPTER VII

CHARACTERISTICS OF AN AGE-VILLAGE ORGANIZATION

a. *The peculiarity of Nyakyusa villages*

VILLAGES in which contemporaries live together permanently have not been reported among any people in Africa other than the Nyakyusa; such villages are not found among their neighbours, and diligent inquiry from Africans of many tribes has not revealed them elsewhere; it is possible that the Nyakyusa system is unique, but we still know too little of Africa to be sure. A similar system might well exist elsewhere without having been noted by Europeans. The fact that Nyakyusa villages were organized on an age basis was not recorded either by the missionaries[1] or the Administration, though the system of Indirect Rule had been in operation for eight years before we began work in the district.

What is common in Africa is for groups of male contemporaries —age-sets—to live together in temporary villages or club houses before marriage. The warrior-villages of the Masai,[2] the regimental barracks of Zulu[3] and Swazi,[4] the cattle posts of Tswana[5] and Pedi,[6] are all occupied by groups of contemporaries; while among the Kikuyu[7] and the Kipisigis[8] local detachments of age-

---

[1] D. R. MacKenzie, *The Spirit-Ridden Konde*, speaks of 'small boys' living in 'tiny houses' of their own (pp. 27–8); J. T. Hamilton, *Twenty Years of Pioneer Missions in Nyasaland*, says: 'The elder boys live together in long oblong houses at the end of the village. When one of them marries he builds a house near the boys' quarter, and in this manner the village extends in this direction.' (p. 40.) He does not suggest any further separation of the generations.

[2] L. S. B. Leakey, 'Some Notes on the Masai of Kenya Colony', *J.R.A.I.*, LX (1930), pp. 185–209; D. Storrs Fox, 'Further Notes on the Masai of Kenya Colony', *J.R.A.I.*, LX (1930), pp. 447–65.

[3] E. J. Krige, *The Social System of the Zulus*, pp. 261–7.

[4] H. Kuper, *An African Aristocracy*, pp. 117–37.

[5] I. Schapera, *Native Land Tenure in the Bechuanaland Protectorate*, pp. 25, 220–9.

[6] G. M. Pitje, *Some Aspects of Male Education among the Pedi and Cognate Tribes*. (Thesis accepted for the M.A. degree in the University of South Africa. Unpublished.)

[7] W. S. and K. Routledge, *With a Prehistoric People*, p. 118.

[8] J. G. Peristiany, *The Social Institutions of the Kipsigis*, pp. 49–51.

sets have club houses in which young men sleep. Among the Cewa, though boys do not move out of the parent village, they have a special hut in which they sleep together from the age of five or six.[1] But among all these people the age-set scatters at marriage, each young man building his permanent home, to which he brings his wife, alongside his kinsmen or, in the case of the Cewa, alongside his wife's kin.

The peculiarity of the Nyakyusa then consists in the fact that contemporaries live together permanently through life, not merely as bachelors: age-villages appear in an isolated area surrounded (so far as we know) by people with no similar institution.

We cannot hope to explain how, or when, age-villages developed among the Nyakyusa: there is no reference to them in such documents as exist, and we could trace no oral tradition regarding their origin. Even the historian Mwandesi (cf. p. vi) had no idea whether age-villages were introduced by the incoming Nyakyusa chiefs, or were found by them among the previous inhabitants of the valley, or were invented after the conquest. We can, however, inquire into the social characteristics associated with age-villages. *What are the peculiarities of Nyakyusa society not found in societies with kinship villages?* In this chapter we attempt to answer that question.

b. *Age-villages and incest*

The Nyakyusa themselves associate living in age-villages with decency in sex life—the separation of the sex activities of successive generations, and the avoidance of incest. When asked why small boys build apart from their parents they refer to the danger of a growing boy overhearing lewd talk between his parents, or seeing them unclothed (*vide supra*, p. 82); and they enlarge on the difficulties of father- and daughter-in-law avoidance were father and son to live in the same village—an avoidance which is consciously related to the fear of incest between father- and daughter-in-law (*vide supra*, p. 85). We may add also the fear of young men seducing their fathers' junior wives, who are often girls of their own age. Nyakyusa informants did not mention this last point as a reason for living in age-villages, but it is significant

---

[1] A. G. O. Hodgson, 'Notes on the Achewa and Angoni of the Dowa District of Nyasaland Protectorate', *J.R.A.I.*, LXIII (1933), p. 129.

that adolescent sons are not permitted to visit their homes after
dark, and when they come by day for their meals they are
often required to eat in the open court-yard and not 'hide in
the bananas or huts' lest they make love to their fathers' wives.
They do not sit about in the men's village. Thus, although the
villages of fathers and sons adjoin until the sons 'come out', the
young men are physically separated from their young 'mothers'.

The feeling that sons should not be cognizant of the sex
activities of parents, and that father-in-law and daughter-in-law
should avoid one another is not, of course, peculiar to the Nyakyusa; all we seek to show is that the extreme elaboration of these
avoidances among the Nyakyusa is dependent upon the existence
of age-villages. Whereas a Pondo daughter-in-law must never
walk across the courtyard of the kinship village in which she
lives, or approach the cattle byre or the men's side of her
mother-in-law's hut, lest she come too near her father-in-law,
yet, living in the same village, she necessarily sees him daily; the
Nyakyusa daughter-in-law, living in a separate village, need not
(and should not) set eyes on her father-in-law after her marriage.
Where the territorial segregation of fathers and sons is blurred
(as at Rungwe) there father- daughter-in-law avoidance is less
strictly observed. The Nyakyusa regard this extreme form of
avoidance as a peculiarity of their culture which has been im-
parted by them to the small groups (such as Ndali, Penja, and
Nyika) whom they are assimilating.

Father- and daughter-in-law incest is clearly a potential danger
in a society in which cattle are controlled by middle-aged and
elderly men, who frequently have to choose between taking
another wife themselves and giving cattle for a son's marriage,
and who are accustomed to marrying young girls of an age suitable to be wives to their sons. But we cannot show that the danger
is *greater* among the Nyakyusa than it is among other patrilineal
cattle people such as the Pondo, Zulu, or Swazi, who do not
find it necessary to segregate fathers- and daughters-in-law in
different villages.

On the other hand the danger (common to all polygynous
societies) of sons seducing their fathers' wives is exaggerated
among the Nyakyusa by the absence of circumcision, the late
marriage age of men, the very early betrothal and marriage of
girls, the high degree of polygyny, and the practice of sons

inheriting their stepmothers. Where circumcision is practised a grown woman scorns sex relations with an uncircumcised boy, therefore uncircumcised youths are not potential lovers of their fathers' junior wives; but with the Nyakyusa there is no ceremony to mark the sexual maturity of a male, and adolescent youths are acceptable to young married women of their own age. And not only does the wide difference in the age of men and girls at first marriage allow of a high degree of polygyny, but the very early bethrothal of girls (over whom their future husbands have exclusive sexual rights except during the initiation ritual) means that there are very few girls available to the unmarried men. The institution of girls' huts (*isaka*) has disappeared among the Nyakyusa owing to the lack of nubile girls who are not already betrothed, and the period of seclusion at initiation (when betrothed girls are available to men other than their husbands) is short. The contrast with Nguni society, in which girls do not marry until sixteen to twenty-two, and have several years of great sex freedom before marriage[1] is marked. We suggest that it is because unmarried girls are so scarce and lusty bachelors so many, that the seduction of the wives of polygynists is frequent, and homosexual practices are general.[2] Nyakyusa insist that formerly seduction was rare,[3] and possibly the impulse towards it was indeed less strong when girls married rather later and *isaka* existed (*vide supra*, p. 87).

Lastly, the Nyakyusa permit the inheritance of a father's widows by his sons, a practice regarded as improper by certain other peoples (e.g. the Pondo[4]) who practise the levirate. A son is required to treat all his father's wives as 'mothers' while his father and father's full brothers are alive, and intercourse with a father's wife is treated as a heinous offence necessitating special purification; but after the death of the father and his full brothers these same women become wives of their former 'sons'—with the limitation that a man cannot inherit his own mother or her kins-

---

[1] Hunter, op. cit., pp. 180-6; M. Kohler, *Marriage Customs in Southern Natal*, pp. 20-44; H. Kuper, *An African Aristocracy*, pp. 135-6.

[2] H. H. Johnston, *British Central Africa*, p. 408 (footnote), hints that similar practices exist among the Nyasaland Tonga and elsewhere *before* adolescence only. The Nyakyusa certainly continue after puberty.

[3] MacKenzie, op. cit., p. 63, states that the acknowledged child of an adulterous union was openly put to death.

[4] Hunter, op. cit., p. 211.

woman. It is scarcely surprising that the seduction of the young wives of an ageing father is a common theme for scandal. We do not suggest that the Oedipus complex involving own mother and son never occurs among the Nyakyusa; what we are concerned to show is that the relationship between a man and his step-mothers is particularly likely to be ambivalent.

It may be asked why there is so much emphasis on the segrega-tion of sons from their parents, and not of daughters. The answer again lies in the sex difference in the marriage age. Betrothed girls pay long visits to their husbands even before puberty, and directly after the initiation which follows first menstruation they leave their fathers' home to join their husbands. During her initiation a girl carefully avoids her father and his contemporaries in the village, and after marriage, when she returns home to visit, she must observe certain restrictions not applicable to an unmarried girl: notably she must not approach her parents' bed, and in-formants interpret the taboo as being due to the danger of mixing the sex activities of mother and daughter.

In short, we argue that there is a connection between the exis-tence of age-villages and the fear of incest between father-in-law and daughter-in-law on the one hand, and between stepson and stepmother on the other, and we suggest that certain features of the Nyakyusa social system facilitate incest of the second type. The incest theme elaborated in one fashion among people organized in clans and practising clan exogamy, and in another among people practising brother—sister avoidance, finds yet a different expres-sion in age-villages, of which the overt purpose is the separation of sons and mothers, of fathers-in-law and daughters-in-law.

c. Good company

The emphasis on the separation of parents and children is matched by the value laid on good fellowship (*ukwangala*) between contemporaries. A main end of age-villages, in the Nyakyusa view, is to allow men the enjoyment of congenial com-pany, that is the company of friends and equals. The value of *ukwangala* is, indeed, directly linked with the age-village organ-ization: to attain it men must build not only in villages, rather than in scattered homesteads, but also with contemporaries rather than with kin, since there can be no free and easy intercourse and sharing of food and beer between fathers and sons. *Ukwangala* implies eating and drinking together frequently, and cannot be fully enjoyed by people who do not live close to one another.

The value of good fellowship with equals is constantly talked about by the Nyakyusa, and it is dinned into boys from childhood that enjoyment and morality alike consist in eating and drinking, in talking and learning, in the company of contemporaries. The solitary and aloof, those who enjoy the company of women (as opposed to direct sexual satisfaction) and those who seek intimacy with members of another generation, are derided.

Now this very emphasis on the value of good fellowship with equals is doubtless a reflection of the difficulty of achieving it. The frequent accusations of witchcraft and movement from one village to another are evidence of friction between fellow villagers. Does the friction turn on the age-village organization?

d. The incidence of accusations of witchcraft

As we have seen, witchcraft is believed to operate primarily within the village, and the typical accusation is against a neighbour.[1] But in other societies also witchcraft accusations are most commonly made against those with whom one is living, and in close daily contact: in Pondoland it is members of the same homestead or of neighbouring homesteads who suspect one another of witchcraft; among Xhosa-speaking people in towns it is fellow employees, or fellow schoolmates; among the Azande it is members of the same small neighbourhood. Therefore it is not only the Nyakyusa who accuse village neighbours of witchcraft.

Of the *frequency* of accusation in different societies we can make no comparison, for statistics on witchcraft are extremely difficult to collect. Few field-workers could be certain that they were cognizant of *every* accusation of witchcraft within a given

---

[1] Over a third of the accusations of witchcraft recorded were against neighbours, as distinct from spouses or co-wives or kinsmen and, if one excludes the modern type of accusation against fellow workers in the same camp, the proportion of accusations against neighbours is almost one half. The thirty-eight witchcraft accusations cannot, of course, be taken as a random sample in the technical sense; we recorded every case that came to our ears, but cannot be certain that inquiries brought to light every accusation in the villages investigated. Nevertheless the preponderance of accusations against neighbours is significant (*vide* Document, pp. 198 ff.).

area, during a given period, so we cannot either assert or deny that accusations of witchcraft are more frequent in age-villages than in kinship villages.

There are two sets of loyalties in Nyakyusa society: those to a kinship group and those to an age-village. Does conflict arise from a clash between them? We have no evidence that it does. It is true that kin may support a sick relative against his age-group, referring to his illness as due to witchcraft, whereas neighbours will attribute it to his own sin and their legitimate anger; but very often the ancestors and the 'defenders' are believed to work together to punish wrong-doers—those who break avoidance and incest taboos, those who insult seniors, those who neglect traditional rituals (*vide supra*, p. 122). Amity between relatives is sanctioned by neighbours as well as by senior kinsmen, and the importance of enjoying the company of village mates is constantly stressed by relatives. Where a village does appear to support a member against his kin, it is usually on the side of the ancestors and 'justice', in terms of the Nyakyusa code, as when neighbours share a father's anger at the insolence of his son, or after his death protect his son against unjust treatment by the heir. The values of village solidarity and of kinship solidarity are thus coherent.

e. The form of witch beliefs

There is, however, a connection between the age-village organization and the *form* of witch beliefs. As we have seen, great emphasis is laid on feasting neighbours, and it is believed that the impulse to witchcraft comes from the lust for milk and meat. The Nyakyusa argue thus: witchcraft comes from neighbours, and neighbours must be fed or they get angry; feeding a witch on milk or beef pacifies him (*vide supra*, p. 92). An explicit connection is made between neglecting to provide feasts on the proper occasions and suffering from 'the breath' of justly angry neighbours whose blighting power springs from the same root as witchcraft. The contrast with the witch beliefs of the Pondo is marked: among them it is held that the drive to witchcraft is sex lust, and all witches have familiars with whom they have sex relations.[1]

[1] Hunter, op. cit., pp. 275–88.

The Nyakyusa emphasis upon lust for food as the incentive to crime is not due to starvation, for they are among the best-fed people in Africa, with a much greater variety and quantity of food at their disposal than the Pondo. Why, then, this emphasis in their witch beliefs? We suggest that it is directly connected with living with non-relatives who have no share in one's inheritance. The most prized possession of the Nyakyusa is cattle, and cattle are controlled by lineages. Neighbours who are not kinsmen, and who cannot hope to benefit by inheritance or through assistance with marriage and funeral cattle from a fellow's herd, are more likely to be jealous of his wealth in cattle than are his brothers and sons who directly share in it through inheritance, and the gift of cattle at marriage and death. The only profit which neighbours derive from the herd of a rich fellow is the milk and meat on which he feasts them. Jealousy of another's wealth is a common enough cause for supposed witchcraft, but the affront of inequality is greater when it is constantly before one's eyes. Nyakyusa live close-packed in villages and can hardly be unaware of what next-door neighbours eat. The statement that the pythons of witches are roused by the *smell* of meat cooking and the *smell* of milk (*vide supra*, p. 92) suggests the envy of a poor neighbour when he smells the roast beef and curds next door. Where the local group consists of a lineage (as among the Pondo) people are not necessarily aware of what non-relatives eat. Among the Pondo the pressure to kill cattle for meat comes from within the lineage, and is associated not with the witches but with the ancestors. Sickness is commonly attributed to the *hunger* of the ancestors (*balambile*), who 'want to eat by means of him' who is ill (*bafuna ukudla ngaye*),[1] a notion quite strange to the Nyakyusa.

In short, we argue that it is because people who do not benefit from each other's herds by inheritance and the provision of marriage and funeral cattle, live close to one another, that so much emphasis is laid on the lust for milk and meat as the drive to witchcraft among the Nyakyusa.

And why the Pondo emphasis on sex? Are they more inhibited than the Nyakyusa? At first sight the Pondon sex code seems a freer one than that of the Nyakyusa. The marriage age of men is no later than among the Nyakyusa, while the marriage age of girls is considerably higher, and unmarried men are free to

[1] Hunter, op. cit., pp. 232, 245.

enjoy limited sex relations with a relatively large group of unmarried girls.[1] But the Pondo have exogamous clans number-ing, on the average, 3,000 to 4,000 members; marriage into the clan of either parent or either grandmother is prohibited; and clans, though not strictly territorial groups, have a territorial basis. Therefore very many of the adolescents growing up in one area are forbidden to flirt together or marry. Moreover, clan incest is regarded with great horror and is associated very closely with witchcraft. A pregnant woman (who must confess her sins and her dreams that she may have safe delivery) is specifically in-structed to confess any flirtations within the prohibited degrees, and to confess if she has had witch-lovers.[2] Even in town, where so many traditional taboos are disregarded, clan exogamy is still insisted upon by Xhosa-speaking people.[3]

Furthermore, in Pondo belief the 'familiar' commonly appears as a European or light-coloured person,[4] and South Africa is a caste society in which sex relations between white and black are very strongly disapproved. We conclude, therefore, that the 'familiar' stands for the embodiment of sex temptation, of for-bidden lust, and that the reason why there is so much emphasis on sex in Pondo witch beliefs is that Pondo live in a society in which sex relations between members of certain large groups who are mutually attractive, are regarded with horror.

In Nyakyusa society the pattern is quite different. Sex rela-tions are prohibited only between the descendants of a common great-grandfather, who are in any case scattered in different villages and not constantly meeting one another. And not only are Europeans very few in Nyakyusa country, but the taboo on sex relations between the colour groups is much less strong than in

---

[1] Hunter, op. cit., pp. 180-4.

It has been suggested by European doctors that limited sex relations are in themselves psychologically disturbing (cf. M. Kohler, M.D., *Marriage Customs in Southern Natal*, p. 33-5), while Africans have argued that such a practice prevents psychological disturbance (cf. J. Kenyatta, *Facing Mount Kenya*, pp. 155-60).

[2] Hunter, op. cit., p. 148.

[3] Hunter, op. cit., p. 483; R. Levin, *Marriage in Langa Native Location* (Communcations from the School of African Studies, University of Cape Town), pp. 13-14.

[4] Hunter, op. cit., pp. 282, 491. My further investigations since *Reaction to Conquest* was published indicate that the 'familiar' is usually described as a European when it takes human form.

South Africa. Sex hunger obviously exists in the large group of bachelors and among the wives of elderly polygynists, but its satisfaction through adultery is not regarded as shameful or horrible. Adultery was formerly extremely dangerous, and is now expensive, but it is not disgraceful. Thus desire, being fully conscious, is not transformed into dreams and fantasies.

It is possible that all witch beliefs are an expression of lust, directed by jealousy, envy, and hatred. Certainly sex lust and the lust for good food appear in the accounts of witch beliefs in one area after another in Africa. The Zande fear that a glimpse of the cats associated with women witches, and particularly with Lesbian practices in the harems of princes, will kill a man, is a classic example of the one;[1] while the Lovale,[2] Thonga,[3] and Nyanja[4] belief that witches kill in order to eat the corpses of their victims is an example of the other. We do not suggest that the Nyakyusa alone believe that the lust for prized food is a motive for witch-craft, or that they think it is the sole motive,[5] but that their emphasis on lust for food, and the particular form it takes, is directly related to the age-village organization. It is significant that the stress laid on sharing food in the village diminishes along with the belief in witchcraft, and a rigid insistence on living with age-mates.

f. 'The breath of men'

And what of the belief in 'the defenders' of the village and the chilling 'breath of men'? Is the idea that contemporaries have a mystical power over one another a function of their living together—a correlate of an age-village, as opposed to a kinship village, organization? The Nyakyusa concept of witchcraft is similar in many respects to that of the Azande, the Thonga, and the Lovale, but, as we have shown, the Nyakyusa differ from these other peoples in the emphasis they lay on the lust for food as a motive for witchcraft; they differ also in the belief that a power

---

[1] E. E. Evans-Pritchard, op. cit., pp. 51–57.
[2] C. M. N. White, op. cit., pp. 96–7.   [3] Junod, op. cit., Vol. II, p. 506.
[4] B. Malkebu, A. Kumbanga, G. Chipengule, B. Chisunzi *Makolo Athu* Nyasa-land Education Department, Zomba (1945).
[5] For the sex associations in Nyakyusa witchcraft *vide supra*, pp. 94–5. There is a hint of the lust for food among the Pondo in the idea that the baboon familiar milks cows, and Thikolose steals food. Hunter, op. cit., pp. 275–81, 287.

akin to witchcraft and distinct from the power of senior relatives is used to punish wrong-doers and to protect[1] the village from witches, and in the belief that village headmen are foremost among 'the defenders'.

The closest parallel to the Nyakyusa concept of 'the breath of men' of which we have evidence in Africa is the belief in the 'conditional curse' among the Meru, Embu, and Kikuyu people. Lambert shows that the main sanction enforcing the judgement of the Council of Elders among the Meru people was the belief that its curse brought misfortune, and he was told in Embu that the Warriors' Council has a similar power over warriors.[2] Kenyatta shows that among the Kikuyu the conditional curse was used to protect beacons, to enforce the judgement of the Council of Elders, and to guard against bribery.[3] As we have seen, the Nyakyusa of the plain also use a word *ikigune*, which is best translated as 'the curse', when the people of the hills use the phrase 'the breath of men' (*vide supra*, p. 101), and whatever phrase is used the implication is that misfortune comes from the shocked astonishment and the anger of neighbours (or father's neighbours) which has been expressed in 'murmuring'. In the Nyakyusa view a formal cursing is not necessary to bring down misfortune, but the anger must be *expressed* (*vide supra*, p. 106). A belief in the legitimate exercise of mystical power by contemporaries or seniors to punish non-relatives thus appears in four societies with highly developed age-organizations, and further field-work may show that the two are always coincident.

However that may be, the belief in 'the curse' (or 'the breath of men') among the Nyakyusa is shaped by the fact that villages are occupied by age-sets. The social function of 'the breath of men' in a Nyakyusa age-village is strictly parallel to that of the mystical power of senior relatives in a kinship village. Where, as among most African peoples, the neighbours are kinsmen, no distinction is made between the mystical effects of the legitimate

---

[1] There are indications that the power of witchcraft is thought sometimes to be used for defence among the Thonga (Junod, op. cit., Vol. II, pp. 510, 516), and the Azande (Evans-Pritchard, op. cit., pp. 129-30) but the idea does not apparently bulk large, and there is no suggestion of a similar power being used to punish wrong-doers.

H. E. Lambert, *The Use of Indigenous Authorities in Tribal Administration* (Communications from the School of African Studies, University of Cape Town), pp. 9-10, 14-15.

[3] J. Kenyatta, op. cit., pp. 39-40, 221-2.

anger of neighbours on the one hand, and of kinsmen on the other.

The idea that a Nyakyusa village headman has the mystical power called *amanga*, and leads the attacks of justly enraged neighbours, gives him a position in his village comparable to that of the headman who, among many African peoples, is the senior kinsman in his village. Each has mystical power over the members of his village, and the fact that the Nyakyusa headman's power is derived from 'a python in the stomach', and operates like witchcraft, while the power of a senior kinsman derives from his birth, and operates through the shades, makes relatively little difference to the relations of the village headman with his people.

The Nyakyusa system is peculiar in that the village headman is foremost as the discoverer of, and defender against, witches; he combines the functions fulfilled elsewhere by the village headman and the witch-doctor. The protection which kinship villages in other African cultures seek on the one hand from their ancestors, and on the other from the witch-doctor,[1] the Nyakyusa look for from their village headmen. Doctors who claim to discover witches, and provide medicines for protection against them, exist in Nyakyusa society; some, at least, of them are spoken of as having *amanga*—the same mystical power as the headmen have —through which they are enabled to see and fight the witches; but witch-doctors play a much smaller part than they do among the Azande or the Pondo; in the battle against witches they are quite overshadowed by the village headmen. Defence against witchcraft is a village affair, and the foremost 'defenders' (*abamanga*) are the political authorities. Village rituals directed to the ancestors are conspicuously absent among the Nyakyusa, and our hypothesis is that this absence, together with the belief that the 'python power' of village headmen and others is used to punish wrong-doers and defend the innocent within their village, is dependent upon the age-village organization, in which neighbours are not kinsmen and the position of village headman is not hereditary.

[1] cf. Evans-Pritchard, op. cit., pp. 161-82, 251; Junod, op. cit., pp. 505, 516–8. The Thonga 'magician' is also believed to fly and know the witches, because he shares their power.

g. Kith and kin

The tendency to identify neighbours and kinsmen—kith and kin—appears not only in religious belief, the two groups being credited with somewhat similar mystical power; but also in verbal usage—'fathers of the village', 'mothers of the village', 'sisters of the village', etc.; in the obligation to respect a father's fellows, to run errands for them and obey their orders; in the belief that a father's neighbours are insulted by an insult to the father, and must be pacified as well as the real father; and in the responsibility of villagers for certain torts of a fellow. The distinction between neighbours and kinsmen is, however, clear-cut in marriage, in rituals, and in the control of cattle. Fellow villagers marry each other's daughters; they neither perform the elaborate ritual at death or twin birth believed to be necessary for the safety of relatives, nor are they required to help each other with cattle for marriages, funeral rites, and fines, as are kinsmen.[1]

Kinsmen are bound together by their common interest in the inherited stock of the lineage and in the cattle coming in for its daughters; by co-operation in cultivation and building; and by the belief that they are mystically interdependent—the contagion of defilement and of certain diseases caused by sorcery travelling along the roads of kinship. Village neighbours are bound together by occupation and ownership of common land; by co-operation in herding and cultivation; and by common defence against enemies 'by day and by night'. In both groups discipline is thought to be maintained by mystical as well as material sanctions, the anger of neighbours bringing ill-health like the anger of senior relatives; and both groups have certain responsibilities for their members in relations with other like groups.

h. Relative social status

The Nyakyusa material suggests certain further connections between the age-village organization and other aspects of the social structure which comparative study shows to be false. For example, it might be argued for the Nyakyusa (as it has been for

[1] Monica Wilson, 'Nyakyusa Kinship' in *African Systems of Kinship and Marriage*.

the Kikuyu)[1] that the equalitarian emphasis is related to the emphasis on age-organization. As we have seen, hereditary office exists among the Nyakyusa but the power of chief and hereditary priest is limited at every point by the power of the leaders of age-sets who are chosen each generation from among commoners. That democratic (i.e. non-hereditary) leadership is not a necessary concomitant of a developed age-organization is, however, proved by the fact that among the Zulu, Swazi, Pedi, and Tswana, whose military organization was based on age-regiments, rank is stressed, and the leaders of age-sets are always sons or kinsmen of the chief.

It is possible, however, that the low status of Nyakyusa women relative to men is partly dependent on the age-village organization. It is most obviously related to the high degree of polygyny, and the fact that the position of the various wives is not clearly determined by date of marriage, birth, or allocation of property. For a commoner the first wife betrothed is his great wife, who takes precedence in ritual, but there is no ranking of houses and allocation of the bulk of property to different houses as among the Nguni, nor the same strong pressure on a husband to visit each wife in rotation. Instead there is acute competition between a man's various wives for the position of favourite, with a disportionate share of milk and meat and of her husband's attention. We do not suggest that there is no competition among the wives of a Pondo or Zulu polygynist, but we argue that competitive tendencies have freer play among the Nyakyusa,[2] and that this competition depresses the status of women in relation to men.

Like the kinship organization, the age-village organization favours men. As we have seen, a main end of age-villages, in the Nyakyusa view, is to allow men the enjoyment of congenial company, that is the company of friends and equals. A village consists of a group of male contemporaries and their dependants; ideally, the men live together all their lives and form a close-knit group of equals, between whom mutual loyalty, hospitality, and affability is fostered from childhood. Those who move tend to go to villages in which they already have close friends. The women,

[1] J. Kenyatta, op. cit., pp. 186–9.
[2] Unfair division of milk between wives is said by some Nyakyusa to anger the ancestors who cause the cows to give blood in place of milk; nevertheless unequal allocation of milk is a much commoner cause of complaint than it is among the Pondo.

on the other hand, come from many villages, and they move from village to village more than men, because most women are inherited at least once in their lives. Nor do the women form an age-set, for men inherit wives as old, or older than themselves, and they continue to marry young brides until they themselves are elderly. A village thus contains women of all ages, the older ones often being quite late-comers to it. There is neither the unity of a kinship group, with leadership of mother or grandmother, as among a matrilineal people like the Bemba, nor the leadership of the mother-in-law as among the patrilineal Nguni and Sotho peoples. It is true that among the latter peoples the leadership of women devolves on a man's senior wife when his mother is dead, but the pattern has developed in a society in which daughters-in-law usually live for a long time in the same homestead as their mother-in-law, whereas among the pagan Nyakyusa a woman rarely joins her own son until she is decrepit, long after his marriage. When the Nguni or Sotho chief wife is obeyed by her co-wives it is as the successor of her mother-in-law; indeed on the latter's death she is often referred to by junior wives as 'mother'. Where women have authority in a patrilineal society it is usually as mother, or grandmother, or father's sister. But there are none with such positions in the context of the age-village; the office of headman is not hereditary so there is no mother of the heir, and the headman's own mother and sisters normally live elsewhere.

Such solidarity and leadership as exist among women in pagan Nyakyusa society are within the group of women of the same lineage who live together. Great emphasis is laid on the propriety of a wife bringing a younger sister, or brother's daughter, as a junior wife for her husband (*ukusakula*): this is felt to be a compliment to the husband and a comfort to the wife, proof that the marriage has been a success. Co-wives who are of the same lineage are very closely identified, their children being treated almost as full siblings, and they themselves co-operating in everything.

One of the marked changes in contemporary Nyakyusa society is the development of leadership among women in the Christian congregations.

i. Constitutional form

Two other negative points are worth noting. First, the Nyakyusa fought among themselves and honoured a brave warrior, but they never developed a military kingdom, nor did they regard battle as the chief end of man. Emphasis on the value of war is not, then, a necessary concomitant of a developed age-organization, as a study of the Masai, Zulu, Swazi, and Pedi material might suggest. Secondly, the constitutional division of a chiefdom once every generation is not dependent upon the age-village organization, for such a division was common enough among the southern Nguni whose age-organizations were of relatively small importance. Among the Pondo and Xhosa the 'great son' and the 'right-hand son' of a chief very often both became independent; the main condition of their separation and independence being that there should be ample land in which they might live, each with his own followers.[1] Nyakyusa chiefdoms could divide in each generation because the Nyakyusa were an expanding population in relatively empty country.

j. Necessary conditions of age-villages

The limitations of the connections we have attempted to show must be realized. None of the characteristics cited are *correlates* of age-villages, for in each case either the age-villages could exist without them, or they could exist without age-villages: e.g. fathers- and daughters-in-law could not avoid one another completely if they lived in the same village, but the separate villages in which they live need not necessarily be age-villages; age-villages might be established though father- and daughter-in-law did not avoid one another; and so on. We claim only that these characteristics of Nyakyusa society which have been cited *partly* determine, and are themselves partly determined by, the age-village organization.

There are, however, certain other characteristics of Nyakyusa society without which age-villages such as we have described could not exist at all. The first of these is the redistribution of

[1] J. H. Soga, *Ama-Xoṣa Life and Customs*, pp. 25-49; M. Hunter, *Reaction to Conquest*, pp. 379-80,

land in each generation. The territorial segregation of fathers and sons is directly dependent upon the shifting of the old men after the 'coming out' ceremony, without which the young men would not have sufficient land to establish themselves as a compact group on land adequate to support their growing families. Where no redistribution of land takes place, as on mission land and in the chiefdoms where the 'coming out' ceremony has been dropped, the territorial division between age groups becomes blurred within a generation.

Redistribution of land in each generation depends upon two further conditions: the existence of ample land to support the population, and relatively little development of land. As soon as land becomes scarce those in possession of it are reluctant to agree to redistribution. It is significant that the most valuable land of all in Nyakyusa country—that in old craters—is *not* redistributed at a 'coming out' ceremony, but is retained by an individual until his death, and then inherited by kinsmen. And as soon as improvements are made in the form of planting long-term crops, or building durable and expensive houses, the difficulties of redistribution are increased. Nyakyusa land-law recognized the right of an elder who had moved, or of his son, to the bamboos and *imisyunguti* trees he had planted (*vide supra*, p. 46). But such rights become much more complicated when it is not only an odd clump of bamboos or two or three trees which are at stake, but a large patch of coffee; or when, in place of the old-fashioned long hut (*ikibaga*) built with the co-operation of kinsmen and neighbours, there is a more substantial house with expensive doors and windows made by an expert carpenter. It has been shown that where individual rights over trees or other long-term crops are recognized and such crops are planted on a large scale, individual tenure of land, as opposed to a temporary right of usufruct, tends to develop.[1]

Secondly, the solidarity of the Nyakyusa age-village, as of kinship villages in other African societies, is a function of a small-scale society. Fellow villagers have been hitherto, and are still in a large measure, dependent upon one another for land, for aid in economic undertakings, for sympathy and good fellowship, and for protection 'by night and by day'. But such mutual dependence is visibly decreasing. In the economic field co-opera-

[1] C. K. Meek, *Land Law and Custom in the Colonies*, p. 28.

tion is already as important beyond as within the village, and village control over the main cash crops has not been established, as it was over certain food crops. With increasing centralization the village headman, embodiment of the solidarity and relative autonomy of each village, is losing power to the chiefs and courts, on the one hand, and to the specialist agriculturalists, school teachers, elders, and ministers of religion on the other.

Friendships beyond the age-village are fostered by common experiences at a boarding school or a labour centre, and by common interests as members of a church or a coffee co-operative which does not necessarily include fellow villagers. And most important of all, fellow villagers are not bound to one another in resistance to external dangers as they were formerly. Lion, leopard, and buffalo still exist in the district, but we heard of no recent case of a village combining for defence against dangerous (as distinct from destructive) game: if action were necessary a European sportsman was usually glad of the chance of a bag. With the cessation of cattle-raiding and inter-village warfare, the curtailment of the right of self-help, and the development of courts with power to enforce judgement in cases involving members of different chiefdoms, dependence on fellow villagers for protection from material dangers and the responsibility of a village for the actions of its members, virtually cease. A sense of dependence upon neighbours for mystical protection lingers, but as elementary education, belief in Christian dogma, and the solidarity of Christian congregations increase, this supposed dependence upon the *amanga* or mystical power of neighbours also lessens. Many men who fear sorcery (including poisoning) do not fear witchcraft, and it is only against witches that neighbours are believed to protect one. Thus change in the form of beliefs is correlated with the development of more intense relationships beyond the village.

An age-village organization is probably dependent upon isolation in another fashion also: by their own account the Nyakyusa feeling that close association between successive generations is improper has been blunted by the example of Europeans and Swahili who do not share this feeling (*vide supra*, p. 69). The missionaries teach that avoidance between father- and daughter-in-law is unnecessary, if not in itself sinful, and the implication is that only 'superstition' maintains the taboo (*vide supra*, p. 84). The Nyakyusa pattern of avoidance has undoubtedly influenced that of the small groups absorbed by them, but they in turn have been influenced by these groups, and by the example of Christians of neighbouring tribes. In Ilolo avoidance between father- and daughter-in-law is much less strict than in Selya. This was attributed partly to the influence of neighbouring small groups of Nyika and Penja, who had not the same tradition of strict avoidance as the Nyakyusa, and partly to the influence of the Christians, whose number was proportionately greater in Ilolo than in Selya. As Nyakyusa informants argued: the pagans see Christian women disregard avoidance taboos, and they see that nothing dreadful happens to them (as the result of their neglect), so the pagans, too, begin to think that avoidance is of no importance.

The relationship between the generations is also modified among the Nyakyusa, as among other African people, by the power of young men to earn money and so command wealth. As we have seen, sons are in a position to *invite* their fathers to drink beer in the father's own homestead. Once fathers and sons have begun to *ukwangala*, drinking beer together, and once the horror of a woman seeing her father-in-law has diminished, then there is much less insistence on the need to buttress separation of the generations by territorial segregation. When convenient, fathers and sons will continue to live apart, but if a building site and arable land near his age-mates is lacking a son may suggest that avoidance does not really matter after all, and his father (if a Christian or a sceptic) may agree to the son building near him.

Nyakyusa age-villages still flourish, but they are hardly likely to survive many decades with increasing pressure on land, the planting of coffee and other long-term crops, the development of trade and migration, and a diminishing isolation from the ideas and values of the outside world. Age is no longer the sole basis for village grouping in Rungwe district—common belief and common occupation now provide other grounds for building together. There are Christian villages, an administrative station, a military station, and trading centres such as Mwaya, the Lake port. Tukuyu (the administrative centre) has its police lines, quarters for hospital attendants, traders' quarters, and so on, while Masoko has soldiers' and traders' quarters. This account of age-villages may therefore have some significance as a document illustrating one of the infinite variations of social form which will not long be available for study. If it is agreed that an understanding of social processes can only proceed from the systematic comparison of many societies, then the recording of vanishing forms, such as that of Nyakyusa age-villages, has some urgency.

SELECT DOCUMENTS
RELATING TO
NYAKYUSA AGE-VILLAGES

1. VILLAGES IN MWAIPOPO'S CHIEFDOM (1938)

Information from numerous informants

Generation	Chief	Sub Chief	Senior Headman	Headman	Village	Category	Legal Authority	Remarks
I[1]	*Mwaijonga*[2]		Njobakosa		IPENDA	Senior village of Mwaijonga[a]		Village survives only ritually—there is no group of men living together as Ipenda. Njobakosa is senior priest of Mwaijonga and eats sacred meat of cow sacrificed in Mwaijonga's grove
				Kissogota	Itiki			Not surviving
			Ngulyo (inherited from his father, Mwaikibilingwa)		ITEBE	Second senior[3] village of Mwaijonga	Ngulyo settles disputes but is subject to senior headman of next generation, Mwansambe (below)	Village survives with 11 members (original or their heirs). Ngulyo is a priest of Mwaijonga and eats the sacred meat in Mwaijonga's grove
				Mwaisumo ('Mwakyusa')[4] inherited	Bukeba			Not surviving
				Mwaikibilingwa ('Kasebere')	Itumba			Not surviving
II	*Mwaipopo I* (son of Mwaijonga)		Mwansambe ('Mwegama') inherited from his father		BUJEGE	Senior village of Mwaipopo. Sons of Ipenda and Itiki	Mwansambe. Mwenenganga settles disputes during Mwansambe's absence, and subject to him	'Coming out' of Mwaipopo I and his brothers was in this village, Mwansambe at present living in another chiefdom but returns for ceremonies and to hear cases

[1] The names of villages of Mwrakagile, father of Mwaijonga, have perished: the names of Ipenda and Itebe will be forgotten when Mwaipopo (generation II) dies.

[2] Italics indicate that the person named is dead.

[3] Informants were not all agreed about the relative status of villages and headmen of Mwaijonga's time.

[4] Most individuals are known by more than one name—we include two when two were in common use.

VILLAGES IN MWAIPOPO'S CHIEFDOM (1938)—contd.

Generation	Chief	Sub Chief	Senior Headman	Headman	Village	Category	Legal Authority	Remarks
II	Mwaipopo II (younger brother and heir of Mwaipopo I See Plate V)			Katotile ('Mwakakalembo') inherited	Bujenga[1]		Katotile	Kikuku who buried Mwankuga I lives here
					Lupaso[2]	Older section of Bujenga	No separate leader	Consists of 10 men who moved at 'coming out' of Mwankuga from Bujenga. The older men moved, leaving their younger contemporaries (Kikuku, etc.) in Bujenga. Katotile lives here, also Kasitile, the rain-maker. Strictly a section of Bujenga
					Busikali	'Younger brothers of Mwaipopo who eat with him', i.e. are of his generation	Mwainyobolela (Tandale) settles disputes	Tandale buried Mwaipopo I
						'Offshoot of Bujenga'		Not established as a separate village at 'coming out' of Mwaipopo. Is strictly a section of Bujenga
				Mwasota	Bulindanajo	Much younger than men of Bujenga and Kyemo	Mwasota?	Mwaipopo II originally lived here. There was once a battle between Bulindanajo and Bujege (vide p. 150).
		Likosyela		Mwakikato	Kibonde		Mwakikato	

1 Besides having direct authority over his own village, each senior headman has authority over other villages established at the 'coming out' with their own headmen (see p. 31). The villages subordinate to each senior headman are listed in column 6 immediately under his own village.

Generation	Chief	Sub Chief	Senior Headman	Headman	Village	Category	Legal Authority	Remarks
II	Mwaipopo II		*Mwaikofu* Mwakwese ('Mwaisumo') inherited from Mwaikofu		LUPANDO	Second senior village of Mwaipopo. Sons of Bukeba	Mwakwese	Old men have moved to one side. Lupando was originally established as two villages but when the headman of the senior (Mwaikofu) died, the villages coalesced under Mwakwese
		Mwakakole		Kanyeka ('Mwasibata')	Kyemo	Younger brothers of Lupando	Kanyeka	Very, very small. Old men have moved to one side
		Mwakipesile		Mwangoba	Kisyelo			
				Mwakitwange ('*Kasele*')	Kitole			Mwakabole 'came out' here
					Kabula			
III	*Mwankuga I* (son of Mwaipopo I)		Mwambuputa ('Mwafungo')		IGEMBE	Senior village of Mwankuga. Sons of Mbujege	Mwambuputa	Mwankuga I 'came out' here. 'Mwambuputa is the greatest (headman) in the country.' Was driven out and later fetched back
	Mwankuga II (younger brother and heir of Mwankuga I)				Katumba	'Younger brothers and a few sons of Igembe.' Mwambuputa's own son built here	Mwambuputa (no separate leader appointed)	53 men. Established *after* the coming out of Mwankuga I. Strictly a section of Igembe. 'Betwixt and between' generations III and IV. Some near contemporaries in Mpuguso
				Nsusa	Lugombo		Nsusa	Nsusa was driven out, later fetched back. Acted for Mwambuputa in his absence. Lugombo has a small sub-division, Itiki.
				Kabolile ('Mwaseba')	Ipoma	Younger than men of Igembe. Sons of Bujenga and Busikali	Kabolile	20 members. Took over land from Bujenga. They 'came out' when very young men. Includes a Christian section under Akimu

VILLAGES IN MWAIPOPO'S CHIEFDOM (1938)—contd.

Generation	Chief	Sub Chief	Senior Headman	Headman	Village	Category	Legal Authority	Remarks
III	Mwankuga II				Ndongoti	Younger brothers of Ipoma	Kabolile. Mwakibilingwa (appointed by Kabolile) settles small disputes	28 members: 27 married. One informant suggested that Ndogoti might be established as a village of the *next* generation at the 'coming out' of Mwanyilu. Others regard it as of generation III and strictly a section of Ipoma. Its members include junior sons of Mwaipopo II
		Mwaseba	Kakuju	*Mwakileka*	Kilwa		Kabolile (no separate leader appointed)	At present a section of Ipoma. May possibly be established as a village of generation IV
					Kibonde (junior section)	Sons of Kibonde	Mwangalaba tries small cases. Others to Mwambuputa	
					NJESI	Second senior village of Mwankuga. Sons of Lupando	Kakuju	
				Mwakatika ('Mwansope')	Mponga	Younger sons of Lupando	Mwakatika	
				Mwakabombe ('Mwaitebela')	Isuba	Youngest sons of Lupando	Mwakabombe	Mwakabombe had moved on account of a quarrel. He was recently brought home
		Mwakibwele		*Mwambegeja*	Lukwebo	Sons of Kitole		
		Mwakipesile		*Kasele*	Ndobo	Sons of Kabula		

VILLAGES IN MWAIPOPO'S CHIEFDOM (1938)—contd.

Generation	Chief	Sub Chief	Senior Headman	Headman	Village	Category	Legal Authority	Remarks
IV	Mwanyilu (about 10 years old)			None yet appointed as Mwanyilu has not yet come out	Mpuguso	Sons of Igembe	Mwambuputa	'Mwanyilu will come out here'
				„	Nsanga	Younger sons of Igembe and Lugombo	Mwambuputa	'Mwanyilu will build here first'
				„	Itinga	Sons of Njesi and Mponga	Small cases to Mwakatika. Serious cases to Kakuju	Some members are married
				„	Ipyana	Younger brothers of Itinga	„	None yet married
				„	Kungwe	„	„	
				„	Isuba (junior section)	Sons of Isuba	„	None yet married

Nineteen independent villages established at the 'coming out' ceremonies of Mwaijonga, Mwaipopo and Mwankuga survive.
There are five village sections treated in some respects as practically independent villages. There are other village sections as Itiki which are not so independent.
There are six boys' villages, not yet established, but likely to be recognized at the 'coming out' of Mwanyilu.
The dividing line between village and village section is difficult to determine when villages have split *after* the 'coming out' at which they have been established, as did Bujenga. Our recognition of Busikali as a separate village and not Itiki is somewhat arbitrary.

It is to be noted that villages not only sub-divide but occasionally coalesce. Two independent villages established at the 'coming out' of Mwaipopo coalesced as Lupando, after the death of the headman of one of them.
The traditional organization is modified in that Mwaijonga's country has not been divided or sub-divided into independent chieftainships.

2. THE 'COMING OUT' (*UBUSOKA*)

Mwaikambo (clerk and son of a chief).[1]

'The village headmen begin to talk among themselves, saying: "Our sons have grown up, should we not establish them?" So they go to tell the chief, saying: "Our sons have grown up, let us show them to the country." Two chiefs always "come out". We call them the senior and the junior. It is an old custom which is still followed that two chiefs should "come out".

'So the village headmen seek a doctor to make them a medicine horn and treat the tails of chieftainship with medicine. The village headmen take council together and choose two senior headmen to "come out" with the chiefs. These senior headmen drink medicine (*embondanya*) with the chiefs.

'When many people, together with the two young chiefs, have come together the doctor gives powdered medicine (*embondanya*) to the chiefs and the senior headman chosen for each chief. They give a spear of chieftainship, and a horn, and tail to each of the men chosen as senior headmen—one for each chief. Each senior headman then binds the horn to the blade of the spear, and standing with his own chief and many men and women, raises the spear to the sky. The women trill and each party goes to its place of "coming out" on the pasturage. Each chief, with his followers, goes to his own place. The men dance; sometimes they have drums, sometimes not.

'Then when each party has reached it own place they make fire with fire sticks. The chief just simulates the action of fire-making then his senior headman takes the sticks and makes fire by friction. When they have built the shelters for sleeping in they warm themselves at the fire they have made; they do not take fire from the houses of men. If there are many of them then there will be three or four shelters, if few, then only one shelter. The men and their chief who has "come out" sleep in these shelters and enjoy themselves together (*nukwangala*). The first day they kill two head of cattle. Also they plant "the tree of coming out" (*umpiki gwa busoka*) which is called *ulupando*. They plant it with a man who has come out previously, a man of their fathers' generation, he begins to plant, then he explains to them what to do, saying "plant", then the new senior headman plants it.

'While they sleep in these shelters with their cattle, they eat food which they take from their fathers, bananas, and milk, and other food.

[1] For a note on conspicuous informants see p. vi.

From time to time their father, the chief, gives them a bull to kill. During the "coming out" food is very plentiful. If people pass on the road they honour them and give them food, and make love to them that they may build there. They remain in their shelters, they do not go about much. If the chief is stingy they teach him a lesson by taking bananas; they say: "Know that we are important people, we are those who have 'come out' and we are your parents." Later on they play drums—I think only in recent years. And the village headmen seize a woman, the daughter of a commoner, as a wife for the chief.

'The horn is the luck of the chiefs, that many people may come to build. Binding the horn to the blade of the spear is to show that the chief is one who has "come out" (*unsoka*); it is as if he were carried aloft (i.e. "chaired")[1]. We show his greatness ("seniority") to people, then we trill.

'The fire made with fire sticks is to symbolize the new chieftainship. We do not take the old fire of the old men.

'The medicine is to make the chief heavy (*nsito*), that it may be apparent that he is a chief.

'The *ulupando* tree is a memorial of the "coming out", that men may come and say: "So and so planted this tree when he came out." Some say it is to show the power (*amaka*) of the chief, because if it does not grow it is said that his chieftainship will perhaps not flourish; then they will say: "Let us move and plant elsewhere." It is said that the spear of chieftainship is to fight battles; it is strength, manhood; it is treated with medicines.

'The tails are those with which battles are fought. When men go to war the senior headman grasps the tail. If the tail does not lead them well they return from the fight. It, also, they treat with medicines.'

---

[1] A bride at a puberty-marriage ritual is carried about shoulder high.

3. A LAND DISPUTE BETWEEN VILLAGES OF
THE SAME CHIEFDOM

This case was discussed with a great number of informants. We first quote the account written by Mwaisumo (our clerk) which sums up the earlier discussions. 'Mwansambe and Mwakalembo are quarrelling over the land of Ipoma. Both are village headmen of the older generation of Mwaipopo (the chief). Mwansambe is the senior, Mwakalembo the junior. Mwansambe is senior village headman of Mwaipopo. Mwakalembo is the next on his side (see table, pp. 181–2).

'At the "coming out" of Mwaipopo the old men gave Mwansambe the land of Bujege, and said that his junior Mwakalembo should build on the land of Busikali. He (Mwakalembo) built with Mwakwese, the man of Seba.

'When the "coming out" of Mwankuga, Mwaipopo's son, was held, Mwansambe sent to his junior Mwakalembo, saying: "At your place here we are going to build the house of our wife Kalinga, that is to say we are going to plant the *ulupando* tree of our child Mwankuga here." Mwakalembo agreed, but in secret he thought to himself: "My senior wants to seize my village! See he is building the great house at my place, and I am a junior!" So they brought out Mwankuga with Mwafungo as his senior headman, and Mwaseba Kabolile as a junior, and they planted the *ulupando* tree. Mwafungo built with his people and Mwaseba Kabolile with his. Later on Mwansambe arranged for his "sons", i.e. Mwafungo and his fellows, to go to his side, and Mwakalembo thought that his land was saved. He had thought that his senior was taking his country, but lo, the latter had moved!

'At that time Mwafungo went to enter into an inheritance[1] in MuNgonde (i.e. on the Lake-shore plain). On his return he went to the side from which he had come. He sought a bull with which to say: "Fathers, I have arrived." Mwansambe called his junior Mwakalembo saying: "Our son has arrived, they are eating the meat there without our having discussed together where we should kill, or where we should eat the meat." (cf. pp. 271–4.)

'So now Mwansambe wants to give his child Mwafungo a homestead site in which to build, he wishes to give him one at the *ulupando* tree where he first established him, and he has told his junior Mwakalembo so. Mwakalembo objected, saying: "How can you give him my homestead? Where shall I go?"

---

[1] Another reason for the departure of Mwafungo (Mwambupta) is given on p. 230.

'Mwansambe said they could both build there together.

'Mwakalembo said "No."

'Mwansambe said: "How can you refuse? The site is mine, and I am your senior. Do you not see the *ulupando* tree which I planted for my child Mwafungo?"

'Mwakalembo replied: "Yes, I see it, but you went away and left it, you and your children. I gave thanks thinking my land had escaped capture."

'Mwansambe said: "And the *ulupando* tree, do you tell us that it was seized also?"

'Mwakalembo replied: "No, I don't deny the *ulupando* tree, but when you pray you pray in your homestead, in the house of your wife. If you wish you can plant again at your place."

'Mwansambe said: "Why do you quarrel with me, Mwakalembo, I, your father, your senior, I who gave you land on which I said your fellow, Mwafungo should also build, since you are both my children?"

'Mwakalembo replied: "The land about which we are quarrelling is mine, it is the place of my blood. I spilt blood, I seized it from Mwaipaja when I fought with him."

(For originally this land about which they are quarrelling was Mwakwese's, it was where Seba's house was built. Then that Mwaipaja of whom they speak was the assistant village headman—a senior man. The followers of Mwakalembo made love to the wives, they approached them when they (the women) went to draw water. Mwaipaja was angry and called out his men to fight with the followers of Mwakalembo. Mwaipaja was defeated, and fled. The followers of Mwakalembo took his homestead. Mwaipaja was driven out: he built at Lupata where Kalunda and his men are now.)

'It is here that Mwansambe planted the *ulupando* tree. It is this land that Mwakalembo means when he says that his land escaped seizure by his senior when he went away again with his followers! Mwansambe says: "See, it is mine also, my father moved Mwaipaja aside, that my junior should build here."

'Mwakalembo says: "I got it by conquest, I spilt my blood."

'People commenting on the case in private say that Mwansambe is wrong, the country is really Mwakalembo's. Many say that although the case is put off it is not finished, Mwansambe will be overcome, and so Mwaipopo himself thinks.

'Mwaseba Kabolile and Mwafungo Mwambuputa are those who hold the country now, they are the children of Mwansambe and Mwakalembo. Mwenenganga, who began speaking (at the trial in court), is the junior ('brother') of Mwansambe but he holds all the seniority of Mwansambe because Mwansambe himself is not in the country, he has moved. The Mwakalembo who is standing there is not Mwakalembo himself, but his son. And the Mweneganga Mwakoloma who is speaking is a junior, but he speaks because he knows how to speak—he has a "good tongue" (i.e. is an orator). And Ngulyo also is a junior—he is speaking because he knows how to speak. All of these are village headmen, senior men, fathers of Mwafungo and Mwaseba Kabolile.'

The case was twice discussed at greath length in Lupata Court but no judgement was given. Some maintained that were a judgement given war would result, because the losers would attack. Mwaipopo himself, as president of the court, was said to be afraid to give judgement lest he suffer from 'the breath' or witchcraft of the offended parties. He refused to hear the case a third time and, as Kasitile pointed out, sixteen months after the second hearing Mwaipopo was sleeping in the village of Bujenga (Mwakalembo's village), and it was Mwakalembo and his men who were in possession of the disputed land. Mwaipopo feared the witchcraft (or 'breath') of Mwansambe and his men.

4. A BOUNDARY DISPUTE

Heard by the Lupata Court (president, Mwaipopo), 18/3/35.

Man A brought case against man B for assault.

Plaintiff and defendant gave their accounts, and also Mwangomo, chief of the country concerned.

A and B had quarrelled over the boundary of their adjoining homesteads, which are in different villages of the same chiefdom. There was an old quarrel about the boundary of the village. Mwangomo stated: 'The week before this quarrel I went with my brothers and the young village headmen (leaving behind the old village headmen because I thought they would quarrel) to settle the dispute. We walked over the boundary and said to the people concerned: "It is here."

'A and his two friends (not in court) were not satisfied with my demarcation and grumbled openly saying: "Who is Mwangomo to take from us the place where our fathers lived, and from which they ate the bananas, and give it to our neighbours? We will take it and not care for Mwangomo" . . . or again: "We do not believe that Mwangomo really decided like this, we shall act as if the line was as before." So when I heard that they were talking like this I asked all the people to watch for any man who might do anything against the decision, and I told one man in particular to watch.'

A and B gave evidence, telling much the same story.

A went to cut the banana leaves (i.e prune) on the old boundary, with a bill-hook (*isenge*), and B came and told him to stop. They quarrelled, each claiming that the land had been his father's, and that his father had eaten the bananas off it. Then B caught hold of the bill-hook, and in the struggle A was cut. A now brings a case for assault against B.

Mwangomo: 'B is in the right, and what makes it worse is that since his father died A has never been in the country. He has lived in MuNgonde (the Lake-shore plain); he has only been back a few days in my country and he brings war into it and spoils it.' Mwangomo spoke angrily, and asked that A should be imprisoned.

The Court: 'We follow what you, the chief, say; if people resist you and speak against you it is very bad, but we disagree about imprisoning him, he has only just returned to the country and it is not a good custom to imprison a man who has only just come to a country. Bring his two friends who have lived long in your country.'

Mwakisisya (another chief sitting in court): 'What about the other man you drove away without bringing him into court? Mwangomo has aggravated the quarrel, he should have called all the men from both villages together and judged the case there.'

The Court, to A: 'Where have you been staying since the fight? Where have you put all your things?'

A: 'In Mwangake's country.'

Court: 'You mean that Mwangomo had driven you out?'

A: 'Yes.'

The Court: 'Then if you have left the country why do you bring this case, troubling us?'

Mwangomo then decided to drive A and his two friends out of the country and said nothing more about punishing A. So the case ended.

5. SUMMARY OF LABOUR HISTORIES — Information from men concerned

| Category | No. of Cases | Worked | Average Total Period (those who worked) | Working One Year and over at a stretch | Schooling | | Skilled and Semi-skilled (of those working) | Place of Work | | | |
					Illiterate	Beyond Village School		In District only	Lupa Gold-fields	Out of Province
Pagan: Middle-aged and over	13	85%	5 months	23%	100%	Nil	10%	10%	—	8%
Christian: Middle-aged and over	10	100%	12 years, 4 months	90%	50%	Nil	80%	60%	—	Nil[1]
Pagan: Young	24	92%	—[2]	17%	63%	4%	5%	10%	70%	20%
Christian: Sons of pagans, young	11	91%	—	40%	9%	36%	40%	30%	70%	Nil
Christian: Sons of Christians, young	21	100%	—	38%	5%	19%	81%	5%	66%	29%
Total	79[3]	94%	—	38%	50%	12%	44%	27%	50%	17%

[1] Four worked on other mission stations of the Province.

[2] As many of the men are quite young, a record of the total period worked is insignificant. We lack material here on the *proportion* of time spent at work.

[3] This is not a true random sample for informants were selected haphazard; therefore, the percentages have no exact significance, but a correlation between Christianity, literacy, skilled work, and long-term employment is suggested.

6. CHANGE IN THE RELATION OF FATHERS AND SONS

Record of G. W.

Mwambuputa, the headman, was building himself a new house with the help of six other men. He invited us to wait and join in the beer and bananas, which were about to be served.

A boy came to call two of the builders to enjoy the company (and food?) of some other friends. They went off. It turned out that these two were from the boys' village, Katumba, one being a 'son' of Mwambuputa, and the other a friend of this 'son'. They had been eating and drinking with the rest of us.

Q.: 'In the old days, would these two have eaten and drunk with you—boys with men? Would you have called them to help you build?'

'No, formerly that was not the custom. Though we should have called them to help us build, they would not have drunk beer, and they would have eaten their calabash of milk separately, over there (pointing to a corner of the hut), while we men were here with our food and beer.'

Q. 'How is it then that the customs have changed, that now you eat, and even drink, with them?'

'You brought it yourselves, you Europeans. You sit down with your children at table and eat together, and the Swahili do the same. So we say: "He! Formerly we hated our children!" We said: "Eat over there." Let us eat with them!'

Q.: 'No, that does not convince us at all. The Europeans are strangers. How many of you have been into a European's house and seen them eating? Only the house-boys!'

Mwambuputa: 'All right, ask the others!'

Mwalubunju: 'Let me speak! In the old days, because there was war, we objected very much to the young men drinking beer with us. If we all drank together and the war cry was raised we should all be defeated. And men did not begin drinking in the morning, never! They began in the late afternoon when the cows came home . . . and in the evening each went home to his own house . . . but now, since the country is at peace, the young men also drink beer.'

Q.: 'Yes, but still I don't see why you drink *with* them. Why not give them a separate pot? And you eat with them, too.'

Mwambuputa: 'Because, as Mwalubunju has said, the country has fallen to you. It is at peace and there is no war, so the young men buy their own beer.[1] Sometimes my son brings his pot to my place and calls his friends, saying: "We will take the pot to mother's house. She will pour in water for us." Then they come to my place and they invite me to drink and I accept and we drink together. How then can I grudge my son beer when I have some? Did he and his friends not entertain me'?

[1] This, of course, is not so much a result of peace as of new opportunities of gaining wealth on the Lupa gold-fields and elsewhere, but to the Nyakyusa the two things go together as 'European times' (*ikisungu*).

7. HOMOSEXUALITY

X (an exceptionally reliable informant)

'When a boy sleeps with his friend they sleep together; it is not forbidden. Everyone thinks it all right. Sometimes when boys sleep together each may have an emission on the other (*bitundanila*). If they are great friends there is no wrong done. If a boy has an emission on his friend in his sleep without the friend knowing there is no case. Boys sometimes agree to dance together (*ukukina*) and work their evil together and that also is no wrong. But they fear very much to dance thus because their parents will be angry, saying: "You are learning adultery; you will be fools when you grow up." Boys do this when they are out herding; then they begin to dance together and to have intercourse together. But there is something which is a great wrong—if one boy, perhaps out herding or perhaps in the boys' village at night, catches hold of his fellow and has an emission on him (*nukutundila*) then it is a great case, involving a fine. One who has been forced by his fellow will tell his parents and they will take him to the village headman to inform the headman. It is a great case and the boy who forced his fellow pays a bull or perhaps a cow. They say that to force a fellow thus is witchcraft (*bo bulosi*); he is not a woman. But when they have agreed and dance together, then even if people find them they say it is adolescence (*lukulilo*), all children are like that. And they say that sleeping together and dancing is also adolescence.

'This custom is mostly among children, it is forbidden for men to sleep together. They do not fear lest when they have soiled a friend they will pay; no, they fear to be shamed. Not many cases of grown men having intercourse together come to light, but only of boys together or of a man and a boy. Some, during intercourse, work in the mouth of their friend, and have an orgasm; those do very, very great wrong. Some have intercourse in the anus, some between the legs—there are many who practise this latter form and this is what boys mostly do. That of the mouth people do very rarely when they dance together, because one who does it may have a great case against him.

'A person never dreams of making love to another man but only when two youths sleep together on a mat, then something evil may take place between them, at night during sleep. Perhaps when one has dreamed that he is having intercourse with a woman but he has been caught and not finished, he soils his friend.

'And when out herding, some of the older boys do evil with the young ones, the older ones persuade the little ones to lie down with them and to do that which is forbidden with them between the legs. Sometimes two older boys who are friends do it together, one gets on top of his fellow, then he gets off and the other mounts. All this which they do together or with a junior is a small wrong. When their parents find them they reprove them and tell them it is forbidden, they beat them a little. But when a little boy is caught hold of by an older boy against his will, and he tells that so and so caught him and had intercourse (*ukulogwa*) with him then the older boy will be fined, perhaps a bull.

'It is altogether forbidden to do evil to a fellow by night. The boy who has been so treated will be angry and run off to the court, and he who did evil to him will be fined. He will pay one cow, because they say it is forbidden to do evil to your fellow by night. There are some who, when they have dreamed at night of a woman, wake up and catch hold of a friend, and have intercourse with him.'

A and J.

A and J agreed that homosexuality occurred frequently in boys' villages. 'A boy has intercourse with his fellow, but a grown man? No, never, we've never heard of it. They always want women; only when a man cannot get a woman he does this, only in youth. A few men do not marry but they are half-wits who have no kind of intercourse at all.

'And there is one famous case in the hills of a man who, though not mad, dresses as a woman; but he has no intercourse either with men or women.'

A case was also quoted of a doctor in Tukuyu who 'is a woman; she has borne children, now her body has grown the sexual organs of a man and her feelings have changed also; but she keeps it very secret, she is spoken of as a woman.'

8. MISFORTUNES ATTRIBUTED TO MYSTICAL CAUSES[1]

(a) Witchcraft

Total number of cases 92

Information from numerous informants

No.	Category of supposed victim	Category of accused	Category of accuser	Spatial relationship of victim and accused	Charge	Grounds of suspicion	Investigation	Upshot of case	Structural relationship of accuser and accused
1	Village cows	Married woman (Mother of Mwaisumo)	Neighbour, a very poor man and a stranger to the village	Same village	She bewitched village cows	Cows went dry	*Mwafi* ordeal (drunk by her son Mwaisumo who vomited)	Accuser had nothing to pay as fine, so beaten	Village neighbours
2	Boy	'Village father' (Mwantibe)	Parents of victim	Parents of victim and accused in same village. Boy in attached boys' village	'Eaten' son of village neighbour	Accused sent boy on a message. Boy refused to go. Accused threatened boy who died shortly afterwards	?	?	Village neighbours
3	Man	Village neighbour (Moses)	Victim	Same village	Bewitching his neighbour	Dream of victim	None. Dream related to neighbours who asked accused to move	Accused moved to another village of same chiefdom	Village neighbours
4	Man	Village neighbour, a doctor	Village neighbours	Same village	Caused neighbour to fall ill	Doctor threatened victim after a quarrel, saying; 'You may sleep'. Victim fell ill. Recovered when treated by doctor who had threatened him	None	Doctor forced by neighbours to treat man he threatened, then driven out of village	Village neighbours
5	Men and cattle	Village neighbour, Kagesya	Village neighbours	Same village	'Ate' people. Bewitched cattle	Death of men. Reduction of milk supply.	Autopsy on victims	Accused driven out and his food seized. He returned to his home village	Village neighbours

No.	Category of supposed victim	Category of accused	Category of accuser	Spatial relationship of victim and accused	Charge	Grounds of suspicion	Investigation	Upshot of case	Structural relationship of accuser and accused
6	Young men	Village neighbour, Kagesya's son	Victims	Same village	Prevented road on which they were working being completed quickly			Accused driven out	Village neighbours
7	Village cows	Man of the village	Village neighbours (public accusation made)	Same village	Bewitched cows	Decline in milk supply	*Mwafi* ordeal. Accused did not vomit	Accused driven out	Village neighbours
8	Child	Man, neighbour of victim's father	Father of deceased	Same village	Killed child by witchcraft	Death of child. Accused did not attempt to persuade father of victim to remain, when he was packing to go after victim's death.	Autopsy on victim. *Mwafi* ordeal. Accused did not vomit	Accused driven out. Chief seized his cattle	Village neighbours
9	Child of visitor	Host	Village neighbours	Same homestead	Made child ill	Child very ill with ear-ache. Host angry because visitor feasted neighbours. Child worse after such a feast. Host did not express good wishes for recovery (cf. p. 110 ff).	Discussion before assistant headman and village headman	Accused driven out of village	Village neighbours
10	Child	Men, neighbours of victim's father	Victim's father	Same village	Killed child by witchcraft	Father of victim wanted an unreasonable amount of land. Given one field when he joined the village. Wanted another which was refused him by the villagers	None known		Village neighbours

MISFORTUNES ATTRIBUTED TO MYSTICAL CAUSES—contd.

(a) Witchcraft—contd.

No.	Category of supposed victim	Category of accused	Category of accuser	Spatial relationship of victim and accused	Charge	Grounds of suspicion	Investigation	Upshot of case	Structural relationship of accuser and accused
11	Man	3 neighbours (men)	Victim (before his death)	Same village	Speared victim internally (by witchcraft)	Illness and death of victim. He dreamed before his death that 3 neighbours (whom he recognized) had speared him	Autopsy. Internal 'wounds' found	No case made. Agreed by village that 'friends' he saw were responsible, but their names were not made public	Village neighbours
12	(a) Cows (b) Child	Neighbour of child's father	Victim's father	Same village	Bewitched cows killed child	Death of child. Accused boasted of his witchcraft	?	Accused driven out	Village neighbours
13	Two men	Neighbour (a man, Kimbila)	Victims	Same village	'He had destroyed their potency' by witchcraft	?	?	?	Village neighbours
14	?	Christian elder	Pagan fellow villagers	Same village	?	'Proud'. 'Does not look at people when he greets them.' Built a very big house in a pagan village	?	?	Village neighbours
15	X Labourer on the Lupa gold-fields	Fellow labourer (a Christian) William	Victim	Same camp	Had injured X's eyes by witchcraft	X had eye trouble. William was seen in a dream by a third labourer. William had recently found gold	Meeting of all the workers	William driven away from the camp	Fellow employees

MISFORTUNES ATTRIBUTED TO MYSTICAL CAUSES—contd.

(a) Witchcraft—contd.

No.	Category of supposed victim	Category of accused	Category of accuser	Spatial relationship of victim and accused	Charge	Grounds of suspicion	Investigation	Upshot of case	Structural relationship of accuser and accused
16	Young man, labourer in Lupa gold-fields	Fellow labourers		Same camp	'They stamped on his belly' (a kind of witchcraft)	Alleged that he ate their rations by means of witchcraft. Illness while at work and finally death after returning home	Divination (twice)		Fellow employees
17	Clerk A	Fellows in work camp, especially fellow clerk B	His friends	Same camp	A made ill by *matila* (a form of witchcraft)	A had replaced B as interpreter and B was jealous. A was greedy when eating with his fellows. Illness began when he choked over a piece of food. He was eating with his fellows	None		Fellow employees
18	Labourer on Lupa gold-fields	Fellow labourers	European employer (sic)	Same camp	Fellow workers had 'eaten' him	Sudden death of labourer. He was lucky in finding gold and his employer's favourite	None	Fellows agreed that one of them had 'eaten' the victim but culprit not found	Fellow employees
19	Labourer on Lupa gold-fields	Fellow labourers	?	Same camp	Fellow workers bewitched him	Died morning after he had received 100s. in prize-money from his employer (cf. pp. 229–30).	?	?	Fellow employees

MISFORTUNES ATTRIBUTED TO MYSTICAL CAUSES—contd.

(a) *Witchcraft*—contd.

No.	Category of supposed victim	Category of accused	Category of accuser	Spatial relationship of victim and accused	Charge	Grounds of suspicion	Investigation	Upshot of case	Structural relationship of accuser and accused
20	Headboy of European employer on Lupa gold-fields	Fellow employees. Individual not named but cook hinted at	Victim	Same camp	'People' had bewitched him	Acute illness of victim after sleeping with concubine of his European employer. This woman was given in charge of the cook when the European visited other Europeans, but she and the headboy were lovers. Victim and cook hated one another on account of this woman. Victim hated by his fellow employees because he was headboy and looked after everything during his employer's absence	A doctor gave victim medicine which would enable him to see the witches in dreams. He saw two men who hated him, and employer's concubine carrying a knife	Slow recovery of victim. He told the dream to his lover	Fellow employees
21	Nyakyusa employer of 31 men on Lupa gold-fields	Employees	Victim	Same camp	Employees had 'speared him' (with witchcraft)	Acute stomach pain. Weakness. 'He had been angry with his men.'	Divination	Victim recovered	Employer/employee
22	Village headman working as a labourer on Lupa gold-fields	Fellow labourers	?	Same camp	Fellow labourers killed him by witchcraft because he darkened their eyes so that they should not find gold. He	Sudden death of headman a week after he began work. Gold was scarce and he alone had found some, earning 10s. prize money	?		Fellow employees

MISFORTUNES ATTRIBUTED TO MYSTICAL CAUSES—contd.

(a) Witchcraft—contd.

No.	Category of supposed victim	Category of accused	Category of accuser	Spatial relationship of victim and accused	Charge	Grounds of suspicion	Investigation	Upshot of case	Structural relationship of accuser and accused
23	Husband	2 wives (not favourites)	Victim	Same homestead	Wives summoned the witches to 'eat' him. Opened the door for them. One herself was a witch	Illness of husband. Wives jealous of chief wife who was the favourite	Divination	Treatment with medicine. Divorce impossible because one suspect a sister of the favourite wife	Spouses
24	Husband	Wife	?	Same homestead	Caused illness in husband	'He hated her and he fell ill.'	Divination		Spouses
25	Husband	Wife	?	Same homestead	'Eaten' husband	Death of husband	?		Spouses
26	Co-wives	Wife (Kajonga)	Husband (first)	Same homestead	'Bewitched loins of co-wives'	Husband did not sleep well with other wives	?	Divorced for witchcraft	Spouses
27	?	Wife (Kajonga)	Husband (second)	Same homestead	?	?	?	Divorced for witchcraft	Spouses
28	Husband's cows	Wife	Husband	Same homestead	Bewitched husband's cows	Cows gave little milk when wife at home, much when wife away	Mwafi ordeal. Wife vomited	Husband paid a cow and a bull to his in-laws	Spouses
29	Adulterer	Husband of woman seduced				Adulterer began to squint after he had run off with the woman			Husband/wife's lover

MISFORTUNES ATTRIBUTED TO MYSTICAL CAUSES—contd.

(a) Witchcraft—contd.

No.	Category of supposed victim	Category of accused	Category of accuser	Spatial relationship of victim and accused	Charge	Grounds of suspicion	Investigation	Upshot of case	Structural relationship of accuser and accused
30	Adulterer	Husband of woman seduced (no. 29)				Adulterer was very ill with a poisoned hand. Husband of his lover had been previously accused	Divination		Husband/wife's lover
31	Senior half-brother (different mother)	Junior half-brother	Victim	?			Mwafi ordeal. Junior brother vomited	Junior brother judged innocent	Half-brothers
32	Father (pater and genitor)	Middle son (Mwalyale)	Brothers (half?)	?	Killed father	Death of father	Mwafi ordeal	Accused driven out of chiefdom. He became rich and brothers later made friends with him. They said 'Mwafi had been mistaken'	Brothers (half?)
33	Child	Father of child an assistant headman	Village headman	Same homestead	Made child ill	Child ill. Father did not report illness to village headman	?	Accused driven out of village	Village headman/assistant headman
34	Chief's child	Village headman (Mwamila)	People of the chiefdom	Same chiefdom	Caused child to have sore eyes	Mwamila had gone to the chief alone and said 'witches are eating the child'. He would have gone with other village headman, had he been innocent	Mwafi ordeal	Chief took Mwamila's 4 cows. He was driven out for one year	People of chiefdom and village headman

MISFORTUNES ATTRIBUTED TO MYSTICAL CAUSES—contd.

(a) *Witchcraft—contd.*

No.	Category of supposed victim	Category of accused	Category of accuser	Spatial relationship of victim and accused	Charge	Grounds of suspicion	Investigation	Upshot of case	Structural relationship of accuser and accused
35	Chief	'People of the north'	?	Same chiefdom?		Chief sick	?	Said that chief and his fellows fought and defeated the attackers in dreams	Chief/People?
36	Chief?	Rich man owning 30 head of cattle (Mwatusa)	Chief	Same chiefdom		Chief 'did not sleep'	*Mwafi* ordeal. Mwatusa did not vomit	Chief seized all Mwatusa's cattle. Neighbours seized his crops. He moved with his wives to another country	Chief/rich commoner
37	Anthropologist	A man who had been refused 1s. when he asked for it as a present	Servants and friends of victim. (Nyakyusa)	Same neighbourhood	Caused attack of malaria (by witchcraft)	Attack of malaria day following refusal of present. Accused did not come to inquire for victim as others did.	None	None	European/African
38	Anthropologist	'The witches' individual not specified	Servants and friends of victim. (Nyakyusa)	Same village	Prevented normal recovery from malaria	Prolonged attacks of malaria, not cured by ordinary treatment. 'It was not just malaria—see you drank much medicine for malaria, but still did not recover.'	None	Formal welcome by wife of chief who lived in village on anthropologist's return, and *apology* for the illness	European/African

MISFORTUNES ATTRIBUTED TO MYSTICAL CAUSES—contd.

No.	Category of Sufferer	Symptoms	Alleged sin	Diagnosis	Ritual performed
1	Village headman (Mwambuputa)	(a) 2 children died	Grudged neighbours certain food		Fled to Lake-shore plain (Mu Ngonde)
		(b) Further deaths among his children after he moved	Failed to perform death ritual of children before leaving		Returned home. Killed bull. Admitted fault in not performing ritual
2	Widow	Widow ailing	Ritual not performed for her at inheritance	Illness due to 'the breath of men'. Diagnosis by divination	Heir killed beast. Feasted neighbours and relatives. Told of illness. People admitted their anger.¹ Said the illness was finished. She continued ill.
3	Widow	Widow ill	Heir of chief's family had not killed bull or cow at inheritance ritual	Illness due to 'the breath of men' Diagnosis by divination	Heir called neighbours and relatives. Killed. Neighbours admitted their anger
4	Enesi	Enesi ill	Father failed to send a gift of food and beer, when she was taken back to her husband, and she is the daughter of a chief's sister	'The breath' comes from her husband's friends. 'They are angry because of the quarrel over food'	None mentioned. The girl died shortly afterwards and her death was attributed to sorcery
5	Chief	T.B.?	Refused to hold 'coming out' of sons	'The country was angry'	Killed 3 cows for people to feast
6	Married woman	Bore no more children	Ran off with lover three times. Finally husband forced lover to eat filth	His father's village 'shocked' because she had 'soiled a man so much'. 'Breath' of village effective because she visits there frequently to see a grandparent. This the diagnosis of the doctor to whom she went for medicines that she might bear children	None mentioned
7	Man (a doctor)	Begotten no child for 10 years	Did not come to bury elder brother with whom he had quarrelled	'The men (of his elder brother's village) were angry. Illness due to the curse (ikigune) of men'	Killed a cow in elder brother's village but did not tell the men of the village about it properly (i.e. admit his fault)
8	Man (A)	Man ill for 2 years (with syphilis), eye came out of socket	Incest—man lover of father's sister	All men were astonished and cursed A	A killed 4 cows at father's place. Relatives and neighbours ate after swearing at him, A recovered quickly. (He had also been treated in a nursing hospital.)

MISFORTUNES ATTRIBUTED TO MYSTICAL CAUSES—contd.

(b) 'The Breath of Men.'—contd.

No.	Category of Sufferer	Symptoms	Alleged sin	Diagnosis	Ritual performed
9	Senior Village Headman	Paralysed	He encouraged chief to expel junior headman from country when latter refused to hoe road	'Illness of senior headman due to the breath of his junior colleague. He was cursed because he was reputed to be the favourite of the chief.' Diagnosis by divination	Bull and beer provided by junior headman. Ate and drank with senior headman and made friends
10	Woman	Unable to walk	Told by villagers (*amafumu*) to choose heir of her brother. Refused to do so, asking them to choose	'They (villagers) cursed her'	Nothing yet done. Thought that villagers will deny responsibility, saying: 'It is not our illness' if offered a cow
11	Woman	Her baby ill	Insulted husband's mother	Illness diagnosed as '*ingoto*,' a disease due to "the breath of men'. No divination; 'knew themselves'.	Woman and child given medicines by a doctor. Woman's father brought a cow for the mother-in-law she insulted.
12	Headman of young men	Ill a long time and still ill	He and his young men built in the village of their fathers before fathers had moved	Illness due to 'the breath of men' (the fathers) because he seized another's office as headman by building in his village. Diagnosis by divination	Nil. Should have asked old men to bless him
13	Heir (son)	Ill a year. Died the next year	Did not drink father's funeral beer in father's village. 'Others ate the food'	Village angry. Their breath fell on him when he came to fetch away property. Diagnosis by divination	After a year's illness, killed a bull. Ate with friends and relatives in father's village
14	Man	Died	Killed large bull for his children (sacrifice to ancestors) and gave only one leg to neighbours	'Perhaps (he died) because he grudged his fellow villagers meat. Neighbours are shocked if a man kills and does not call them to feast'	
15	Woman	Her child ill	Swore at her husband	Illness diagnosed as *ngoto* (an illness due to 'the breath of men'). Diagnosis by divination	Admission of sin. Woman's father gave her millet to brew beer. Her husband called his fellows to drink and admit their anger and speak about the child's recovery (cf. p. 236)
16	Younger brother of chief	Died	Claimed to be a chief	People said 'breath of men'. Family said witchcraft. Diagnosis by divination	

(b) 'The Breath of Men.' contd.

No.	Category of Sufferer	Symptoms	Alleged sin	Diagnosis	Ritual performed
17	Village headman	Hurt his hand on a stone directly he reached the Lupa to work	Had left for work without the agreement of his people	'Country was angry because he was a headman' (and had gone to work)	None. Died shortly afterwards. Death attributed to witchcraft of fellow workers (cf. cases of witchcraft No. 22)
18	Young chief Mwankuga heir of his deceased senior brother and so heir to chieftainship	Did not beget a son by his inherited wives	Not specified	Village headmen angry so medicine chief has taken not effective. The headmen showed their anger by not taking chief to doctor as they should have done. He went alone	None when case recorded
19	Kasitile, hereditary priest (of chief's lineage)	Kasitile ill	Did not cook for his village neighbours. 'They complained because I, a great chief, did not cook food for them'	Fell ill night after attending a beer drink at a neighbour's house	Feasted neighbours. Treated by a doctor
20	Kasitile	Kasitile had worms	Provided 1 pot of beer for fellow priests when he should have provided 4 pots or a calf	Sickness due to wrath of men. Diagnosis of a doctor	
21	Kasitile	Kasitile ill	Cut down a sacred tree which he should not have cut	'The whole country is angry'. 'Priests and village headmen are angry'	Feasted other priests on meat and beer
22	Village headman, Nsusa	His cow drowned	Ordered to pay a fine for slander or move, and refused. Complained to the District Officer	'All the village headmen are angry'	Nsusa moved. Later brought home (cf. pp. 268–9)
23	Man (junior brother of chief)	Died	He had cut one branch for an axe-handle from a self-sown tree growing in the cultivated land of a village in which he was a new-comer. He had not asked the villagers' permission to cut wood as he should have done.	The "owners" of the village were angry and killed him'	None recorded

(c) 'The Curse of Christians'

MISFORTUNES ATTRIBUTED TO MYSTICAL CAUSES—contd.

No.	Category of Sufferer	Misfortune	Alleged sin	Category of individual or group believed to have called down a curse
1	Ex-schoolboy	Cannot get a job	Disobeyed his Nyakyusa teacher	Teacher
2	Ex schoolboy	Dismissed from government job. Reason unknown. Unemployed	Sent to boarding school with mission money, then refused to work for mission. Later married 12 wives. He also stole	The congregation
3	Teacher, son of elder	Eaten by a crocodile (seven years after sinning)	Committed adultery with daughter of chief. Spoke against the church	The congregation
4	Son of elder	Died of venereal disease	Committed adultery	The congregation
5	Pagan man	Died	Refused food to travelling Christian elder	The elder
6	Mohammedan man	Cut his leg with his hoe	Hoed on Sunday	Two Christian men
7	Ex-schoolboy	Always lost his job though clever and good English-speaker. Now a fisherman and 'talks English to the fish'	Not known	European missionary
8	Ex-boarding schoolboy	Cannot get a job, 'Just hoeing like uneducated people'	Eloped with a girl betrothed to a fellow Christian	European missionary
9	Christian woman	Paralysed for sixteen years	Took an unfair share of meat at feasts	Christian neighbours
10	Man-servant of missionary	Married several times. Each time his wife died	Dressed in missionary's clothes and sat at table pretending to write with his pen	European missionary
11	Rich man	Property disappeared	Caught with a woman and denied having committed adultery	European missionary (said to have uttered a conditional curse: 'If you are lying all your property will disappear')
12	Woman	Became a wanderer	Stole things from loft of mother-in-law's hut. Disobeyed husband and complained of him to neighbours. Asked for divorce	European missionary
13	Young man, newly married	Did not beget a child	Did not make a wedding feast for his neighbours in Christian village	Christian neighbours (complaining they had eaten no meat). Young man's pagan 'mothers' inquired of diviner and this was the diagnosis

MISFORTUNES ATTRIBUTED TO MYSTICAL CAUSES—contd.

(d) *Sorcery* (Ubutege)

No.	Category of victim	Category of accused	Category of accuser	Spatial relationship of victim and accuser	Charge	Grounds of suspicion	Investigation	Upshot of case
1	Chief	'People'	Chief and one of his village headman	Other chiefdoms	Made chief ill	Envy of chief having a court. Illness of chief.		
2	Conquered chief	Conquering chief (pre-European)		Different villages but same country (after the conquest)	Conquered had killed conqueror by sorcery	Mwamakula had taken Mwaseba's country. Death of conqueror		
3	Christian who became very popular by feeding men. People said he would 'kill' the accused because of his popularity	Senior village headman X		Same village	X sought medicine to work sorcery against the Christian	X envied popularity of new-comer. He was overheard by neighbours saying he would work sorcery. Serious illness of Christian followed		
4	Child of P.	Classificatory brother of P.	P., father of victim	Different chiefdoms		Quarrel over inheritance of cattle. P's brother claimed cows from him. Case went to court of defendant's chief. Decided in his favour		
5	Man (Mwanyilu) and his wife	Not specified	Son of deceased (Mwambete)			Death of Mwanyilu and his wife	Autopsy on Mwanyilu. Found a powder, thought to be *ubutege* medicine, in his stomach. No autopsy on wife but 'know that she died from the same disease'	Family drank protective medicine
6	2 wives of X. Sister of X. 1 married daughter and another child					All died within a short time of one another. Sorcery ...	Autopsies	Family drank medicines provided by a doctor and the ...

No.	Category of victim	Category of accused	Category of accuser	Spatial relationship of victim and accuser	Charge	Grounds of suspicion	Investigation	Upshot of case
7	Daughter of A. Son and daughter of A's full brother B	A accused X, his parallel cousin (child of A's father's brother). X accused A	A, father and brother of victims		Use of sorcery against one another	Junior brother's son wanted inheritance divided. Elder brother's son (A) did not. This was followed by illness of victims	Suggested by doctor that trouble due to sorcery or to anger of ancestors over family quarrel	Open discussion of quarrel (ukwiputa). Drank medicine against sorcery. Also prayer to ancestors
8	Child of neighbour B	Man X	Neighbour B.	Same village	Sent his leopard to kill the child	Child killed by leopard on day after X had quarrelled with accuser B, saying B's cattle were eating his crops	X asked for ordeal. This refused	X driven out of country by chief. Later returned
9	Foreman and clerk A, very lucky in striking gold and favourite of his employer	Fellow clerk B.		Same camp	B accused of killing A by sorcery	A died suddenly at his house. B was very jealous of A's wealth, and had spoken in secret of his desire to kill A by sorcery, saying 'may he die at his house'		
10	Wife of village headman					Death	Autopsy. Symptoms of sorcery found	
11	Man who had run off with another's wife	Injured husband	Victim	Victim on Lupa. Injured husband in Iringa (300 miles distant)	Husband blowing medicines at the seducer of his wife—ubutege. The husband's friends might have classed this as vengeance magic	Continued illness of victim	Divination by a doctor	Victim treated with medicines. Moved to another house. He finally recovered, but his host fell ill

(e) *Vengeance Magic* (Ulupembe—*the Horn*)   MISFORTUNES ATTRIBUTED TO MYSTICAL CAUSES—contd.

No.	Category of Victim	Category of accused	Category of accuser	Spatial relationship of victim and accuser	Charge	Grounds of suspicion	Investigation	Upshot of case
1	2 brothers M1 and M2	A doctor (Makikoje)			Accused used the horn. Did not tell M1 that he was doing so	Accused said M1 had stolen his millet. M1 and M2 both died	Autopsy revealed death due to 'the horn'	Chief drove accused out of country for not bringing case to court but revenging himself. The doctor had used the horn in his own case
2	1. Seducer of woman 2. Child of seducer's elder brother	Husband of woman seduced (Mwakikulu)	Relatives of deceased seducer		Accused used the horn. Relatives of victims spoke of deaths as due to sorcery (*Ubutege*)	Victim 1 had eloped with accused's wife. Accused boasted that he had revenged himself. Both victims 1 and 2 died suddenly		Woman returned to husband lest others of the family should die
3	Child of A and children of other wives of A's husband	Co-wife B.	A, mother of victim	Same homestead	B used the horn	A had stolen B's bananas and not admitted it when case was taken first to husband and then to chief. B was dissatisfied. The death of child A and children of other wives followed		A paid B for theft. A and other wives went to horn-doctor and drank medicine. They recovered
4	Man C, and woman X, with whom he had eloped	Man A who inherited the woman X	Man B, brother of deceased C	Different chiefdoms	A used the horn	C ran off with X, widow of A's elder brother whom A had inherited. C and X both died. A boasted: 'I killed them with the horn'		B speared A and fled to a distant chiefdom (before Europeans came)

(e) (*Vengeance Magic* (Ulupembe—*the Horn*)—contd.)

MISFORTUNES ATTRIBUTED TO MYSTICAL CAUSES—contd.

No.	Category of victim	Category of accused	Category of accuser	Spatial relationship of victim and accuser	Charge	Grounds of suspicion	Investigation	Upshot of case
5	9 of A's children	B, son-in-law of A	A, father of victims		B used the horn	A's daughter left B. A returned only 2 head of cattle to B. Owed him 10 to 13 cattle. Told him to collect balance from his daughter's second husband. A refused. Told B to come before horn doctor. A refused. Told B to sue in court. Within 3 years children of A died		A speared B. He was convicted in District Officer's court of manslaughter
6	Gwatabile, his wife, and his full sister's husband	Man (Itupa)	Family of deceased debtor, Gwatabile		Itupa kindled the horn	Gwatabile had a cow belonging to Itupa. The relationship not known. The three victims died.		Family paid a cow to Itupa
7	C	Doctor	C ?			A ran off with B's wife. B followed her and found her in C's house. B claimed damages from A, but A objected saying: 'No, she was found with C'. The court gave judgement against A, and he paid damages to B, then subsequently the court gave judgement for A in his case against C, ordering him to return to A the cows A had paid to B. C delayed, so A went to a doctor and got him to make medicine against C. C handed over the cows to A immediately and paid doctor 6s. to counteract his medicine.	Case brought before D.O.	Doctor discharged. Doubt whether or not doctor should be expelled from the chiefdom in which he lived. Opinion of the Nyakyusa divided on this point

9. METHODS OF WITCHCRAFT

Mwaikambo (*clerk*).

'We people think that the witches have pythons (*isota*) in their stomachs. It is these which have power to change so that they fly. We say a man cannot work witchcraft without a python, but only when he has one. The python can come out of the stomach and enter again. When the python has gone to throttle someone only the witch's body remains. It is said that this body has no strength, and cannot get up; sometimes it can speak a little, sometimes it cannot speak. It is referred to as "a hide".

'When the pythons have come to the place where they are going to eat people, they are said to take out the teeth of others which they use to eat with. They do not eat with their own teeth. When they have "eaten" someone they return the teeth. It is said that if a person wakens before they return his teeth, and cries out that his teeth have gone, then his teeth will disappear all together. He will only have gums in his mouth. The witches do not carry spears with which to bewitch. I, and others also, are surprised at this, for when an autopsy is performed I have never heard it said that tooth-marks have been found, but always that spear wounds have been found. And some, when they wake up in the morning, have said: "My teeth are loose." Then others tell them: "The witches ate with your teeth in the night."

'Witches fight a very fierce war in their supernatural strength (*kumanga gwabo*). It is said that they fight with spears. Those of one village do not fight, but the village of one chief (*sic*) fights against the village of another chief. When the witches of one chief try to kill another chief the latter's men fight them and save their chief. Hence it sometimes happens that the chief kills cattle for his people to thank them for having fought for him.

'Sometimes witchcraft is directed at food or a brewing of beer, causing it to rot. When the witches have spoiled the beer it is not nice. The witches spoil other things like this by means of their witchcraft with pythons.

'When the witches go to "eat" a person, two or four may go together or one may go alone. When they go they travel with the strength of the python; they leave a "skin", or body only. When they come to the person they throw away their teeth; they take the teeth of him whom they are going to eat, and eat with them. And one whose teeth have been returned knows in the morning that the witches used his teeth. We are warned that if ever we find no teeth in our mouths we must not cry out, because then the teeth will disappear altogether, but to be silent, then they will reappear.

'And another activity of the witches is to take sickness from one country and cast it on some home they choose. So when people die they say this sickness was brought by the witches to so and so.'

Mwandesi (a very old man famous as a historian).

'The witches are always naked when they go to choke a person in dreams. A witch leaves his skin (ungubo) on his sleeping-mat and goes naked. When his neighbours, "the defenders" (abamanga), see him they may snatch his skin; then when he returns he trembles and sits down naked, ugly-looking. He looks as if he had a curse on him. But after a little while he gets another skin.'

Mwaisumo (clerk).

'The man of whom we have spoken twice (vide pp. 124, 252) is sometimes said to be a witch, he throttles the cattle of the village and men say that he throttles them also. But he is especially notorious for throttling the cattle of the village so that their milk disappears. Once they caught him for witchcraft, saying: "You are throttling us" and they drove him away. He moved to another village but in the same chiefdom, and there also men continually said: "We do not sleep on account of our fellow! If he brings witchcraft to us here he will die, we shall hit him with fists" (meaning that "the defenders" will hit him with fists) when he goes out to throttle his victims. If their cows dry up they say: "We shall hit his python, he will die." For it is said that if a person has a python which throttles the milk, men strike the python and he dies. The python means the witchcraft of throttling cattle or food. Saying "We shall strike his python and he will die" means that we shall strike him when he is throttling our cows and he will die.'

Ntulanongwa (pagan man).

'When the chief is good the cows are many and there is much milk. And when the village headman is good, when he forbids witches to come into his village, milk is plentiful. When we say a chief is good (nnumu) it means that he never goes to throttle cows, or if we say that the village headman is good it means that he does not go throttling. Formerly chiefs and village headmen were good. If they were great witches, no one came to them. I come from Penja country over there,

Mwalukasa was good. We knew he was good because people came to him and cattle increased and people loved him. Some who are quarrelsome lose all their men and are left alone. . . . . A village headman or chief *gwa ifugo* is one who always preaches to his fellows that "food should be plentiful among us here, friends; none should bewitch others." "A man of plenty" (*ugwa ifugo*) is a village headman or chief who is angry at witchcraft in his village, and forbids it, who allows no one there who is "clever". The cunning of a witch, of one who has the bowel of witchcraft, is to go around throttling cows and eating people. When they go to throttle they go on high, they fly, they go like the wind. If they went on earth they would be killed by "the defenders". It is said that they eat the meat (flesh) of people, truly they eat it. When they go to "eat" a man, they spear him; they take his meat and eat it. A man does not recover when they have taken his meat; he dies. Those whom they have only speared and whose flesh they have not taken, recover. They roast this human meat and then they eat it; in this their cleverness lies. When they go to "eat" a man and have speared him and taken some of his flesh, they do not roast it at his place, they go to their homes, and there they roast it.'

10. A MYTH OF WITCHCRAFT

Mwaisumo (clerk).

'This story is often told us by our mothers: A woman once went to bewitch (*ukupita*) leaving her child in her bed. While she was away the child began to cry. So the father woke up and came to see what the trouble was, and he found the mother was not there. When she appeared again he asked her where she had been and she replied: "I was here. I did not go anywhere." This happened several times. One night the father took the crying child to his own bed and made it sleep, but he himself sat awake watching. Then the woman came in and lit her fire and began to cook the human flesh, and he caught her and asked: "Where have you found this meat?" Then she admitted that she'd been to bewitch people and that that was where she had got her meat from. And he said: "You are a witch. You always leave my child crying to go to bewitch people." So he divorced her and sent her home. But people usually say that when a witch goes to throttle people he leaves his skin. The skin stays in the bed, but doesn't feel anything.'

11. WITCHCRAFT AND LUST FOR MEAT AND MILK

Mwaisumo (clerk).

'Some "defenders" (*abamanga*), when they smell something delicious in the house of a relative or a close friend, say: "The meat (if it's meat) smells nice, give me a little to eat, I am a witch, the pythons will rouse up and carry me off to throttle someone." This can only be said (and it is said quite seriously) in the house of a relative or great friend, because in no other house can a man ask for meat. Shame prevents him. People think a man who asks for food is a fool.

'Some people, when they have eaten a little and finished, say: "Give me a little more, if we witches are grudged food the pythons rouse up!" It is said that throttling is in order to eat delicious food (*ukupita ko kulya ifinafu*). The witches say human flesh is delicious, and the milk of cows is also delicious.

Some people will eat cooked food which has been left over-night; others refuse it, and when asked why, say: "It is forbidden for us witches to eat cooked food which has stood over-night." I have heard this said often. "The defenders" say it spoils their pythons. Chiefs do not eat kept food either; it is said to spoil their *ifingela* medicine. People say that it is bad for chiefs or witches or "defenders" to eat left-over food because it has been touched by the ancestors at night. This is often said by "defenders" as well as others.'

12. INHERITANCE OF WITCHCRAFT

Bwilile (*elderly pagan man*).

Question: 'How does a mother give her child witchcraft? How does a father give a child witchcraft?'

'It starts when a woman is menstruating; then she begins to give a child her cunning (*ubugalagala*). It is said that when a woman is menstruating she should avoid certain things (*ukutila*), particularly she should not pass behind people. For when a woman is menstruating a child has begun in her belly. People know that a certain woman is cunning when they see that she does not avoid people at certain times. Then they say: "Friends, this woman is spoiling the child. Why does she not observe the avoidances? Look, we have seen that she is fruitful (meaning that she is menstruating)." For it is that dirt which creates witchcraft. When a woman does not avoid, then she gives the child in her belly witchcraft. It is from this that witchcraft really comes. When a woman is not cunning, then she always observes the avoidance taboos; she does not go about anyhow. From of old it has been thought important that a menstruating woman should observe certain avoidances. A woman avoids certain things because she fears to spoil the child in her belly. When a woman does not avoid these things, the dirt, that is to say the menstrual blood, goes to where the child is. That is how she spoils the child. On this account women fear to go about anyhow, to pass behind people; they fear those medicines with which we men smear our bodies, all those for good fortune and others. Especially they fear a fierce medicine, that of fire. For there is a medicine with which some people smear themselves which causes a person to faint if the user strikes him once with the flat of his hand. It is this medicine which spoils the child in the belly of a menstruating woman if she passes behind a man. This is the lineage of witchcraft. It comes especially from this, from that dirty little thing (i.e. woman) who does not observe the avoidance rules. Hence, we say she has given her child witchcraft.

'A father gives his child witchcraft because the man's blood goes into the woman, for a woman is a pocket.'

Ntulanongwa confirmed the above statement of the origin of witchcraft, and explained:

'A woman does not menstruate when she is pregnant, but some menstrual blood remains in her, which may "spoil" her. We all think that when a woman is menstruating some of the blood remains in her belly, and it is this which spoils the child when a woman does not avoid certain things. There is no other way in which a woman gives her child witchcraft.'

Mwaikambo (clerk).

Some people have witchcraft implanted in them (*ukupanda*) by their parents. Some children are witches; they are born with it in their stomachs. When a child is small, even a tiny baby, the witches may take it with them to bewitch (*kumanga*) in order that it also may learn the business of witchcraft. Hence sometimes it is said that a mother, or perhaps a father, shielded himself behind her (his) child, meaning that he fought with other witches and when they were going to spear him he put his child in front of him. When such a child grows up he will be skilled in witchcraft.'

13. ACQUIRING WITCHCRAFT FROM FRIENDS

Bwilile (elderly pagan man).

'We have heard it said that sometimes, when a woman plays with a friend's child who is growing up a little, she may give it something in food, or offer it something to taste, which causes the child who has eaten it to become a witch. Hence people say: "A stranger gave him (or her) witchcraft; there is none in our family (*ikikolo*)."

'Some make children climb up the walls or hut pole when they wish to give them witchcraft, hence when a child slides down it is said, "He (or she) is pure; he has no trace of witchcraft in his stomach." If he has any in his stomach, then he clings to the walls or pole, and it is said, "He is giving him mystical power (*amanga*)", meaning the witch is giving him the cunning of witchcraft that he also may be "clever". If there is a girl at home who is cunning, her friends shun her. They admonish her, saying: "Don't do those things. It's forbidden at a husband's place. You will always be driven out." She gives her friends things saying: "You eat that, and you that." And boys do likewise. We knew the custom of old. When boys are out herding cattle one friend tells another to dig up a certain plant, saying it will give him cunning. Hence it is said that a cunning boy wants to make his friends cunning also. When girls are secluded at puberty they always play with younger girls, and if one makes another climb the hut pole or wall the mothers are very angry, saying: "No! That's forbidden. Don't do (bad) things to others. It seems as if you were cunning." '

Commenting on this text, Mwaisumo said: 'The witches learn to enter a house by climbing up the wall, instead of going through the door, so that people don't see them come in. If a child has *no* witchcraft in its stomach at all, no one can give it witchcraft, but if the blood of the mother is dirty with witchcraft it becomes a witch.'

14. CONSCIOUSNESS OF WITCHCRAFT

Mwaikambo (*clerk*).

'Witches act consciously. That is to say a person caught for witchcraft is not startled at being a witch. And in their business of going to bewitch (*kumanga*) when they "eat" people, they go willingly; nothing compels them. We hear that sometimes when witches go to "eat" people some of them are satisfied. The milk is plentiful for though some of the witches say: "Let us drink it", others disagree. When they have agreed between themselves they leave a person alone.'

15. THE ASSOCIATIONS OF *UKULOGA* AND *UKUPITA*

Mwaisumo (clerk).

'*Ukuloga* is like *ukupita* but not the same. It is said that when some-one is angry with you and has drunk a medicine to give him power to bewitch (*amaka ga kuloga*), he greets you and the word alone has power to bring illness. You will be very ill.

'It is said that when a woman is pregnant and walks round a person who has many medicines, one of them being a medicine *ukuloga*, she will have a miscarriage. There is no case (against the owner of the medicines).

'It is said that when the owner of pythons, or the owner of medi-cines, passes when food has been spread out to dry, the food will disappear. He bewitches it (*ukuloga*). It is as if he hankered after the food in his heart; it disappears and becomes less. When a python man ("he of pythons")—they speak much of python men, little of medicine men—passes cattle and hankers after milk, he bewitches the milk (*ukuloga*). It disappears. He does not throttle (*ukupita*) the cattle; no, the milk just disappears.

'It is forbidden to say of a child that it is beautiful. It is all right to a close friend but not among ordinary people. To do so is to bewitch (*ukuloga*) the child. The child will fall ill. It is forbidden to say of a cow that its udder is big. If the owner hears he says: "You are be-witching it" (*ukuloga*), meaning the milk will disappear. Everyone fears to admire children or cows in this way; if such a sign is followed by sickness or failure of milk people swear at the man who has ex-pressed admiration, but do not bring a case.

'The work of pythons is especially to steal away the milk, to throttle (*ukupita*). It is reported that some say: "I am a witch, but I have not got a python. I do not throttle the cows." They might mean they "eat" people but do not steal milk.'

Kakugu (pagan man).

'*Ukupita* is to throttle (with hands round the throat).'

In reply to a question as to the further meanings of the word *ukupita*, Kakugu said: 'When my relatives are there I say: "Have you *kupita* with my wife?" But when we are alone I say: "Did you sleep with my wife?" or "Did you have intercourse with her (*gwalogwa nagwe*)?" We only liken intercourse and witchcraft; witchcraft is quite different. When a woman is an adulteress I say: "You are a witch (*undosi*); you kill me," but it is just a metaphor (*fyo fifwani*). Adultery involves paying for cattle for all of us; it differs from witchcraft. And when I ask a man: "Why, why did you *kupita* with my wife?" that means: "You are like a witch." It is just a metaphor. But (he volunteered), if I catch an adulterer with my wife, even if he has practised *coitus interruptus*, I am angry and kill him from jealousy, though I do not suffer from diarrhoea.'

An adulteress is spoken of as an *undosi* 'because she brings illness upon her husband' by her adultery, if intercourse is complete, but not, it is thought, if *coitus interruptus* is practised. The illness commonly thought to be caused by a wife's adultery is diarrhoea.

16. THINGS ASSOCIATED WITH WITCHCRAFT

Mwaisumo (clerk).

1. 'Bestiality. This is associated with witchcraft (*sya bu losi*) because, it is said, witches eat the flesh of human beings which an ordinary person does not eat—ordinary people all avoid human flesh. One who has intercourse with an animal, a thing which an ordinary person does not do but avoids, is like one who eats human flesh.'

2. 'Intercourse with a very young girl. This is associated with witchcraft because no one desires it, only this person' (i.e. such a desire is abnormal).

3. 'Intercourse with a very old woman. This is associated with witchcraft because no one desires old women.'

4. 'Intercourse between a grown man and a boy. This is associated with witchcraft because grown men always desire women.'

In reply to a question: 'No, it never happens that two grown men lie together, but youths do. That is not associated with witchcraft; that is adolescence.'

5. 'If a woman takes something very dirty (such as excrement) and puts it on her husband's bed, or in his food, because she hates him, that is associated with witchcraft because it is very, very dirty. No one (normal) does such a thing.'

In reply to a question: 'No, if children play with excrement, that is not associated with witchcraft.'

6. 'In Selya we do not eat the meat of a leopard though in Kukwe country they do. If a Selya man tastes it people say: "How can he eat leopard meat which no one eats? It's like witchcraft." Leopard meat is forbidden because leopards kill and eat people.

'So with the meat of a dog or rat or monkey. A dog is not eaten because it's our friend—a person—and a monkey is a person.'

17. DREAMS AS EVIDENCE OF WITCHCRAFT

Mwaisumo (clerk).

'Suppose I dream we are fighting, and that you knock me down, or that you come to beat me, then I will say to my friends that you bewitched me last night. Men talk with their friends and tell their dreams. If several people dream like this of one man, they say: "Why should we dream of him? He must be a witch (*undosi*)." More than one person must dream of the same man before they will say this. If I dream of you, my friend, like this I will not tell you in the morning that I dreamed so, or else you will say to me: "Why do you accuse me of witchcraft?" and you will take it first to the headman, and then to the chief, and make a case. We Christians do not believe this; we say: "It is just a dream" and we tell it to each other, but the pagans tell it to their friends, and if two or more dream of the same man they say: "He is a witch."

'There are a number of dreams—dreams of fighting, of being chased, being beaten, of the house burning, of one coming to the door and weeping for me as if I were dead—which are signs (*ifimanyilo*) of witchcraft. There are other signs, too. An owl (*ingwita*) may come at night and cry on my roof. I go out and chase it away, watching the direction in which it flies; it flies towards your house. Then the next night it comes to another man's house, and he again goes out and chases it and watches its flight, and again it flies towards your house. Then we shall say that you are a witch. Or if you meet a man in the road and stare at him, and that night he falls sick, he will remember and say: "Why did so and so stare at me like that? He is bewitching me."

'A man may dream of a woman, like this, or a woman of a man—of being beaten, etc., and will say it is witchcraft (*ubulosi*). But if they dream of each other and desire each other that is not witchcraft. (Here he laughed.) They will seek each other out. He will tell her: "I dreamed of you last night", or she, if she has any love for him, will say: "I dreamed of you." Yes, that is an invitation. It is queer but it often happens that a man and a woman will dream of each other on the same night.

'Women dream of each other, of fetching firewood and fighting.'

Ali (a young man, a Christian).

'The pagans say that if I dream of flying that means that the witches came and tried to eat me. If I do not dream at all, but wake up in a sweat, then they say: "They came to bewitch you by night." They say that the sweat is the water with which the witches wash their hands before eating. Again, if I dream that someone comes and holds me down so that I cannot get up, they say: "The witches came to kill you." They say a man is a defender (*gwa manga*) if he does not merely dream, but sees in his dream who it is that came. So with dreams of fighting, if I recognize that my opponent is so and so, then they say I have mystical power (*amanga*), not otherwise. We Christians have all these dreams but say they mean nothing and do not fear them.'

18. GROUNDS OF ACCUSATION OF WITCHCRAFT

An elderly Christian man.

'The pagans are afraid of what they dream, and secondly, if they have quarrelled with a man and they fall sick they at once think he is throttling them.'

'Without dreams of him?'

'Yes.

'Then again, if a man is given milk by his neighbours and yet goes round in other villages, complaining: "They grudge me milk. I don't drink their milk", and his neighbours hear of it, they say to him: "What do you mean by saying we grudge you milk? Scandal-mongering is bad. Indeed, you are a witch." And then, as soon as the cows fall sick, they point to him: "That is the witch who is throttling the cattle." And they drive him out. Yes, without dreams.

'What our parents used to say to us when discussing these things was this: "Pride! If a man is proud and is not sociable with his neighbours; if he boasts, saying: 'I am someone, and others are not people at all,' then we say he is a witch." And if ever the cows fall sick or go dry, then we point to him as the witch who is throttling them and drive him away. This happens without dreams, too.

'And then again, if one man has quarrelled with another and the other falls sick, they may say the one is a witch and drive him out. Perhaps if he was a man of Mwaipopo he goes to live in Mwangomo's country (that of a neighbouring chief). Then one day a man of Mwaipopo's goes to his new village and talks to the people: "I see that you have received so and so here. We drove him out as a witch. He's a great witch, that man." And so when next the cows fall sick or someone dies, they point to him as a witch and drive him away again. Then he goes right up to Mwangoka's (twenty-five miles away) and again someone from Mwaipopo's or Mwangomo's comes up there and repeats the story. A little later the same thing happens and he is driven out again.'

19. THINGS WHICH ARE SAID TO ANGER THE WITCHES AND MAKE THEM THROTTLE US

Mwaisumo (clerk).

'Carrying very heavy loads, frequently. They (the witches) wonder (*ukukiba*) at a person and he (or she) falls ill.'

'Hoeing a very large field, surpassing others.'

'Being more wealthy, as by earning money on the Lupa, like Bingibamo and Kiputa.'

'Boasting at work, saying: "I am the senior" like Ramsay and Isiah at Tukuyu.'

'Eating fine food alone. This may be meat, when you have killed a bull or cow, or beer or gifts of food from in-laws, or any other fine food. Mwambuputa was accused of doing this.'

'People are always afraid to carry very heavy things because they think that others will be angry and wonder at it (*ukukiba*). Their astonishment causes illness. Women especially speak of this a great deal when they are fetching firewood. If they carry a very big load others express wonder saying: "It is God who has given you strength surpassing us all." This astonishment brings on serious illness. People fall ill and some even die. Formerly people feared very much to speak to someone who carried a heavy load, saying: "You carry a very heavy load"; they were likely to be fined if they did, because the person to whom they said it would complain, saying: "He wondered at me. He brings down illness on me; he brings the witches by saying I am a strong fellow."

'It is like this also in hoeing; if a man has hoed much he fears lest they (the witches) will kill him; if people say: "He has surpassed us in strength" and are angry, that is what happens—the man falls ill and may die.

'Surpassing others in possessions is said also to anger other people, witches, who kill their fellow because they think that he has a medicine (*unkota*) which enables him to surpass them in wealth. The medicine for surpassing others is the medicine of good fortune (*unkota gwa lusako*). There was a case like this among the Nyangomo—the case of a young man who died quite recently. His name was Bingibamo, the son of Kiputa. This young man was in employment on the Lupa gold-fields . . . and he sent back money to his father to buy cattle. When he had been working for a certain European for a short time only he surpassed the other workers as they searched for gold, and found a very big nugget. He saw it first and picked it up immediately. All the others wished to share it; they all went together to their European (employer) to say that their fellow did not find this nugget alone, but that they had all got it. The employer said: "Yes, of course I shall pay you all for sifting, but he found it. He picked it up. I shall give him something separately." So he gave Bingibamo 100s. and to each of the others he gave 6s. The next morning Bingibamo was ill; the following day he died and they buried him. It is said that his fellows "ate" him, they were angry about the nugget he had got. And those who work there (on the Lupa) regularly say that no one who gets a nugget ever escapes; those who get money always die.

'It is said that one who boasts at work saying that he has surpassed his fellows in wisdom and seniority dies like Ramsay, who was a clerk at Tukuyu, and Isiah Mwagomba. They died. Some say privately that the sin (*inongwa*) which killed them was boasting—they boasted very much to their fellows. Some say that there is one man among them (the clerks at Tukuyu) who always kills his fellows if they seem likely to surpass him in seniority (i.e. importance). A boastful man (*gwalwitufyo*) is always proud (*gwamatingo*), and as for enjoying the company of his fellows he does not keep on good terms with them at all (*atikwangala nabo kanunu*).

'Eating fine food alone is said to kill a man. If you have killed a bull to eat you must give your fellows some, because if you grudge them they will summon the witches to "eat" you. That is to say the people who saw you will tell of it and at night "the defenders" will be angry and summon the witches to "eat" you. Or when your in-laws bring something when they visit you, and you do not call your fellows, but grudge them a share they will "eat" you, as happened in the case of Mwambuputa. It is said that Mwambuputa grudged his fellows certain food, so they were very angry and two of his children died at home. When he found that sickness was spreading at his homestead he fled to the Lake-shore plain (MuNgonde), but there also he found that death pursued him and he returned home again. It is said that sickness pursued him to the plain because he went off without performing the death ritual for the children who died. So when he returned he found two bulls and killed them, saying: "Friends, I have come. I did wrong because I did not perform the ritual for your children with you." '

20. THREATS OF WITCHCRAFT

Mwaisumo (clerk).

'It is said that some witches show themselves openly. When he is angry with his fellow a witch may say openly *"Uligwaki?"* (literally: "What are you?") and his fellow takes ill in the evening, sickness falls on him. Or one who makes love to a woman repeatedly and is refused by her, may say: "Woman, what are you? *(uligwaki?)* You are very proud, you fancy yourself, thinking that you are more beautiful than all others. Dance and show off—we shall see in what a pleasant fashion."

'It is now forbidden, as it was in the past, to swear at *(ukufinga)* a person without cause, saying: "What are you?" If someone speaks before others, and the person sworn at is quarrelsome, the man who swears is fined. The man sworn at will go to law, saying: "My fellow swears at men; I do not know what I have taken of his, he wants to make me ill by swearing at me." Sometimes, also, if he does not wish to be paid, he calls one before the court, or before neighbours to say: "This fellow of mine has sworn at me, if anything happens it is he who is responsible." Meaning that if he falls ill that evening it is this fellow who has caused the illness. And some, when they have recovered, make a case, saying: "It is this fellow", and bring him before the village headman accusing him. If he is found guilty he will pay perhaps a bull. Such tales are told, especially by our mothers, teaching us in childhood that it is forbidden to threaten a friend with witchcraft *(ukumfinga unnino bulosi).*[1] If you swear at your friend and he falls ill that evening then he will say it was you who swore at him.

'But there are some who wish to be feared and thought witches who constantly threaten people. Such a man says: "What are you? You *may* sleep or may not *(ulikagone)*, I do not know!" but in great secrecy. Or perhaps sometimes he speaks, saying: "You! Leave me!" He knows that those who are there will tell (his enemy)'

Andambike (a young Christian man).

'Some boast of witchcraft, they praise themselves on account of knowledge, or food, or their homestead . . . saying that no one else has built so well; others praise themselves on account of their fields,

---

[1] *Ukufinga* means to swear to a statement. In this context it is better translated 'to threaten'.

and many things of that sort. . . . I once asked an elderly pagan if it were really true that witchcraft existed. The old man replied: "No, it does not exist, and the reason why I say that is this: Once a man hated his fellows and they were angry, and met at his place. (According to the pagan custom when your fellows are angry they gather at your home and they cut leaves; if you do not move you will die, or perhaps something will happen.) When they had met together at his place they said: 'Perhaps you may sleep or may not!' (implying you will not sleep on account of witchcraft.) When they had gone the man threw away all the leaves on which they had been sitting, the leaves which they say bring sickness to a home.[1] He slept, but those who talked about it said: 'He will not escape, for the custom which has been carried out against him is fatal.' He waited and slept again. The next day he was still well. Then I, for my part, understood that witchcraft does not exist, those men boasted, saying: 'Perhaps you may sleep or may not', but nothing happened. They just wished to frighten him. And one day I myself tried to frighten a certain man. His cow had eaten my seed so I went to his house and complained that his cow had got into my food. The next day again the cow ate my seed again. So then I was angry and said to myself, 'I'll frighten this fellow.' When I said: 'Why is your cow in my seed again?' he replied: 'I don't know. Do *I* herd?' So I said: 'My child, perhaps you may sleep or may not when you answer like that!'

"He said: 'Are you a witch then?'

"I said: 'You thought I was just talking. Know that I am talking to you here angry enough to wish to fight with you, so if you are strong in body you will overcome me at night in dreams.' And I went to tell a neighbour that my child perhaps might sleep, or might not, and not to be startled the next day if something happened to that child of mine. That night I blew a calabash trumpet that he should think I was coming and tremble. When he heard it he set off by night, saying:

[1] Mwaisumo commenting on this said: 'When, as boys, we went round in groups eating at one another's homes we were told by our mothers not to cut too many leaves, but just enough for us to use (to sit on). It's forbidden, they said, to strew leaves at a home. It looks as if there were something against the owners of the homestead, you foretell bad fortune, perhaps sickness or death. So, likewise, if I go to visit a sick friend that does not affect his recovery, but if I shed tears because he is sick men say: "It is forbidden (to weep), you foretell misfortune, perhaps he will die (because you weep)." And here (in the case recounted) the the leaves were a sign that this man had a case against him. Others wonder, asking: "What has happened, what has happened?" It is said that when people wonder something will happen on account of their astonishment. If they know that there is a ritual or a funeral all is well, but if nothing is known then questions are asked, something will happen because people wonder, that is people from other villages, not the neighbours of those who have a case against them.'

'Wives, let us die from our own disease, not this one, pick up the pot and leave it with someone else immediately, we are leaving this home, he is not going to find anyone.' They hid the pot by night, and they moved. A child died after they had arrived at the place to which they moved.

"So I began to understand that witchcraft does not exist but that we die of fear. See, I am not a witch at all, I just tried to frighten that man, but their fear killed them. As for frightening people with witchcraft, we frighten them that they may respect us, or that we may get what we want to eat, they think that if they grudge us they will be throttled by witches."

'The old man who told me (Andambike) this is still alive, living in the country of Kilwa, MuNgonde, in Korosso's chiefdom.'

21. CHILDREN LEARNING OF WITCHCRAFT

Mwaikambo (clerk).

'I learned about witchcraft from the accounts related by the elder boys in our boys' village. There we tell about witchcraft; of how the witches fight with people of another village, of their way of travelling to where they commit witchcraft (*kwa kumanga*), that is flying. We tell how they eat people and that the strength of witchcraft is in pythons. And we speak of some who are dead, who each had a python, or perhaps four, and of village headmen who have protective pythons (*isota sya buketi*). We relate cases which always appear true, and make us afraid.'

22. 'THE BREATH OF MEN'

Mwaisumo (clerk).

' "The breath of men" is a very serious illness; if a person is ill from "the breath of men" he is in great trouble. Such a person never recovers until they pray (*bikwikemesya*). This illness comes especially when a man enters into his inheritance but does not perform the ritual, perhaps to bury him from whom he inherited—his father, or elder brother, or perhaps his mother's brother. As in the case of the estate of our mother's brother, Mwakaliku. When Mwambilike (informant's elder brother) inherited the woman Kyando, he did not perform the ritual for her. The woman was constantly ailing, but no one knew that she was suffering from this illness until they went to divine and found that she was ill from "the breath" because no ritual had been performed for her from the time she was inherited until now. So Mwambilike found a cow and called together all his dependants and his fellows in the village, and he killed the cow and told everyone about this illness. Then people "complained" (*ukwijaja*), and said: "Indeed, may this illness finish." (It was neighbours who complained, not relatives.) From that time the woman concerned has never been ill again. So everyone says: "In truth, 'the breath of men' is very great."

'This illness is very serious, but it never kills people, though they are ill for a long time. If it is not discovered that this is the cause, the patient will be ill for a very long time, perhaps for two or three years. Yes, sometimes it kills when it has spread in the homestead, but people very rarely die from this illness.

'It is often seen in connection with inheritance. Another case occurred in my country. A certain man built with us who was of a chief's lineage. He inherited from a relative but he did not kill a cow at the death ritual. The wife he inherited was constantly ill until they went to divine and found that it was "the breath of men" (which was making her ill) because he had not performed a ritual since he entered into his inheritance. So he also found a cow and called people (non-relatives) and all his descendants, and killed the cow, and his fellow villagers "complained" (*ukwijaja*). But I do not know whether the illness finished or not. What I do know is that he found a cow—I saw it myself when it was lying there dead and people gathered, relatives, descendants, and neighbours.

'*Ingoto* is a disease of children. It comes from the insults used by the mother of the child. It is commonly said that when a married woman has been angry with her husband, and perhaps quarrelled with him, and has sworn at her husband by "the things"(i.e. the sex organs) of his mother, or perhaps his father, the child she bears will fall sick with *ingoto*. It becomes very thin and does not grow. The disease is recognized when a child is very ill from infancy, and it is very thin but does not die. Then they say it is *ingoto*. Sometimes they inquire of a diviner and the diviner reveals that it is ill of *ingoto*.

'I remember a certain woman who was married to a man, Akay-amba. This man had married two wives, and she of whom I speak was the third. This woman was very proud (*namatingo fijo*) and was constantly quarrelling with her husband and her co-wives. When she quarrelled with her husband he got angry and beat her. Then she swore at him horribly, about "the things" of his mother or father. She said: "You! So and so of your father! So and so of your mother!" Then this woman bore a girl child and when it had grown a little it became very ill. It was very ill for a whole year. When it began to recover she quarrelled again with her husband and swore at him insultingly, and the child got ill again. So her husband (the father of the child) and she went to inquire of a diviner. The divination revealed *ingoto*. It said: "Your wife has sworn at you about the things of your mother when you were quarrelling." When they got home the husband drove his wife away, saying: "Go to your father!" When she got home the woman told her father everything and he took millet and gave it to her to make beer with which to pay. So she brewed beer and brought it to her husband, saying: "I did wrong, my husband." Her husband called his fellows and they all drank the beer and expressed their anger (*ukwijaja*) and said: "May the child recover and grow well!"

'This happened when I was 13 or 14 years old. The girl (who was ill) is still alive; her body shows signs of not having grown properly.

'The disease comes from "the breath of men" because these insults were made publicly and others heard them. I do not think anything would happen if the insults were private, I am not sure.'

A curse of neighbours for neglect of rituals.
Angombwike (young Christian man).

'If I do not do the (death) ritual properly for my father the death of my children is due to the case against me, the dispute with relatives and the curse of people—non-relatives (*nongwa mbukamu, ikigune mbandu*).

'Sometimes the villagers (*amafumu*) bind a man's loins so that he cannot beget children with his wife. They are both sterile. Mwakanámale, the doctor in Selya, is a case of this. He had quarrelled with his elder brother and did not come to bury him. Later he came and killed a cow, but did not tell the men of the village (*amafumu*) properly, and they were angry, and so for the last ten years he has had no child. His wives do not conceive at all. That is due to the curse of men (*ikigune kya bandu*).'

A curse for 'soiling a man'.
Angombwike (young Christian man).

Angombwike cited a case of sterility attributed to *ikigune* because a woman had 'soiled' a man.

'She had run away three times with X. Finally her husband forced X to eat her filth and drink her urine. X was very ill but recovered. She bore no further children on her return to her husband. She went to Lyandeleko (the informant's mother) for medicine but the latter said she could not help as it was *ikigune*. Her neighbours were shocked because she had "soiled the child of someone". Also the neighbours of X's father were shocked. Their "breath" takes effect because she visits frequently in their village, going to see a grandparent. They say: "This is the woman who soiled our child." '

N.B.—It is the woman who is held to have suffered, not her husband or X.

A curse due to incest.
Grant (young Christian man).

'A, son of B (a chief), made love to his father's sister X. X's husband, C, had married (*ukusakula*) a full sister, Y, of Λ. Λ lay with X. Λ had syphilis and X and her husband C both fell sick of it. C asked X where the disease came from. She accused A. C complained to B. B was very angry and all men were astonished at it. It is forbidden. How could he have intercourse with his mother, the sister of his father! B took four of A's cows and gave them to C. People cursed (*ukuguna*) A, who was very ill for two years. His eye came out of its socket. He went to a mission hospital.

'The villagers (*amafumu*) gathered at B's and said: "This sickness of A is because of that case of his when he lay with X. It is because of that he is sick." So B sent to A and told him to bring four cows, which he did. B called his people and brothers and sisters and said: "Bless your child." They swore and swore at him, and they caught hold of the woman and swore, saying: "How did you agree to sleep with your child? You have both sinned greatly." Then they killed the cows and ate them. I was there. Very quickly A recovered and his eye is all right now.'

A curse on a senior village headman due to the anger of a junior village headman.
Mwandeba (Pagan man).

'A young chief, Mwaidemale, called his men to hoe a road at the order of the Government. The third village headman of the country and his men refused to come, saying: "Not we, we have been once already", and they beat Mwaidemale's messenger. So Mwaidemale was very angry, and reported the village headman to his father, who was also very angry and told the headman and all his men (a very big age-village) to move to another chief. And the senior headman agreed, saying: "Indeed, my junior is a proud fellow. Let them go." So they all went to the country of Mwansasu.

'Now the senior headman has fallen ill with the "breath of men". He is unable to walk. The diviner said his illness was due to "the breath" of his junior colleague—he had been cursed because he is reputed to be the favourite of the chief. He was very ill and moved to Korosso's country where he has begun to recover.

'After being away for a year the third headman brought a cow to pay to the chief (Mwakabolofu). The chief refused it, saying: "No, indeed, my country is quarrelsome. Perhaps you think it was you who built it? I do not wish that you should return. Go with your cow." Some of the third village headman's men came back and then Mwaka-bolofu allowed to build, but he said that he would never let the banished headman back. Many men stayed with their headman and refused to return until he did. Only two years ago (1937) the headman brought two cows to Mwakabolofu who forgave him on the condition that he found something to take to the senior headman, who was ill, to fetch him back from Korosso's country. So the third headman fetched his senior with a huge bull. They came back with it and killed it and drank much beer and made friends. Most of the beer was pro-vided by the third headman, who had spent two years in exile, but some by the senior.

'The mystical power (*amanga*) of the third headman and his men was able to reach the senior headman because a whole village had moved, but had a single man moved he would not have been able to send "breath" to another country, because when "the defenders" come at night in the power of *amanga* (*mmanga gabo*) the owners of the country who remain in it ask them: "Where are you going?" and they reply: "We are just walking about in our country, to our homes", and the owners of the country do not drive them away; but of a single man they ask: "Why are you walking about here?" and they drive him off.'

'The breath of men' and witchcraft.
Mwambuputa (Senior village headman).

' "The breath of men' (*embepo sya bandu*) and witchcraft (*ubulosi*) go together. If all the members of a village murmur that a certain man is evil then the words of the innocent (*abelu*) have no weight, no strength at all, but those of the heavy ones (*abasito*) have. It is the heavy ones who carry that breath into his body in dreams, they chastise him, but the innocent just talk and murmur against him, that is all.'

Question: 'Then that breath comes from the pythons inside them?'

Mwambuputa: 'Yes, that is where it comes from, it is one with witchcraft, identical. Sometimes they just chastised him a little, he did not die, but just fell sick; and in such a case there was never any drinking of *umwafi*; if he killed a beast for them they would pray (*ukwiputa*) and pray, they would let out all their anger, saying: "Certainly we were angry, it was us, but now it is all over." Then life came back to him and he recovered. That is the curse (*ikigune*).

'But sometimes they would kill him—and then they had to drink *umwafi* . . . if a man died and they found spear-marks, wounds, in his entrails the chief would get angry and say: "You have killed your fellow, drink the *umwafi*." So then the *umwafi* would convict one of witchcraft and he would be expelled from the country. For we said: "It is forbidden to kill a man." We others were afraid, although we had disliked the victim ourselves, we feared that at some later time the witch would kill us.'

23. RITUAL OF RECONCILIATION

Mwakionde (*doctor, brother of a chief*).

'If my son has sworn at me, my friends in the village are angry and say: "Why has our child sworn at his father?" Then the youth falls ill, and people say: "It is the curse (*ikigune*). It was we who were angry, because he swore at our fellow." Then he seeks something with which to pay—perhaps a bull or cow. If I, the father, am a rich man I brew beer for the people coming to instruct my child and to say: "It was we who were angry, young man, because you swore at your father. Now may you recover!" While they are drinking the beer they kill the bull, which he found, and eat it.'

Mwambelike (*pagan man*).

'A junior relative who has wronged a senior and later wishes to make friends has to satisfy not only him but his neighbours. For example: A man X seduced a widow of his father who was regarded as the property of his senior half-brother, Y, the heir. (She was not Y's wife, because she was a sister of his mother, but given to deceased's younger half-brother.) Later X paid Y one cow as a fine "for seducing his mother". Then X brought him a bull to re-enter the family and ma e friends, saying: "Indeed, I wronged you, my father." Y said: "If you wish to make friends again you must also bring a cow for the village to eat, so that all shall know that I am satisfied." X brought a heifer calf which was eaten by the village.'

There was no mention of sickness in this case.

24. PROCEDURE IN A WITCHCRAFT CASE (TRADITIONAL)

Mwakionde (doctor, brother of a chief).

'The custom was that if a man was accused of witchcraft he always went to the chief and said: "They have accused me of witchcraft. Please give me witnesses." The chief would send off the man with his accuser and with witnesses to the doctor. If the accuser was proved wrong he had to pay four or five cows, or if he had no cows, a girl, and then after she had borne a child the accused would come to pay cows and be a relative in the end.

'If the ordeal (*umwafi*) convicted both, neither vomiting, the chief would be angry and say: "You are both witches." Then each would pay four cows to the chief who would kill two from each of the four for his men to eat, and both men would move from the country. If both vomited the chief would say: "You are fools; be friendly," and the village headmen would say: "Yes, but the accuser must pay cows to the accused for accusing him."

'Men never went to drink the ordeal without first going to the chief.

'Sometimes the one convicted as a witch was speared and all his cows taken by the chief—none went to the accuser. If the accuser was caught and the accused vomited, four cows went to the accused, and the others to the chief because the accuser was himself a witch. Some who were great witches died of the ordeal.'

Mwaisumo (clerk).

'There was a nasty little chap (*kaliko akandu kamo*[1]) who came from the hills to live at Bijilila, and who built next door to father. This chap was very poor; mother and the other villagers always gave him food. I remember the chap very well—he was very dirty in his person.

'Well, once there was complaint (*ukwijaja*) because the milk supply in the village was small. So this chap fortified himself within and said: "Do not go on complaining, sons of Kihabia, I have seen the witch who is throttling the cows. It is Kimpunga! Catch her, and let her drink *umwafi*." Mother was astounded at being taken; she was dumbfounded at being "caught" for witchcraft, for in her lineage no one had ever been caught. So then she also said: "Indeed, my husbands,

[1] Mwaisumo speaks of him as a thing rather than a person.

take me to the ordeal, and let me drink (*umwafi*)." Mwankaje, my older brother next to me in age, went to drink the *umwafi*. He vomited immediately after he had drunk it. So that nasty little chap, Mwasulama, was defeated. He escaped paying a fine for he was so poor—they beat him a little with sticks. Had he been rich he would have paid mother a cow, for it was customary for one who had been accused of witchcraft but had vomited the *umwafi* to claim compensation for slander in court, and to be paid a cow.

'Long ago when I was a child, when the AbaMpulo were young men, the homestead they built was very rich. Ngemela and Mwasalutaba, and Mwakinene, and Kyula, and Swita, and all the others built there. Swita was a witchfinder. He had power (*amanga*) to catch witches when they throttled the cows. He always went out to the pasture when he knew that there were people who wished to throttle the cows. On one occasion the cows in the village did not give milk. Everyone was called together to complain (*ukwijaja*), and Swita (Mwaitulo), the man who caught the throttlers of cows, was among them. When they were speaking he, Swita, fortified himself with medicines within and said: "Why are you complaining all of you? I, I have seen him who throttles the cows. Let us all come together again here to-morrow, and no one must stay behind." So they all met together there. . . . Formerly it was the custom to call out names. They met together and one man who shouted the names stood a little distance off and the witchfinder who responded stood a little distance off, separately. The first man shouted the names and the witchfinder responded, saying: "Yes!" All the names were called out, but when they came to the name of Mwasalutaba the witchfinder was silent; the name was repeated and he was still silent; the third time the whole company groaned together. Mwasalutaba then said: "Friends, I am astonished, I am not a witch, I do not throttle the cows, so I ask for the ordeal." So the witchfinder said: "Yes indeed, drink *umwafi*, and if it does not convict you then I will pay a cow." So they went with him and told everything to a certain doctor who had built in the country of Mwambebule, in the hills. When they got to the doctor's Mwasalutaba drank the *umwafi*. They addressed it, saying: "We think that our fellow throttles cows, but if we are wrong tell us, you medicine." While they were yet speaking the sun went down, so they said: "The *umwafi* has caught our fellow." They returned home, and they drove him away. His cattle escaped capture though it was the custom when someone was convicted of witchcraft for the chief to take his cattle, and if he chose, to kill for those of that village who were innocent to eat meat. But Mwasalutaba escaped— they only drove him out, for the village was not really his own village, he came from another side. And he has never moved back to the village, nor has he ever been accused again of witchcraft.

'Swita really knows how to catch those who throttle cows for witchcraft. Here is another tale about it: One of the fellows of the AbaMpulo had begotten a child, and the child died. When they had done the autopsy "the owner of the child" said: "They (the witches) have eaten him", and he prepared to move. Then Swita began to speak in secret saying that the so and so's had killed the child. And they of whom he spoke did not come to persuade their fellow, who was preparing to move, to remain. When the chief heard that a man was preparing to move, and his fellows the so and so's did not come to persuade him to stay he called together the whole village, and was very angry with them. When he found that they all agreed he went to Ngemela (the village headman?) and said: "I think that it is they of whom Swita spoke who have killed the child, their cattle will be taken." Ngemela objected very much to taking their cattle, and the chief went to Ngemela's junior saying the same thing, that it was they (of whom Swita spoke) who had killed the child and he, the chief, would take their cattle. But Ngemela's junior also objected and reported to his senior Ngemela, who agreed that he did not wish to take anyone's cattle. The chief agreed, saying: "All right, I shall not take their cattle." But they, in their foolishness, when they heard that the chief had said that it was they who had killed the child of their fellow, and that he would take their cattle, themselves started the matter saying: "We want the ordeal." Their request was agreed to; they were given *umwafi* to drink, and addressed. But they were killing themselves. When they drank the *umwafi* convicted them; they did not vomit. When this happened and chief said: "See! It is as I thought, it is indeed they who killed the child." And he took their cattle and killed some, and people ate the meat. One cow which he took on account of this case is still there, I know it myself, we call it "Lyakakata". Formerly when people were convicted of witchcraft their goods were taken, or they were driven from the village. This tale was told me by a man belonging to the country in which it happened.'

25. THE ORDEAL (*UMWAFI*)

Mwaisumo (clerk).

'I was once given *umwafi*. It was long ago but I remember it very well. It was at the funeral of my mother's younger brother my *umwipwa unnandi*; he died suddenly, and when he was dead some people of the family said that the disease was from my father's side (i.e. from my father's younger brother, *tata unnandi*, my own father was dead at this time); and others said, no, it was from the side of the deceased's new wife—this was his third wife, recently married—he had run away with her from her husband. Those concerned were the deceased's sisters (and their husbands), brothers, wives, and fellow villagers. They said: "Let us drink *umwafi*." So they took two children, I and another, a girl—she was a daughter of the dead man and represented his own house; if she did not vomit then the disease came from within the house (i.e. from one of the wives); I, in the same way, represented my father's house.

'The doctor took some banana leaves and prepared medicine, putting some into each leaf; after a little while they called us and told us to stand apart, a bit away from the house. First the doctor gave the *umwafi* to the girl from her leaf, and then to me from mine. The leaves are kept separate and there are several for each person. All the family drew closer and sat around us. The doctor addressed each of us in turn. I do not remember the words exactly, but it was something like this: "If it was you that has brought sickness, let us see. We are sure it was you that brought the disease." Then we both vomited, she a little before me. If one does not vomit it may be very serious; the poison stays in you and you may die. Then they said: "Well, we do not know where the disease came from." Then they gave us water to wash in and some meat to eat—food is specially put aside for those that drink *umwafi*. This was the end.

'Afterwards it was said that it was the man who was the woman's first husband who had poisoned my mother's brother. We were being tested for sorcery, not witchcraft, as the autopsy had shown that it was a case of sorcery. Having heard this, we did not spread the news; we kept quiet, waited, and watched. And then after a week the dead man's son, my cousin (*untani*), was dead; and that woman ran away. She was frightened. Then we knew it was her former husband who had killed both by sorcery.[1] The family sought the doctor to get

[1] In another text (quoted on p. 256) Mwaisumo explained that the injured husband had used 'the horn', i.e. vengeance magic. Being of the family which suffered Mwaisumo calls it 'sorcery'.

the medicine for the prevention of the disease, and then it was finished. The wife was taken back by the first husband, so the disease could not kill us any more.

'When she went back to him he could not come to us again. (True, he had no reason to do so.) Nothing happened to him. It is not our custom to accuse such people to the chief; we do not exactly know if it is the man, and still we have taken his wife. We were all concerned in this because of my mother. It happened four years before my brother died; there were four years between my uncle's death and his. I was in Tukuyu during the influenza after the war—in 1918—and then I went to Selya the next year, 1919, and my uncle died.

'The procedure is similar in an accusation of witchcraft.'

Mwaikambo (clerk).

'*Umwafi* is always used when someone denies practising witchcraft or theft, or denies that he is a liar. When they[1] have "caught" their fellow in the village and say that it is he who is throttling their cows so that they do not get milk, and the accused man denies it, then they take him to drink *umwafi*. When they have come to the doctor's place they tell him their tale. Two men support the accused and two the accuser. They do not eat when they are going to drink *umwafi*. The doctor first says to the accused: "If you are really guilty of throttling the cows, don't trouble the *umwafi*, but confess." And he replies: "Had I been seen as a witch I would not have come here." And both his supporters say: "Our friend is falsely accused; he has never practised witchcraft."

'The doctor questions the accuser in the same way, saying: "Did you really see your fellow as a witch?" and he and his supporters reply that they saw him.

'So then the doctor gives them *umwafi* to drink. He sprinkles a little powder in tepid water; or sometimes (so they say) he sprinkles the *umwafi* on two freshly cut stumps of banana stem, one representing one side, and one the other. Then the stump in which the "new growth" (? sap: *ulufyogo*) first appears is the one that has "vomited". The "growth" appears the same day that they cut it. The doctor addresses the *umwafi* (*ikupangililaga*) and the others present assist, the supporters of each man addressing him. Then one vomits and those on his side trill, but he who has not vomited is very sad. Then they go home and he who has vomited pays the doctor.

'There is very little drinking of *umwafi* nowadays, but much divination (*ubulagusi*).

[1] i.e. 'the defenders'. Mwaikambo explained, 'A witchcraft accusation always begins with "the defenders" seeing the witches in dreams.'

'There are some in our country who were caught for witchcraft, for "eating" people and throttling cows. The name of one of them was Sumali, but now he is dead; another is Mwaimama. They denied the accusation very strongly; they were brought before the chief (my father) for their case to be judged, and when he had given judgement they said they wished to go to *umwafi*. So they went to the *umwafi*, and when they had drunk it Sumali vomited and Mwaimama was conquered. Nothing happened to him—he was not driven out, they just told him to stop doing such things—but continually, even now, he is accused of witchcraft whenever anything happens. He's not gone to *umwafi* again.

'This happened before I went to school, when I was still herding cows, about 1925 or 1926. I did not see the trial (before the chief) with my own eyes, but I was there when the *umwafi* was administered.

'On another occasion a woman was "caught" for witchcraft when her child died. When they do an autopsy they sometimes find wounds on the right side or on the left. The right side is the side of the man, the left that of the woman. This time they found them on the side of the woman. The woman (i.e. the mother) denied that it was she who had "eaten" the child so they went to *umwafi* and the woman was "conquered" (i.e. proved to be lying). It was not she, in her own person, but a member of her lineage who had "eaten" the child. After the *umwafi* had "spoken" they went to a diviner to discover exactly who the individual was.

'I heard about this from others, but Mwasintobile, the father of the child who died, is a man of our country—I know him.'

26. THE AUTOPSY

Note.—It was not easy to see an autopsy among the Nyakyusa—
one never knew beforehand when such an operation would be held,
and since imputations of witchcraft and sorcery are punishable
offences, people were often reluctant to perform it when Europeans
were there. There was only one European doctor in Rungwe district,
and he was a very busy man with a hospital and dispensaries to super-
vise. All the operations witnessed were performed over twenty-five miles
from his headquarters and far off any road. Therefore, we were never
able to arrange for a qualified practitioner to be present at a Nyakyusa
autopsy, as we wished. The following layman's accounts, though
lacking any anatomical detail, explain the method of procedure, and
the Nyakyusa reactions.

Autopsy (ukupandula) *witnessed by G. W.,* 16/3/37.

Funeral of the wife of Mwampiki: Mwampiki himself is dead, but
his homestead and wives have been inherited by a younger half-
brother, Mwisalwa. The dead woman is a wife of another half-brother,
Mwalemba. Kakuju, the village headman, called me to the funeral.

The body was carried apart, away from the crowd of women, behind
a clump of bananas, by five or six women, who then washed it and put
on a bark-cloth and a cloth (folded tight like a bark-cloth) round the
loins. Then the young man, Mwaijumba, and I were allowed to come
and watch.

The doctor, a woman, had five little knives of bamboo, made for
the autopsy, and thrown away with the rubbish afterwards. Before
she began to cut the stomach open another woman, a wife of Mwampiki (wearing mourning belts and smeared with mud) came and
crouched down with her face close to that of the corpse, and a cloth
covering her head and that of the corpse. 'That is the Nyakyusa
custom', the young man explained. 'She is helping the doctor. The
fearsomeness (*ubusisya*) of a human body is less when someone else
is at the head.'

Then the doctor, using the bamboo knives, made an incision across
the stomach, and cut through the flesh until the intestines showed.
The stomach was swollen up. Mwantembe, a classificatory brother of
Mwampiki, had joined us by this time. He was fetched by Mwaijumba
to come and examine the corpse. He urged the doctor to make the
incision wider and she did so. Mwantembe also insisted on Mwai-

jumba coming close and looking, too. 'Come, Mwaijumba, look, so that another time you will know.' He did not give direct instruction—he was far too much worked up—but he insisted on the other coming to see what was being done and discussed.

At several points the doctor was clearly under the stress of emotion and reluctant to do more than was absolutely necessary—she had to be urged on by Mwantembe. 'Now,' Mwantembe said, 'let us dissect, mother! Let us look well. Let us dissect! Do you say it's a person? No, it's just a log, a piece of firewood!' And several times these words were used by Mwantembe and others to urge her on. 'Do you say it's a person? It's just a log!'

The doctor then pulled out all the contents of the stomach so that Mwantembe and the women could see up into the chest—there was nothing unusual there on either side; then we looked downwards into the loins and found something unusual—a round growth full of blood. I asked if it was a foetus but was told: 'No, it is not; we don't know what it is. We don't ordinarily find that. It is something evil (*lindo*, literally "rubbish"). We are afraid.' The growth was taken out, and also the upper intestine, for there was said to be something unusual about that too, and the liver and something else (*akanongo*). These, I think, are always removed. We were not told of anything unusual about them. The doctor herself made few or no suggestions—it was Mwantembe who did that—she just did the operation silently.

The stench was foul—several of the women put stoppers of banana leaf into both nostrils. Half-way through the woman at the head of the corpse got up, looking overwrought, and went away to a distance. The others said: 'It's all right, it's not a person, just a log' (i.e. there is no need for her to stay). At length the doctor pushed the rest of the organs back into the stomach and tied up the body with a cloth—another was tied over it to make all secure.

The discussion (which had been going on spasmodically all the time) broke out in a flood. People nodded to each other and said: 'Sorcery (*ubutege*)! Look! Look! Sorcery indeed!' The young man, Mwaijumba, told us: 'I dreamed of a medicine. When they were at the funeral [the dead woman had been taken ill while at a funeral at her classificatory father's homestead], before she fell ill, I dreamed in my sleep, I saw someone giving a child a banana, but I caught hold of the banana (all in my sleep). I broke it open and I found a powder there in the banana. So then I sent a message to her (the next day when I was awake), saying: "Come home. You have mourned sufficiently." And that very day I fell ill myself.' He told this with great excitement. Mwantembe also was obviously moved and said several times during the autopsy: 'I'm afraid. I'm afraid.'

Then Kakuju, the village headman, and Kissogata (an old man, a village headman of the previous generation) came to see the results of the autopsy—the things extracted. The doctor had made a small incision in the thing chiefly suspected—the round growth full of blood and measuring five or six inches in diameter. Kakuju got very excited and insisted on her making a bigger incision to see what was inside. 'Look well!' he shouted, 'You are our ordeal (*umwafi*). We know this illness which is killing people in the country. We know it. We know it (passionately). It's sorcery (*ubutege*), is it not?' Mwantembe then said: 'See, it is sorcery, see!' showing him all that had been extracted. Both Kakuju and Kissogota agreed and then Kissogota said: '*Igobe!*' At this word the tension seemed to relax. Kakuju jumped at it. 'Yes, yes (eagerly) *igobe*. Is it not *igobe*, Mwaipaja?' (passionately to me) '*Igobe*,' Mwantembe repeated. '*Igobe*', shouted the women. Kakuju and Kissogota walked away talking. Then all the remains (i.e. the growth, etc.) and the bamboo knives were buried apart in the waste land, and the body was buried in the usual way.

Angombwike later explained that *igobe* was an old word for *ubutege* (sorcery).

Autopsy (ukupandula), *witnessed by G. W.*, 23/3/37.

Funeral of little granddaughter of Mwaihojo (a chief)—daughter of Mwaihojo's son Mwakisisile—aged one year. Child died last night. Funeral at Mwaihojo's homestead.

The doctor, a woman, cut the stomach open crosswise and pulled out the contents of the stomach. 'See that little black thing, branching!' They looked all over thoroughly, up and down. 'Look carefully, people of Selya!' said the doctor. 'You tell lies! You will go and tell lies! Look carefully! See, there is no *ikitasya* (a disease).' All agreed that there was no sign of *ikitasya*, but no positive opinion was expressed till two men had been fetched to look. They came and said: 'Why do you deny it? Why do you not know the disease from ropes (*engoje*)?' 'Yes,' replied the women, 'but we said we should let the men look first.' Before the men came and gave utterance to the word *engoje*, the women had, I think, come to the same conclusion; it was clear from the way the doctor pointed out 'the little black thing, branching' that she was certain what it meant, and they nodded in an understanding way. Only when she asked them: 'Look, what is it?' they would not answer, saying: 'We don't know, you are a doctor who understands these things.' Then, instead of saying what she thought, she asked: 'Aren't the men coming to look?'

The men came back to Mwaihojo and repeated: 'It is the disease from ropes, that binding. The women were uncertain.' 'Yes, indeed,' replied Mwaihojo. 'Whenever did women know how to perform an autopsy? They don't know how to do it. They only know how to close the corpse again, that's all.'

A woman lay down with her head to that of the corpse under cloths. The other women told her to do this, saying: 'At the head, at the head! You are both brave, you, too!'

The doctor removed the liver, two other parts, and the bile sack. This latter she squeezed out on to the leaves, saying: 'Medicine, medicine, she drank much medicine.' All these she wrapped up in leaves and buried in the foot of the grave.

It was explained that the ropes (*engoje*) were those of Mwakisisile. Mwakisisile, the father, had gone mad (*abopaga ikigili*) and had drunk medicine before he had married this woman. 'We forgot to give them both medicine later on. When he went mad we bound him with ropes to take him to the doctor.'

(It is believed that the kinsmen of one bound with ropes will suffer from the disease *engoje* if treatment is not adequate.)

27. WIVES DRIVEN AWAY FOR WITCHCRAFT

Makwelebeja (elderly commoner).

'Many wives are driven away for witchcraft. They are driven away by their husbands. If a man has several wives one may be bad and throttle her husband's cattle, or throttle her husband himself. Then the man goes and complains (*ukwijaja*), saying: "They have destroyed my cattle", or perhaps, "My neighbours have 'eaten' me", whichever it is. When his fellows hear his complaints they say: "Do not accuse outsiders. See! It's your wife." Some women are bad and the husband does not sleep when he is with his other wives; only when he is with her (the witch) does he have a good sleep. She spoils the fertility of her co-wives. Or sometimes all the wives are friendly and agree to spoil the cattle of their husband.

'There is a woman named Kajonga whose husband drove her away for witchcraft because she bewitched the fertility of her co-wives. A long time after her divorce she was married to another man, Mwitoba by name. From that man also she was driven away for witchcraft, but what wrong she had done was not much known. Some time later she died.

'Women who are driven away for witchcraft always remarry; they do not run off with men.'

Njobakosa.

'When a wife was accused she drank *umwafi*. If she was "caught" by the ordeal sometimes her husband drove her away, sometimes he did not. Usually he did not.'

Nsusa.

'Formerly wives were frequently driven away for witchcraft. Such a wife remarried quickly.'

28. FEAR OF HEREDITARY WITCHCRAFT

Mwaisumo (clerk).

'There are some people who, though they wish to marry a certain woman, fear to do so because the mother or father of the girl is a witch. They are afraid to marry because she is the child of a witch. And sometimes a girl loves a particular young man very much, but if his father is repeatedly accused of witchcraft her parents refuse to allow the marriage, because the young man's father is a witch. Such was the case of a certain young man, in the country of Mwaijande, who loved a particular girl very much. Her father was said to be a witch (*undosi*) a maker of wild animals;[1] he was said especially to make leopards. The parents of the young man objected very much to his marrying this girl whose father was a witch, the mother of the young man objected even more than her husband, saying: "No! She is a witch; witches always go in the lineage (*ikikolo*), and she will also be a witch when she grows up and comes to the house" (i.e. her husband's house). The father of the young man and the father of the girl were next-door neighbours, their homesteads adjoined. The matter was only spoken of in whispers, but I heard about it because the brother-in-law of the young man (the husband of his full sister) was my friend, and he told me about it.

'And again, a certain man who was always said to be a witch made love to a woman who was a widow, the husband who had married her having died. They agreed together that they should marry. When the parents of the woman heard they objected very much, saying: "That man is a witch." The women was not yet old—she was quite young. Her husband had died but there was no one to inherit her. So then she refused the man (who had made love to her) saying: "I do not love you." Her parents argued against the marriage, saying: "We do not like it" and they persuaded her to leave the man, saying: "You know yourself that when he beats you you will think, 'I am married to a witch'." For she was grown up and her parents could not compel her if she loved him, though if she had been a child they would have been able to object and compel her to do what they wished. But she (though she was grown up) followed the advice of her parents and left him and refused to marry him.

---

[1] There was some doubt whether this man should be classed as a witch or a sorcerer. In this text Mwaisumo refers to him as *undosi*, but elsewhere he was spoken of as a sorcerer (*vide supra*, pp. 124, 252).

'And again, a long time ago, my brother Mwamoto went to betroth a girl at the place of that man who was a witch. Mwanama objected very much to his younger brother's action, saying: "You should not marry at that man's place, everyone says he is a witch." But Mwamoto paid no attention to any of them—others also tried to persuade him not to marry the child of a witch. He married her and she is with him now, as his wife.

'People fear witchcraft in a husband or wife lest he or she bring witchcraft into the house, and they have children who become witches when they grow up. As I explained witchcraft runs in a lineage (*ikikolo*). It is especially women who object to their children marrying or being married by a witch, it is they (the women) who forbid the children, and their husbands also object. I remember once that a certain man came to make love to my sister. The mother of this man was spoken of as a witch, and my mother objected very much, saying: "Do not desire this young man's cattle, I do not like him even though you do. His mother's witchcraft is much spoken about." He had come to betroth the girl when she was still very young. The others agreed to what my mother said and refused the young man, saying: "We have not got a child yet (ready for marriage), she of whom you speak must first grow up." '

In reply to questions Mwaisumo explained that people fear to marry witches lest their children be witches and be driven from country to country. 'We say it is bad to be driven out. A man is never driven out because of the witchcraft of his wife—he used to divorce her if it were proved—but a girl's parents will refuse to give their daughter in marriage to a young man from a family of witches because if he is convicted of witchcraft she will be driven out with him.'

We were also told of a young Christian who had been refused by a number of women. It was whispered that this was because his father was a sorcerer. Later on, however, he married and the talk died down.

29. CHRISTIAN SCEPTICISM OF WITCHCRAFT

Nsangalufu (Christian Elder, an early convert).

'At first when we repented, the missionaries asked us whether we believed in witchcraft, and we said: "Yes, there is witchcraft", and we told them about it and the wounds found in the bellies of people who have been killed by witchcraft. So the missionaries said to us: "When there is a death tell us, and we shall go and look." I was taken once by Klaus (a missionary) to a death. I was afraid to go near the corpse—everyone was afraid—but the missionary stood over the grave and looked at the corpse and even put his hand inside (the stomach). The person was said to have died of *igobe* (a kind of sorcery), but Klaus said he had died of a disease of the chest. He told people to come and look. Mwaipopo (the chief) was there but he refused to come and look; they all refused. After some time I came and Klaus showed me. In this way we have been and examined corpses, and we have never seen the wounds of witchcraft. . . . Klaus used to go round to funerals, examining corpses. . . . Ndabele here has seen a corpse which the pagans said had a python. Last week Ndabele went to a funeral near Itete and the pagans said there was a python inside; the woman (who had died) had been a witch. He said: "Let's see the python, let's see it", but no one could show it to him.'

30. SORCERY

Mwakionde (doctor, brother of a chief).

'When they open a dead person and find the intestines red, black and white in different parts, they say the death is due to sorcery (*ubutege*). They go to the doctor and get medicine for the relatives.

'Sorcery comes very quickly, especially when they have done an autopsy. Then the one who takes the body in her arms, and the one who buries after the operation, die very quickly. If the body has been opened the disease spreads very quickly. In one case thirty people died, mostly relatives. In another case, a wife, a girl child, a mother, a father's sister, and a son-in-law (husband of the girl child) all died. The wife died one day, next day the girl child and her mother, then the father's sister, then the husband of the girl. Autopsies were performed on the first three.'

31. DEATHS ATTRIBUTED TO 'THE HORN'

Mwaisumo (clerk).

'My mother's brother died from the sorcery (*ubutege*) of Mwakaliku the younger. His death came about in this way: He had run off with a woman whose name I have forgotten now, and the "owner" of the woman continually stirred "the horn" that all those concerned should die, if they did not return his wife. Almost immediately my uncle fell ill and died; shortly afterwards the child of his elder brother, Mwakyando, fell ill and died three days later. Then we understood that it was this woman who brought the illness, for her husband boasted to people that it was he who had killed members of our family. We drove away the woman in order to end the sickness among us. Perhaps if we had not sent her away the illness would have spread and killed many of us and our wives also.'

32. PROCEDURE IN WITCHCRAFT CASES (MODERN)

Nsusa (village headman).

Question: 'How do you manage about witchcraft cases nowadays?'

'We judge them openly but we do not have them written in the court book. When "a defender" has seen his fellow throttle someone, he tells us, and we judge that witch. It is "the defenders" (*abamanga*) who see the witches. Perhaps "the defender" comes out of his house by night and calls out: "I see so and so throttling so and so! Listen to-morrow."

'Yes, that happens nowadays.

'When someone tells us in this way we agree; the witch is driven out. Yes, even though he denies it, we say: "You are a witch. You are a thief. Even though you do not admit it, get out of the country." But formerly they went to the ordeal.'

Question: 'Now you just accept the word of the defender?'

'Yes, formerly if a man denied guilt when he was accused he went to the ordeal, and the *umwafi* "caught" the witch. Now since the Europeans have forbidden the use of *umwafi* we accept the word of "the defenders". Look, they (the defenders) *see* witches. Yes, in dreams.'

Question: 'What about the man who accused the wife of Mwakobela?'

'He denied it. He said: "I did not see her", so on that account we said: "Since you have slandered her you must pay thirty shillings." But had he really seen her and told us properly we would have overcome the woman in argument and divorced her from her husband, but he denied it, saying: "I did not see her", and we all said: "The woman is not a witch; who has seen her?"

'If a woman is divorced for witchcraft there is no fine, the husband gets back his cows, that is all.'

Question: 'And the friend of Mwambuputa?'

'He was really a witch. They said: "You, Mwambuputa, we will convict you of witchcraft yourself if you are friendly with him."

'And if a man is fined because he has accused his fellow of witchcraft without seeing him, really, we do not write that in the book either.

'No, *umwafi* is not used; the Europeans and the chiefs and the village headmen have strictly forbidden it.'

From the Records of the First Class Subordinate Court of Rungwe

Criminal case, 11/1935.   *Heard* 5/3/35 *before P. M. Huggins.*
                                L. Rouquette, prosecuting.
                                Rex v. *Musa, son of Hassani.*

Charge: 'By actions and statement representing himself to have power of witchcraft and supplying instruments of witchcraft (green leaves) to one Mwakalobo, son of Mwakalobo.'
Charge read and explained.
Accused pleaded not guilty.

Mwakalobo, headman[1] *of Kapya, a pagan (complainant).*

'About two months ago a man called Bakowike came to me at Ikapu, stating that he had been sent by the accused to warn me that there was a conspiracy to bewitch me, on the part of one Mwakagiri and Mwaka-tumbula, because I was supposed to have taken some of the former's country. I told Bakowike to tell the accused to come and tell his own tale. The accused came that same day at about sundown. We entered the house and then he called me outside to talk to me. Prior to doing this he told me that Mwakagiri had given him four cows to arrange my death as the former stated that I was in possession of his land. He said that if I gave him a cow he would take no action. I did so. He also gave me some ground-up green leaves which he instructed me to mix with water and drink. He alleged that this potion would render me immune from witchcraft.

'The accused went off with the cow. Kikomile (X), Kyongalala (Y), and Mahandi (Z) and three of my wives were present during the above conversation.

'About a week later Mwakagiri came to visit me—I had sent for him. I did not welcome him—I told him I had heard that he was after my life. He asked me who had said this and I indicated the accused. He then told me that the accused had made the same statements about me to him. I then came and reported to the D.O. I threw away the medicine that the accused had given me. Relations have recently been strained between Mwakagiri and myself.'

In reply to question by accused: 'Yes, I sent for you but only because you sent Bakowike to me first to warn me.'

First witness, a brother of the complainant, confirmed his story, having been present when both Bakowike and the accused came to the complainant. He added these points:

[1] Probably a minor chief (*umalafyale*), not a village headman (*ulifumu*). The report of the case was in English.

'Mwakagiri wished to kill Mwakalobo over a land dispute and sub-chief Mwakatumbula also desired to do so, as he did not obey orders. Mwakalobo said he would not drink the powder (given by the accused) except in the presence of all his sons. . . . Bakowike was known to me, he lives at Isagula in Mwakatumbula's country, and Mwakalobo is married to two of his sisters.'

Second witness, Mwangambo, a classificatory brother of Mwaka-lobo, entirely confirmed Mwakalobo and the first witness. He also was present when both Bakowike and the accused came. Also, he said:

'I was present subsequently when Mwakalobo sent for Mwakagiri. Both of them stated in conversation that the accused had informed them that each had designs on the life of the other.'

In reply to a question by the accused: 'You did not spend the night with us, nor did you drink beer; there was none. We didn't drink the medicines.'

In reply to a question by the court: 'Yes, Bakowike came back again with the accused.'

A henchman ('*capitao*') of Mwakalobo confirmed the above stories.

Bakowike confirmed the other stories. He said: 'The accused and Mwakyangile with whom the accused lived (Mwakyangile is also a doctor) came and told me that Mwakagiri had come and informed the accused that he wanted to kill Mwakalobo, and had given him four cows for the purpose. He asked me if I was a relative of Mwakalobo's. I told him that I was; then he advised me to go and warn him, which I did that day. Mwakalobo then told me to fetch Musa (the accused). I called him and Mwakyangile the same evening.'

In reply to a question by the accused: 'I did not come to your house. I did not give you a goat in exchange for medicine for my wife.'

In reply to a question by the court: 'I had never heard of Musa before. He lives across a stream about one and a quarter miles away.'

In reply to a question by the accused: 'We did not sleep at Mwaka-lobo's.'

Note by the court: Impression that this witness had previously met the accused, probably buying medicine from him as stated by the accused, but is afraid of acknowledging the association.

Mwakagiri: 'It is true that Mwakalobo and I have had a dispute about land. I have never met Mwakalobo on any occasion on which we have accused each other of invoking witchcraft against each other, but on various occasions Mwangambo (the second witness) was sent by Mwakalobo to inquire why I was bewitching him. I told Mwangamo I was doing nothing of the sort. This was about a month ago. No one else was present. I did not learn how Mwakalobo came to suspect me.

I have often met the accused; he came and took a wife from my country. The accused is a doctor. I do not know why Mwakalobo should say that I met him. It is a lie.'

Mwakalobo was called. He said: 'Mwangambo (the second witness) is a nephew of Mwakagiri. I sent him to call Mwakagiri. He came back the same day with Mwakagiri and Nyomilela.'

Mwangambo when recalled confirmed this, adding: 'I live under Mwakalobo.'

Nyomilela: 'I know of no meeting of Mwakalobo and Mwakagiri. They were disputing over land. I heard from Mwakagiri that his nephew Mwangambo had told him that Mwakalobo accused him of exercising witchcraft against him. I am no relative of either party. I never went with Mwakagiri to meet Mwakalobo.'

Note of the court: I am of the impression that Mwakagiri and Nyomilela are hiding something. Their evidence is not given in a straightforward manner.

Accused (Musa): 'I have never received four cows from Mwakagiri. True, I went to Mwakalobo's house. He called me to prescribe for his impotency. He paid me with a cow. I was surprised at this as it is not customary to receive payment till a cure is effected.'

In reply to a question by the court: 'No one approached me with a view to exercising malignant witchcraft. I do not know why I should have been dragged into this. Perhaps Mwakalobo heard I had gone to Mwakagiri's country. I only went there to see my father-in-law. I gave Mwakalobo medicine to cure his impotency. I warned him that it would be no use for his trouble, but he insisted on having it. Yes, he even insisted on giving me the cow as a pledge of friendship. I did not know why he was so positive and wanted to be friendly with me. This is the first gift of that nature that I have received. I have been three months in Isangulu. I am on my way to my home at Mwaya. I stopped at Isangula because I was suffering from a boil. All my relatives live in Sangu country.'

In reply to a question by the prosecution: 'I was myself surprised that as a resident of three months' standing I should have been suspected by Mwakalobo of witchcraft.'

In reply to a question by the court: 'Mwakyangile was present with me at Mwakalobo's. I went to call him.'

Note by the court: There is no question that this evidence is given glibly, and carries no conviction. The demeanour of the accused is that of a man seeking for a way out of a trying situation.

Mwakyangile told a different story from Musa. 'Mwakalobo wanted treatment for his children, who were suffering from *ikitasya* (a disease). He wanted nothing for himself.'

In reply to a question of the court: 'He did not complain of impotence.'

In reply to a question by the accused: 'We did not discuss bewitching anybody.'

Order

'There is in my opinion no doubt that the accused is guilty of practising witchcraft for reward, and is causing fear and annoyance. Section 5 of the Witchcraft Ordinance virtually prohibits any effective and rapid steps being taken to combat witchcraft. Section 5 (i) necessitates the delay of trial by High Court, and the offence disclosed is not covered by it, whereas Section 5 (2) necessitates obtaining from His Excellency the Governor both sanction to prosecute and confirmation of any sentence imposed. Under the circumstances, and in view of the delay that has already taken place, permission is granted by the police to withdraw their request for sanction to prosecute under Section J (2).

'By virtue of the powers conferred on me by Section 8 cap. 21, Musa, son of Hassani, is ordered to reside at Mwaya and to report once a month at the District Office, pending such decision as the Provincial Commissioner shall make, following a request that he should exercise the powers conferred on him by Section 8 (3) to order Musa, son of Hassani, to reside in his own domicile, Usangu.'

The Provincial Commissioner agreed to the request and Musa is now in Sangu country.

33. SETTLEMENT OF DISPUTES IN CHRISTIAN VILLAGES

a. Christian suing a Christian

> Mundekesye (appointed by the Church to settle disputes in villages on Itete mission land).

'Nsangalofu (a Christian elder) accused Jonah's son, Lwimkio, of making love to the wife of Nsangalofu's son, Nkisu. I (Mundekesye) was trying the case between Nkisu and Lwimiko. Lwimiko denied everything, but Nkisu's wife said: "Yes, he was making love to me; he did so on three occasions." I gave judgement, saying: "You Lwimiko, are guilty, because the woman admits it," and ordered Lwimiko to pay a cow. Lwimiko refused, so I took the case to the Court. I reported my decision and Lwimiko's refusal to pay. The Court asked Lwimiko why he refused to pay up when the woman admitted their guilt, and ordered him to pay a cow.

'I reported the case to Mwangomo (the chief in whose country Mundekesye lives), but as it was quite clear I took it direct to Court. Difficult cases I take to Mwangomo before they go on to Court.

'Nsangalofu and Nkisu brought the case to me. I called the elders of the Church to be present at the hearing of the case. The congregation notified Mwakapelela (the European missionary who lives on another station) and he ordered that Lwimiko should move off mission land. Lwimiko and Nkisu had both built in Mpanda (a boys' village on mission land).'

b. Arbitration between Christians

> Asagene (Christian deacon in Itete).

'Mogege accused Amanise of stealing a cloth belonging to him, and brought Amanise before his fellows. He brought him to Rheuben, near whom he lives.

'Amanise denied the accusation, so the case was taken to Mundekesye (vide supra). Mundekesye tried the case with "all the congregation" (i.e. elders and deacons and anyone who cared to attend the court) and found Amanise guilty. The case was then taken before the missionary who ordered that Amanise should be fined 5s. and suspended from membership of the Church. He also ordered that should he refuse to pay he should move off mission land, because this was the second occasion on which he had been found guilty of theft. (The elders of the congregation had suggested turning Amanise off mission land immediately, but the missionary advised giving him a second chance and fining him.)'

34. SETTLEMENT OF DISPUTES BETWEEN PAGANS AND CHRISTIANS

a. Christian suing a pagan

Twijulege (Christian man).

'Anisile (a Christian elder) and Kujobanabatwa (a pagan) had a dispute. Cattle belonging to Anisile and his fellows ate Kujobanabatwa's crop. Anisile went to drive the cattle out of the field and Kukobanabatwa met him as he was driving them out. Kujobanabatwa swore at Anisile. So Anisile got angry and went to the chief; the chief took the case to Court and Kujobanabatwa was found guilty and ordered to pay 10s. He paid up and the case was finished.'

b. Arbitration between pagan and Christian

'L. (a Christian preacher) when he was visiting the Ngoni[1] in the bush country bought rice from a pagan Ngoni, Manana, and promised to pay him later on. He was a long time in paying his debt so the Ngoni went to Ulindula, an elderly Christian living near L., saying: "L. has my shilling. He took my rice." L. agreed that he owed the Ngoni a shilling; he said that he had not yet got the money, but would get it very soon. The Ngoni went home and after some time, as he was not paid, he came again. Ulindula tried to pacify him. The Ngoni said: "If the case defeats you, I shall go to Court." So Ulindula called his fellows Rheuben and Hoseah to pacify the Ngoni, and the latter agreed to wait; but still L. did not pay up. So when the missionary visited, the Ngoni took the case to him. How it was decided (by the missionary) no one knows.'

c. Pagan suing a Christian

Mwaisumo (clerk).

'Mwansepe, a pagan man, has a young son who was once bathing in a stream when Anangisye, a Christian, came down to bathe also. Anangisye said to the boy: "Get out, I want to bathe." The boy replied: "See, I was bathing here first", at which Anangisye got angry and beat the boy.

'Then Mwansepe and his son hastened to Mundekesye's court

[1] There are one or two villages of Ngoni immigrants in the strip of unoccupied bush country between Selya and the Lake-shore plain. They mix very little with the Nyakyusa.

(*vide supra*) and Mundekesye tried the case with his friends and judged that Anangisye should pay two shillings. Anangisye refused to pay, so Mundekesye took the case to Mwangomo (the chief in whose country the land on which the Christian village Anangisye lived in is situated) and there judgement was given that Anangisye should pay three shillings. Anangisye agreed to do so.'

35. JOINT RESPONSIBILITY OF NEIGHBOURS

Mwaikambo (clerk).

'In former times people did not live at peace as we do now. Because they fought frequently they never were friendly with those of other villages as they are to-day. The occasion for beginning a fight was usually a dispute over women or cattle. If a man had made love to a woman of another village he got a friend to steal her for him. Then if the "owners" of the woman saw them they told their chief that men of such and such a village had run off with "their wife". Their chief allowed all his people to go to recapture "their wife". Also those who had stolen the woman told their chief that they had a case against them, they had stolen someone's wife. Then the chief replied that they should tell everyone to be ready.'

Mwamgwanda (old pagan man).

'In the old days if one man A, had "eaten" the cow of another, B, living in a different chiefdom, and failed to repay it, though B came frequently to claim his cow, and if the wife of a village neighbour of A visited in B's country, B might seize her and take her to his chief, saying: "This woman is the wife of C, a neighbour of A, who has 'eaten' my cow." Then the chief sent to the chief of A's country, saying that they had caught the wife of C and they wanted the cow due from A. Then A would send the cow and B would send back the wife of C with a bull to say: "Thank you, you have settled my case." Then the husband, C, might demand a hoe as well. If A denied his debt when the message came, and asserted that B's friends had seized the woman without cause, his chief would send him to B's chief, saying: "My man denies the charge. Let them drink *umwafi*." Then A and B would take the ordeal in B's country.'

36. MOVING

Mwanjala.

'Lukama's father had built in the country of the chief, Mwaikuju, and Lukama moved and went to the country of Mwasyika. He returned to Mwaikuju's of his own accord, and when he had been there a considerable time his wife fell ill, so he moved again to Mwasyika's. After three months his fellows came to fetch him, and they put him into his own old house. They told him to choose whether he would go to his own old homestead, or to another, and of his own accord he chose to build on another site, but he occupied his own old house temporarily. After a year and a half had passed, his wife fell very ill again, and he went to Mwasyika's. He had been there a month when his fellows— those from his other age-village (in Mwaikuju country)—came to fetch him. They put him into another man's house and he lived with him there. He ate his own food for he was the owner of the homestead —a stranger eats of the bananas of strangers. After he had been there some time, but before he had built a house, his wife fell ill again, and he went to Mwasyika's country where he is still.'

In reply to a question: 'It is customary to fetch a man who has moved because people mostly move on account of illness. Hence, the man's fellows say: "If we do not fetch him it appears as if it were we who had driven him away, as if we had done that which caused him to move." '

Kimbolela.

'Mwapefya moved and went to Mwankenja's country. He moved on account of his own illness. Before he had been away long his fellows (i.e. village neighbours) went to fetch him. He was only away perhaps four or five months. When they brought him back they put him into his old house, for no one had taken it. He took his food from where he had cultivated previously, for as he had not been away long there were still sweet potatoes in his field. He came the first time they went to fetch him.'

Details from various informants, in reply to a question about three new huts being built.

'Three young men have just moved from the village of Mwafula to the village of Mwamunda, because someone had accused them, saying:

"You're making love to my wife", and the man who made the accusation was from the family of the chief. On account of this, they said: "The chief is driving us out. Let us move." All three moved because of this case and are building here. Of the three friends who were supposed to be seducing the minor chief's wife, one had been found at night-time in the suspected woman's hut, and had been fined 12s. for "making love to the woman" though they had not been found together.'

Record of G. W., 20/4/35 (from various informants).

'The chief Mwaipopo was sick, and living "in the forest", i.e in a recently settled and cultivated area at a distance from the main population of his chiefdom. Nsusa, one of the headmen of his classificatory son and heir Mwankuga (cf. p. 183) went to see him. On his return Nsusa said to Mwankuga: "Mwaipopo told me that you, Mwankuga, were poisoning him. Mwkanyamale (a doctor) says that your doctors are in the hills, you went to fetch them there." Then Mwankuga went to his father Mwaipopo and asked him: "Is it true that you are accusing me of working sorcery against you? Do you say so yourself?"

'Mwaipopo said: "Who told you of this Mwankuga?"

'Mwankuga: "Nsusa told me."

'Mwaipopo: "It was Nsusa who told me that you were working sorcery against me! Go and ask him about it, and have it out with him."

'So Mwankuga took the case to Mwakisisya (another chief) for arbitration.

'Mwakisisya said: "Nsusa is in the wrong and must pay a cow to his chief Mwankuga."

Nsusa refused.

'So Mwakisysya said: "All right, we shall go to those who know about the case", and he came with all his men to Mwenanganga, Mwaipopo's senior village headman (i.e. the representative of Mwansambe, vide p. 181). There a witness gave evidence, saying: "I was with Mwankuga when Nsusa told him that Mwaipopo accused him of sorcery." Nsusa denied it.

'Mwakisisya said: "I, Mwakisisya, I have finished, Nsusa must pay a cow."

'Nsusa still refused.

'Mwankuga: "Your honour the judge, and others. I have cows, I shall not ask for his cow, but let him leave my country and build elsewhere."

'Nsusa replied that he was hoeing near Mwaipopo in the forest, and sleeping there, and he refused to move. Then Nsusa wrote a letter (he begged a sheet of paper from the clerk of the court and got a Christian, Mbokigwe, to write for him) and sent it to Tukuyu (i.e. to the District Officer.) All the village headmen were very angry.

'Then one of Nsusa's cows fell into a crater-lake and was drowned. An autopsy was done and "wounds" were found in the animal's stomach. It was said that it had been killed by witchcraft. Nsusa moved to Mbambo, because, he said, "They are killing my cows". Then Mwaipopo fetched him to build in the forest. Nsusa replied that he would prefer to go home, and Mwaipopo agreed, but said he must first pay two cows. "I," said Mwaipopo, "am satisfied, but your friends there are angry, you have done wrong to Mwankuga; you can go if you pay two cows." Nsusa refused and got angry and wrote to Tukuyu again, saying: "Mwaipopo never comes to Court. He spends all his time drinking in the forest, and I, Nsusa, have judged all the cases myself in Court. Now that I am away from Court the cases are not judged; all is silent."

'The clerks at Tukuyu recognized that the stamp and the hand-writing were not those of the court clerk, so they wrote to Mwaipopo. He was angry and imprisoned Nsusa for three months. The District Officer advised Mwaipopo not to let Nsusa return to his country, so when he came out of prison Nsusa built in the country of Mwangomo. This was a year or so ago, and the day before yesterday the village headmen went to fetch him. He is here, sleeping in the house of Kasisi, in Igembe. Eight men went to fetch Nsusa, carrying his household stuff and driving back the cattle. (We saw them.) 'Yes, Mwaipopo must have agreed, for if a chief drives away a man no commoner can take the initiative in fetching him back.'

'Nsusa killed a bull and also provided two pots of beer, one for the men of Igembe and one for the men of Lugombo. His own village was Lugombo, together with Itiki (cf. p. 183). He killed the bull at the house of Kasisi where he is staying. He has not yet been given a homestead.'

37. FETCHING HOME A PRIVATE INDIVIDUAL

Ilolo village, 19/9/37.

Five young men ran past our house (which was on the main village street), carrying mats and calabashes.

Angombwike: 'They have gone to fetch one of Porokoto's men who had moved elsewhere. A son of Porokoto (the chief) went with the others to fetch him back. That is as if the chief had gone himself; he loves him. It is customary for people to seize the mats of the man who has moved. If he objects they do not agree to his objections. They say: "You have spent time here. Let's be off!" They just snatch his mats. The man who has moved agrees and tells them to go, he will follow, and he comes later.

'When he comes they put him in a house where he stays for two or three days; then he asks: "How about a home, friends?" Then they point out a homestead to him. If he does not like it he refuses it and they agree and tell him to choose one for himself, which he does.

'But if he does not agree to come perhaps he sends a son to build here; perhaps he comes but after he has spent two or three days he says: "I am going; I want to return to where I was, so he goes."

'When they go to fetch a man they always run off with his mats.'

38. BRINGING HOME A VILLAGE HEADMAN

Mwambuputa's home-coming

Mwambuputa is the senior headman of Mwankuga who had fled to the Lake-shore plain from fear of 'the breath' of his men (cf. pp. 229–30). He was brought back with ceremony. His return also brought to a head an old land dispute (cf. pp. 188–90). For the status of the personalities concerned consult the table of villages and headmen on pp. 181–5.

Record of G. W., 1/5/35.

'I visited Tandale (Mwainyobolela) the village headman of Busikali and the man chosen to bury chiefs. Katolile (the village headman by inheritance of Bujenga, and a brother of Jane, Kasitile's wife) turned up with two others to fetch him to the home-coming of Mwambuputa (Mwafungo)[1] in Igembe. We picked up Kikalango (a junior son of the chief Mwaipopo) on the way and he and Tandale told me the following story:

"Mwambuputa went to the Lake-shore plain (MuNgonde). Then Mwankuga I (the young chief), while he was still alive, found a cow and the village headmen went off with it to fetch Mwambuputa home. Mwankuga did not go himself. This cow was kept by Mwambuputa, not eaten. It was to say to him; 'Come back, my headman.' Then Mwambuputa agreed and said: 'I will return, take my son back with you now.' So they came back. Then Mwankuga I died, and Mwambuputa came up to his funeral and put up temporary huts to live in, and he has not since been back to MuNgonde. Yes, he could have built proper houses before this ceremony, had he wished, it is not forbidden."

'Those who come to this gathering are his fathers (i.e. the men of Mwaipopo) and his friends (i.e. the men of Mwankuga), all commoners—no chiefs come to this ceremony. And in fact neither Mwaipopo nor Mwankuga II was there, nor did I see any of Mwaipopo's brothers. Kikalango and Kititu (junior sons of Mwaipopo) came to accompany me. We arrived at Mwambuputa's huts with Ngulyo, about noon. About 100 men were present. I noticed Mwambuputa himself, Kakuju, Ngulyo, Tandale, Katotile, and Mwaseba (Kabolile).

[1] Some informants used the name 'Mwambuputa', others 'Mwafungo'. To avoid confusion we use only the former.

'I was told: "The meaning of the ceremony is this: Mwambuputa says to us: 'My fathers, you sent for me, I have come'; and then they show him a place to build, saying: 'You, friend, this is your homestead here.' " At noon Kakuju explained: "Now Mwansambe the senior headman of Mwaipopo (actually he has inherited this position and lives in another chiefdom, coming here for cases and ceremonies) has gone to announce to Mwaipopo that: 'Your child has returned'. Mwaipopo will send him back saying to him: 'Thank you for telling me, my headman, do you go and perform the ceremony and ritual (*ukatendekesye, ukanyagule*) he is your child, you are his father.' Then he will return here and say: 'I have told Mwaipopo, let us go and show Mwambuputa his new homestead.' These huts of Mwambuputa's are on the old men's side, it is Bujege here. He will be given a homestead in Igembe. He had no place in Igembe, he was a stranger. So after the funeral of Mwankuga I, he went to the old men and was given a homestead, and bananas to eat here. A man named Mwanbenja had them before, but he moved to Mwangomo's country. Now they will go and give him a homestead in Igembe. He did build before in Igembe, but he spent a long time on the plain, and others have built there." (For another version cf. pp. 188–90.)

'Then Kakujo asked Kikalango: "Have they told Mwankuga?" Kikalango replied: "I do not know." Kakuju explained to me: "They should tell him, 'Your man has returned'." Mwansambe (Mwegama) came back and called the old village headmen together for a discussion. Then he led us off to Igembe, to the homestead of Mbuluko Mwaipopo a cross-cousin (*untani*) of the chief. Just before we got there Mwansambe turned to Tandale and the other senior men and said: "Look after Mwambuputa in the war by night, look after him in dreams."

'Kititu and Kikalango explained that "Mbuluko is Mwakalungu and Mwaipopo;[1] now they have come here he will have to move and give place to Mwambuputa. At first he refused, but they pacified him. He cannot refuse, he will move. They just considered where it would be best for the village headman to be." And, previously, on the way, they had told me that to whatever house we came, the householder would have to move and give place.

'Two bulls, one full-grown, and one a little smaller, had been promised by Mwambuputa, and were brought with us. Mwanjinga, son of Mwansambe killed them both. Mwansambe said to the village headmen: "We give Mwambuputa to you, Mwakwese, and you (here he mentioned other village headmen whose names are not in my notes). He was in exile (*ndisu*), he has returned." A woman, wife of the house-

---

[1] The implication is that Mbuluko inherited through his mother from his grandfather, Mwaipopo I, but we did not pursue this.

holder, brought out a dish of cooked beans and set them down. The two men nearest took and shared them. The division of meat was carried out by Mwansambe in collaboration with his senior colleagues. It was as follows:

1 ribs and saddle (*akakwa*) to Mwaipopo (chief)
1 ribs and saddle to Mwankuga (young chief)
1 hump to Mwaipopo
1 hump and liver to me (sent with me when I went home).

'It was explained that "If it had been an ordinary killing we would have sent both ribs and saddle to Mwaipopo, one for Kalinga, and one for Kalobo (the two chief wives), now we send one to Mwankuga because it is his ceremony."

1 leg to the men of Bujege ⎫
1 leg to the men of Bujenga ⎪
1 leg to the men of Nkyemo ⎬ 4 senior age-villages of Mwaipopo
1 leg to the men of Ndupando ⎭

1 leg to the men of Igembe ⎫
1 leg to the men of Ipoma ⎪
2 legs to the men of Njesi and ⎬ 4 senior age-villages of
  their juniors the men of ⎪   Mwankuga
Mponga ⎭

'Mwakatika of Mponga, the headman of the village immediately junior to Njesi had not come, so Kakuju of Njesi divided two legs, one for his own village Njesi, and one for Mponga.

'I went home with Kititu and Kikalango and two children sent to carry my meat. On the way Kititu said: "The leg of Igembe will be divided up at Mwambuputa's place (i.e. where it was killed) into four parts. The four villages of Igembe will each get their share: each of these four groups will have a pot, but the meat will be no further divided.

Igembe, 1 pot
Lugombo, 1 pot
Katumba, 1 pot
Nkibonde, 1 pot ('They eat with the men of Igembe'.)"

'(This was confirmed the following day by a young man of Katumba who had eaten some of the meat.)

'Kabolile Mwaseba of Ipoma came with his younger men also. Mwalisu Mwaijonga is his assistant headman and he was there, but Kabolile cooked all the meat together, in one pot. It was explained that "While in Igembe we have many villages it is not so in Ipoma.

There is Ndongoti, true, but they always eat with their elders. The men of Igembe are the oldest of all, they are inheriting from the men of Bujege as they die. They are senior to the men of Ipoma who are their juniors. The men of Ipoma did go through the 'coming out', but with their elders. Mwalisu has no separate village."

'About the ceremony I was told "Mwambuputa took the initiative, he sent a message to Mansambe saying: 'I have returned' and Mansambe told the others." And someone else explained that, "Before Mwambuputa killed the bulls we did not see that he had come back; now he has returned." '

BIBLIOGRAPHY ON THE NYAKYUSA-NGONDE PEOPLE

Cotterill, H. B., 'On the Nyassa and a Journey from the North End to Zanzibar', *Proceedings of the Royal Geographical Society*, XII, (1878)

Dixey, F., 'The Distribution of Population in Nyasaland', *Geographical Review*, XVIII (New York, 1928).

Elton, J. F., *Travels and Researches among the Lakes and Mountains of Eastern and Central Africa* (London: John Murray, 1879).

Fotheringham, L. M., *Adventures in Nyassaland: a two years' struggle with Arab slave dealers in Africa** (London: Sampson Low, Marston, Searle & Rivington 1891).

Fülleborn, F., *Beitrage zur physischen Anthropologie der Nord-Nyassalander*, 2 vols. (Berlin: Dietrich Reimer, 1902).

Das Deutsche Njassa-und-Ruvuma-Gebiet, with Atlas* (Berlin: Dietrich Reimer 1906).

Hall, R. de Z., 'Nyakyusa Law from Court Records', *African Studies*, II (1943). 'Local Migration in Tanganyika',* *African Studies*, IV (1945).

Hamilton, J. T., *Twenty Years of Pioneer Missions in Nyasaland* (Bethelem, U.S.A.: Bethlehem Printing Co., 1912).

Johnston, H. H., 'British Central Africa', *Proceedings of the Royal Geographical Society*, XII (New Series, 1890).

British Central Africa (London: Methuen, 1897).

Kerr-Cross, D., 'Geographical Notes on the Country between Lakes Nyassa, Rukwa, and Tanganyika',* *The Scottish Geographical Magazine*, VI (1890).

'Crater-lakes north of Lake Nyasa', *The Geographical Journal*, V (1895).

Lugard, F. D., *The Rise of our East African Empire*,* 2 vols. (Edinburgh and London: Blackwood & Sons, 1893).

MacKenzie, D. R., *The Spirit-Ridden Konde** (London: Seeley, Service & Co., 1925).

Merensky, A., 'The Konde Country', *The Geographical Journal*, II (1893.)

Deutsche Arbeit am Njassa* (Berlin, Berliner evang. Missionsges; (1894).

Moir, F. L. M., *After Livingstone* (London: Hodder & Stoughton, 1923).

Moreau, R. E., 'Joking Relationships in Tanganyika', *Africa*, XIV (1943-4).

Sanderson, M., 'Relationship Systems of the Wangonde and Wahenga Tribes, Nyasaland', *J.R.A.I.*, LIII (1923).

Stewart, James (missionary), 'The Second Circumnavigation of Lake Nyassa', *Proceedings of the Royal Geographical Society* (1879).

Stewart, James (engineer), 'Lake Nyassa and the Water Route to the Lake Region of Africa', *Proceedings of the Royal Geographical Society, New Series*, Vol. III (1881).

Swann, A. J., *Fighting the Slave Hunters in Central Africa* (London: Seeley, Service & Co., 1910).

Thomson, J., *To the Central African Lakes and Back*, 2 vols. (London: Sampson Low, Marston, Searle & Rivington, 1881).

Thurnwald, R. C., *Black and White in East Africa* (London: Routledge & Sons, 1935).

Thwaites, D.H., 'Wanyakyusa Agriculture', *East African Agricultural Journal*, Vol. 9 (1944).

Wilson, G., 'An Introduction to Nyakyusa Society,' *Bantu Studies*, X* (1936).

'An African Morality', *Africa*, IX* (1936).

'Introduction to Nyakyusa Law', *Africa*, X* (1937).

The Land Rights of Individuals among the Nyakyusa* (Livingstone: Rhodes-Livingstone Institute Papers No. 1, 1938).

The Constitution of Ngonde* (Livingstone: Rhodes-Livingstone Institute Papers No. 3, 1939).

'Nyakyusa Conventions of Burial', *Bantu Studies*, XIII* (1939).

Wilson, M., 'An African Christian Morality', *Africa*, X (1937).

'Nyakyusa Kinship' in *African Systems of Kinship and Marriage*,* edited by A. R. Radcliffe-Brown and Daryll Forde (London: Oxford University Press, for International African Institute, 1950).

Young, E. D., 'On a Recent Sojourn at Lake Nyassa, Central Africa', *Proceedings of the Royal Geographical Society*, XXI (1877).

Reference may also be made to Census Reports for Nyasaland and Tanganyika Territory; to the Annual Reports of the Agricultural, Education, and Medical Department in both Territories; to annual Provincial Reports, and to Government reports on specific topics such as the following:

Tanganyika Territory: *Native Administration Memoranda*, No. II, 'Native Courts' (1930); No. III, 'Native Treasuries (1930).

Wilcocks, C., *Tuberculosis in Tanganyika Territory* (Dar es Salaam 1938).

Hornby, A. J. W., *Denudation and Soil Erosion in Nyasaland*, Nyasaland Department of Agriculture, Bulletin No. II (1934).

Nyasaland Protectorate: *Report on Emigrant Labour* (Zomba 1935).

* The more substantial accounts of the Nyakyusa-Ngonde people.

INDEX